STOCK INDEX FUTURES & OPTIONS

WILEY TRADING ADVANTAGE

STOCK INDEX FUTURES & OPTIONS

THE INS & OUTS OF TRADING ANY INDEX, ANYWHERE

Susan Abbott Gidel

John Wiley & Sons, Inc.
New York • Chichester • Weinheim • Brisbane • Singapore • Toronto

Copyright © 2000 by Susan M. Gidel. All rights reserved.

Published by John Wiley & Sons, Inc.

Published simultaneously in Canada.

This publication is designed to provide accurate and authoritative information in regard to the subject matter covered. It is sold with the understanding that the publisher is not engaged in rendering professional services. If professional advice or other expert assistance is required, the services of a competent professional person should be sought.

Designations used by companies to distinguish their products are often claimed by trademarks. In all instances where the author or publisher is aware of a claim, the product names appear in Initial Capital letters. Readers, however, should contact the appropriate companies for more complete information regarding trademarks and registration.

Library of Congress Cataloging-in-Publication Data:
Gidel, Susan Abbott, 1956–
    Stock index futures & options : the ins & outs of trading any index, anywhere/Susan Abbott Gidel.
        p.   cm.
    Includes index.
    ISBN 978-0-471-29539-6 (alk. paper)
    1. Stock index futures.   2. Dow Jones averages.   3. Futures.   4. Standard and Poor's Corporation.   I. Title.   II. Title: Stock index futures and options.
HG6043.G538 2000
332.63'228—dc21   99-15786

To my grandmother, Eunice Abbott, who instilled
in me a fascination with words and publishing.

To my parents, Ed and Dorothy Abbott, who always
have encouraged me to pursue my interests.

To my husband, Jerry Gidel, whose unconditional
support made this book possible.

CONTENTS

CONTENTS

PREFACE

Before stock index contracts came along, futures trading had received a bum rap. You know—cocktail party stories about soybeans in the front lawn and that funny-sounding pork belly contract. But futures on stock indexes brought in big players who used the nice, neat index packages to allocate assets or to protect a portfolio in the blink of an eye. With the blessing of the big-time institutional users, futures trading came into its own in the financial arena.

Today, individuals are more involved than ever with the stock market. Futures traders like the volatility in stock index contracts, which present profit opportunities, as well as the vast number of indexes available, which give them access to every important stock market in the world. Individual investors, with scads of stock investments that have done well in the bull market, may be interested in broadening their scope to the futures and options arena either to gain exposure to market movements around the world or to protect gains in their underlying portfolios.

This book is for both futures traders and individual stock investors and is written on the premise that stock index futures and options markets are one of the most accessible, understandable ways to enter this area of financial markets. Having written about the futures markets as a journalist for more than 20 years, I believe that in order to make good decisions about trading stock index contracts, you need to have good information. You need to know what kind of index you're about to trade—its construction, the market exposure it provides, and details about the contract itself. You also need to understand what makes stock index markets move and who is doing the moving.

However, background information isn't the be-all, end-all. Veterans and new traders alike will benefit from the trading strategy ideas that offer real-world solutions to real-world investment goals.

Ever dream about trading from the beach? It's no longer a dream, and I've devoted an entire chapter to the exciting developments in technology that are behind giving you direct electronic access to the markets.

Stock index futures offer individuals the opportunity to either gain or protect exposure to a variety of stock market niches and world economies on an affordable basis. This book is intended to help you get started on that path. Here's hoping that you'll be one of the first to lead a new trend in cocktail conversation and chat-room discussions—stock index futures and options.

Susan Abbott Gidel
Chicago
June 1999

ACKNOWLEDGMENTS

One person may be considered the author of this book, but that number belies the dozens of people who had a hand in its creation.

Those kindred spirits who got me going down the path and confirmed my belief in the value of good writing and in this project include Bill Falloon, Alan Guebert, Darrell Jobman, Jack Schwager, and Hugh Ulrich. Along the way, Bob Meier stepped to the fore with an open invitation to scour his extensive collection of files and books for helpful information. I, of course, took him up on his offer gratefully.

I must thank deeply the friends that I have gained during many years in the futures industry who very willingly spent their time and expertise reviewing my words. They include Bill Kokontis, who also was a ready provider of encouragement and perspective; Don Selkin, from whom I have learned a lot about the stock market; and Susan Taylor, whose critical editor's eye has never failed me. Most of all, I'd like to thank Leslie Wurman for her extremely generous contribution of time and incredible attention to detail. She was there to lend a helping hand whenever it was needed, and I am deeply indebted to her.

My husband, Jerry Gidel, came to the rescue in the text's final weeks of preparation. It is not an exaggeration to say that without his understanding of this project and his persistence in digging out the details of information that make it a valuable resource, this book would not be in your hands today. We both appreciated the care package that my sister, Jan Abbott Landow, and her husband, Brett, sent to get us through the home stretch, as well as the post-project refuge that they provided.

Because I discovered along the way that writing a book inevitably eats into one's day job and normal life, I'd like to thank my regular business clients for their understanding and my family, friends, and neighbors for their patience.

Among the many exchange staff members who provided answers to a myriad of questions about their respective stock index products, Rick Redding of the Chicago Mercantile Exchange deserves a special thank-you for his very early encouragement in tackling this project and his advice on important aspects of its direction.

Other stock index experts who provided needed information or clarified certain points of confusion include the following:

Huib Vermeulen of the Amsterdam Exchanges; Warwick Sheehan of the Australian Stock Exchange; Gary Ellis of Bates Commodities; Jeff Campbell, Abi Diaz, Gene Mueller, Catherine Shalen, and Katie Spring of the Chicago Board of Trade; Brett Vietmeir, David Lerman, and Ellen Resnick of the Chicago Mercantile Exchange; John Gallagher of Credit Suisse First Boston; Ricardo Manrique of Dow Jones Global Indexes; Frank Hartmann and Thorston Neufeld of Deutsche Börse; Walter Allwicher and Lothar Kloster of Eurex; Mary Ann Burns, Toby Taylor, and Tracy Wahler of the Futures Industry Association; Leslie Mitchell of the Futures Industry Institute; Lynette Berry and Florian Cartoux at FTSE International; Kevin Chang, Ross Lai, and Anthony Yeung at the Hong Kong Futures Exchange; Chiara Rotelli at the Italian Exchange; Hillary Dietz and Steve Harmon of internet.com LLC; and Candice Bowman and Barbara Loftus of the Kansas City Board of Trade.

Several staffers for the London International Financial Futures and Options Exchange on both sides of the Atlantic were incredibly helpful, including George Anagnos, Marco Bianchi, Morgan McKenney, Jonathan Seymour, Richard Stevens, and Martyn Wild. Carol Burns, Carole Huguet, and Huu Minh Mai answered my questions about stock indexes trading at MONEP. Manuel Andrade was a similar source of information at MEFF-RV.

Other contributors of information include Ronald Cherry at Morgan Stanley Capital International; Peter Canada and Miami Delacruz at Nasdaq; James Williams at Nikkei America; Tim Barry, Rick Kaufmann, and Tom Walker at the New York Board of Trade; Dave Ryan at the New York Mercantile Exchange; Bethann Ashfield and Joe Kenrick at the New York Stock Exchange; Annika Hanberger, Marie Ekman Parck, and Sofia Ullman at OM Stockholm; Yuji Ikeda at the Osaka Securities Exchange; Brad Zigler of the Pacific Exchange; Judy Sahler Delen, Tom Ryan, John Szczepaniak, and Tammy Wood from the Frank Russell Company; Lori Nice of the Securities and Exchange Commission; Andrea Fleischmann and Matthew Rian at STOXX Limited; Todd Kennedy, Vicki Kwan, and Steven Mater of the Sydney Futures Exchange; and Vielka Maynard, Rama Pillai, Len Schuman, Bernard Suen, and Gerard Yeo of the Singapore International Monetary Exchange. Bill Jordan and Carol Levine of Standard & Poor's Corporation were especially helpful in providing information and data. The following also deserve my appreciation: David Downey of Timber Hill LLC; Takashi Naito and Hiroyuki Tokimune of the Tokyo Stock Exchange; Steve Kee, Richard Carleton, Glenn Doody, and Patrick McDonagh of the Toronto Stock Exchange and Toronto Futures Exchange; and Harold Levine of Value Line.

Finally, I'd like to thank everyone who created and maintained the web sites that made it possible to collect and confirm on a timely basis the information I needed about the stock market, stock index products, and industry developments. Thank God for the Internet and e-mail!

STOCK INDEX
FUTURES & OPTIONS

1

UNDERSTANDING STOCK INDEX FUTURES

Stock indexes have been a part of the investment culture for more than 100 years, but futures contracts on them did not begin until the 1980s. These contracts continue to develop as the markets enter the twenty-first century. Nearly three dozen countries have developed stock index derivatives products, which represent their domestic stock markets, and the largest economies in the world have several different indexes available that target various market segments. With the advent of the *euro*, the single currency of countries participating in the *European Economic and Monetary Union* (EMU), development of pan-European indexes was a hotbed of activity as the twentieth century came to a close, as were indexes representing the Asian-Pacific region and Internet stocks.

Leo Melamed, chairman emeritus of the *Chicago Mercantile Exchange* (CME) and chairman and chief executive officer (CEO) of Sakura Dellsher Inc., oversaw the development of stock index futures in the early 1980s while he was at the helm of the CME. Nearly 20 years later, he remains a staunch defender of stock index futures and options, and in a 1996 speech in Singapore he explained their importance:

> Indices and index markets have become indispensable tools in equity markets all over the world, and stock index futures have become even more indispensable as equity risk management tools. . . .

1

The world at-large has benefitted from stock index futures and options, which have changed the manner and scope of equity markets. They have led to innumerable new trading strategies, and also to the recognition of the existence of a large liquid pool of risk takers alongside the traditional equity cash markets that can instantly accommodate hedging requirements. . . . There are related benefits as well, like an increase in world foreign investment. This has in turn contributed to an increase in trade, technology transfers, and the development of multinational corporations.[1]

In the United States, where futures and options on futures trade on a dozen different indexes, the investable stock index trend began propitiously. The first stock index futures contract in the world, the Value Line Index at the *Kansas City Board of Trade* (KCBT), opened for trading on February 24, 1982, just six months before the U.S. stock market scored a major bottom. Since then, the popularity of stock index futures and options has risen along with the bull market in the underlying equities market. According to data from the Futures Industry Association, equity index futures in the United States traded 42.4 million contracts in 1998, almost triple the 14.8 million traded in 1990. Options on these futures contracts rose an even greater degree—to 5.6 million contracts in 1998 from 1.7 million eight years earlier. (During the same period, volume in index options at U.S. securities exchanges fell to 74.8 million contracts from 88.2 million at the decade's start.)

Internationally, all but two (India and Russia) of the 21 nations with equity market capitalization exceeding $100 billion in 1997 (see Figure 1.1) boast a domestic stock index product on either a stock or futures exchange, and often on both. In addition, exchange-listed stock index products track the equity markets in the following countries: Austria, Chile, Denmark, Finland, Hungary, Israel, Korea, Malaysia, New Zealand, Norway, Portugal, Romania, Taiwan, and Thailand.

Not all these products are available to U.S. investors, however. The U.S. *Commodity Futures Trading Commission* (CFTC), the governmental regulator of futures products, must pass judgment on a foreign stock index futures contract before it may be offered or sold in the United States. After an exchange applies to have its index available to U.S. customers, the CFTC grants approval by issuing a *no-action letter* to the exchange, meaning that the agency will take no regulatory action against the exchange if it sells the product in the United States. Options on stock index futures contracts have been considered approved simultaneously with the underlying futures contract since 1996. Similarly, the U.S. *Securities and Exchange Commission* (SEC) has jurisdiction in granting no-action letters to exchanges that want to sell foreign stock index options (on the cash index, not a futures contract) to U.S. citizens. As of April 28, 1999, 14 stock index futures con-

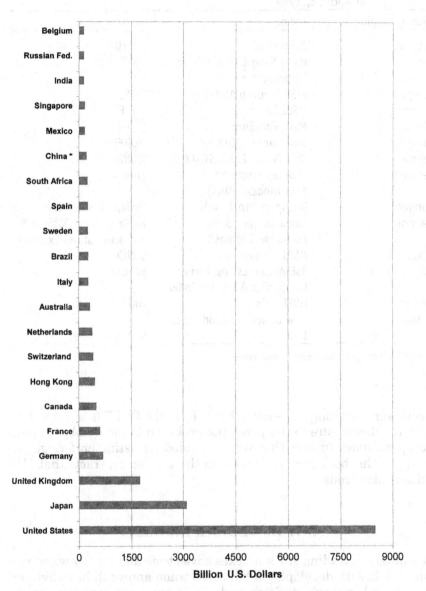

Stock Market Capitalization Levels in 1997

Billion U.S. Dollars

FIGURE 1.1 World stock markets, ranked by market capitalization
* includes Taiwan
Source: World Bank

TABLE 1.1   Non-U.S. Stock Index Futures Contracts Pending CFTC Approval as of April 28, 1999

Country/Region	Index	Exchange
Belgium	Belgian 20	BELFOX
China	Hang Seng China-Affiliated Corporations	HKFE
Europe	FTSE Eurotop 100	LIFFE
Europe	MSCI Euro	LIFFE
Europe	MSCI Pan-Euro	LIFFE
Europe	Dow Jones STOXX 50	MONEP
Europe	Dow Jones EURO STOXX 50	MONEP
Germany	Mid-Cap Deutsche Aktienindex(MDAX)	Eurex
Hungary	Budapest Stock Index	Budapest Stock Exchange
Malaysia	Kuala Lumpur Stock Exchange Composite	Kuala Lumpur Options & Financial Futures Exchange
Singapore	MSCI Singapore Free	SIMEX
South Africa	JSE Actuaries Top Forty Companies All Share Index	SAFEX
Taiwan	HKFE Taiwan	HKFE
Thailand	Dow Jones Thailand Stock Index	SIMEX

Source: Commodity Futures Trading Commission

tracts were awaiting a no-action letter from the CFTC (see Table 1.1). That number is sure to rise given the explosion in the number of pan-European index futures that were intended for listing on foreign exchanges. This book mainly focuses on those index contracts that U.S. citizens may trade.

WHY TRADE STOCK INDEXES?

In a nutshell, trading stock indexes saves time and money when you compare it with developing a balanced trade approach in individual stocks. With a single decision, order, and brokerage commission, as well as less investment capital, you can gain exposure to a country's entire stock market or segments of that market—for example, blue-chip, mid-cap, or technology stocks.

Stock index futures and options markets also make maintaining your current stock portfolio easy—whether you own individual stocks or mutual funds—yet protect you against a potential downturn in value during a correction or bear market. Since the *Dow Jones Industrial Average* (DJIA) was introduced in 1896, most major market tops have held sway from 6 to 13 years before being penetrated decisively to the upside. At the extreme, the 1929 top that preceded the Great Depression was not surpassed for decades, until 1954. Talk about the wrong 25 years to own stocks!

SEC Chairman Arthur Levitt told an investors' seminar in early 1999 that the bullish stock market of the 1980s and 1990s had greatly increased interest in stock ownership. Two years before stock index futures began trading in 1982, about 6% of Americans owned stocks; today about 33% of Americans own stocks, either directly or indirectly, through pension or other retirement plans offered by their employers.[2]

No doubt, mutual funds are a significant portion of those holdings. Statistics from the Investment Company Institute, which tracks the mutual fund industry, show that the number of U.S. households owning mutual funds increased nearly ten-fold from 1980 (4.6 million) to 1998 (44.4 million); of all U.S. households, 29% owned stock mutual funds in 1998.[3] Of course, the explosion in the number of mutual funds available, and the bull market, contributed to the trend as well. In January 1984, investors had to choose among about 400 stock mutual funds, whose total net assets equaled $76.4 billion. Fifteen years later, more than 3,500 stock mutual funds were available, and assets totaled $3.1 trillion.

TYPES OF STOCK INDEXES

The dominant exchange-listed stock index contracts tend to be broad-based indexes that represent a country's entire stock market, although those that focus on only the largest stocks also are popular. In addition, most indexes are *capitalization-weighted*, which means that the stocks with the most outstanding shares at the highest price are weighted the heaviest in the index and thus, have the most influence on index movement. Indeed, of the 10 most popular indexes traded in 1998 (see Table 1.2), only the Nikkei 225 is not capitalization-weighted; instead, it is a *price-weighted* index like the DJIA; whereby the stocks with the highest price carry the most weight. Sometimes, a capitalization-weighted index is modified to reflect only the available shares or *free float* of stocks in the index. Thus, those shares held in firm hands, such as company owners, are not considered available for trading and are not used in calculating a stock's market capitalization. A third way of computing a stock index—*equal-weighting*—assumes that an equal amount of money is invested in each component stock. This method neutralizes the influence of both high-priced and highly capitalized stocks.

TABLE 1.2 Top 10 Stock Index Contracts
(Average Daily Volume, 1998; 252 Trading Days)

Rank	Index (Exchange)	Average Daily Volume	Year-End 1998 Open Interest
1	Standard & Poor's 500 Futures (CME)	124,724	379,062
2	DAX Cash Options* (Eurex)	118,843	957,284
3	CAC 40 Futures (MONEP)	65,251	273,387
4	OMX Futures (OMS and OML)	36,184	240,364
5	IBEX-35 Futures (MEFF RV)	34,236	72,363
6	Nikkei 225 Futures (OSE)	32,504	217,474
7	Hang Seng Futures (HKFE)	27,737	37,571
8	FTSE 100 Futures (LIFFE)	27,600	194,586
9	DAX Futures (Eurex)	27,528	55,492
10	MIB 30 Futures (IDEM)	23,398	23,927
	*not approved for U.S. investors		

Source: Futures Industry Association

The depth of the U.S. equities market allows for development and active trading in several types of stock index contracts. Broad-based indexes include hundreds or thousands of stocks and are considered representative of the market as a whole. U.S. stock index contracts also are based on market capitalization for those who want to focus strictly on large-, medium-, or small-cap sectors.

In the mid-1990s, the type of exposure available through exchange-listed products drilled down even deeper, with indexes for growth and value stocks listed. The technology sector was hot for both price movement and index development, spawning revitalized versions of the PSE Technology 100 Index and Nasdaq-100 Index in 1996, both of which had first been listed in the 1980s but failed to sustain trading then. In 1999, the futures industry's first Internet stock index was introduced at the KCBT, home of the original stock index contract.

Another popular twist on U.S. stock index contracts in the late 1990s was to offer the same contract with various contract multipliers, thus making the index affordable and suitable for everyone from individuals to institutional users. The CME was the first to take this approach on its flagship Standard & Poor's (S&P) 500 contract, offering the E-mini version at one-fifth the contract multiplier in the fall of 1997; in 1999, CME did the same for the technology-oriented Nasdaq-100 Index. Just weeks after the E-mini S&P 500 opened in

TABLE 1.3　Top 10 U.S. Stock Index Contracts (1998)

Rank	Contract (Exchange)	Average Daily Volume	Year-End 1998 Open Interest
1	Standard & Poor's 500 Futures (CME)	124,724	379,062
2	Standard & Poor's 500 Options (CME)	19,788	179,776
3	E-mini Standard & Poor's 500 Futures (CME)	17,722	8,723
4	Dow Jones Industrial Average Futures (CBOT)	14,157	15,688
5	Nasdaq-100 Futures (CME)	4,220	8,668
6	NYSE Composite Futures (NYBOT)	2,342	9,299
7	Standard & Poor's Mid Cap 400 Futures (CME)	1,230	15,981
8	Russell 2000 Futures (CME)	1,098	14,486
9	Dow Jones Industrial Average Options (CBOT)	974	13,775
10	Nasdaq-100 Options (CME)	506	6,295

Source: Futures Industry Association

Chicago, the *New York Board of Trade* (NYBOT) listed a large version of its flagship product, the *New York Stock Exchange* (NYSE) Composite Index, which doubled the original contract's multiplier; in 1998, it added a small version at half the original multiplier.

At the same time it introduced smaller-sized contracts suitable for individual traders on the S&P 500 and the Nasdaq-100, the CME went a step farther and listed them on its electronic trading platform. Both indexes trade primarily on the GLOBEX$_2$ platform, virtually 24 hours a day. (Large orders are traded in the traditional open outcry forum but only when pit trading is open for the regular-sized stock index contracts.) Trading in the E-mini S&P 500 has been quite successful, vaulting to third place behind the S&P 500 futures and S&P 500 futures options in terms of total trading volume among all U.S. stock indexes listed on futures exchanges in 1998 (see Table 1.3).

HOW ARE STOCK INDEX FUTURES PRICED?

As its name implies, a stock index futures contract is an instrument that reflects the market's current belief about the future value of the underlying index. For example, when you're trading a March futures contract in January, you and all other market participants are trying to determine what the underlying stock index value will be when the futures contract expires in two months. Thus, the current futures index level represents expected *carrying charges* for holding the underlying stock portfolio.

The expected return from a stock portfolio includes price appreciation of the stocks, the stocks' dividend yield, and the reinvestment return from the stock dividends. However, the vast majority of stock index futures contracts track price-return indexes that do not reflect stock dividends. Instead, a stock index futures valuation is based on the expected price appreciation of stocks in the index plus the current risk-free rate of return. This is because you can control the entire stock portfolio represented by the index with about 10% of the funds it would take to buy it in its entirety and can put the other 90% in T-bills.

The stock index futures value will equal the value of the underlying cash market index at the futures contract's expiration because all futures contracts are designed to settle to the value of the underlying stock index. Therefore, the current value of a stock index futures contract essentially compares the risk-free rate of return with the return expected from stock dividends. Generally, a stock index futures value will be greater than the current value of the underlying index as long as short-term interest rates are greater than dividend yields.

WHAT IS FAIR VALUE?

Buying low and selling high are the goals of every trader, and that concept enters into play when trying to decide whether a stock index futures contract is cheap or rich compared with its theoretical *fair value*, or break-even point. To determine fair value, you take into consideration current interest rates, expected dividend yields from the component stocks, and the amount of time until the futures contract expires. Capturing the difference between a futures price and its fair value provides *excess return* (often measured in basis points, or 1/100th of a percentage point) beyond the benchmark return of the index that money managers are trying to outperform.

Although fair value may be an interesting tidbit of market information for individual traders, it remains primarily in the arena of professionals, who may have varying incentives for tracking fair value and varying results in its calculation depending on their cost of money, dividend forecasts, and transaction fees. Indeed, a 1996 study from the CME says, "no single break-even price is universally appropriate," and outlines how five different investment objectives produce five different fair-value calculations.[4] Rest assured that these market professionals are keeping a close eye on the fair value of a stock index futures contract and will trade accordingly when futures are out of line with the underlying cash market, selling futures and buying stock baskets when futures rise too far above fair value and buying futures/selling stock baskets when futures drop too far below fair value. In either case, the action will bring the futures market closer to its fair value versus the cash index.

Information about current calculations of fair value for a stock index (typically assuming no transaction costs and equal marginal borrowing and lending rates) sometimes is posted on the web site of the exchange where the index is listed or on sites that provide market research.

HOW CIRCUIT BREAKERS WORK

Market *circuit breakers*, which halt trading in stocks and stock index futures, grew out of the stock market crash that saw the DJIA drop 508 points, or 22.6%, on October 19, 1987. Traditionally, stock markets had not restricted daily price movement of listed stocks (and thus, stock index values), allowing prices to rise or fall without limit. (Interestingly, it is equally traditional at futures exchanges for nearly every contract to have a daily price limit.) During the October 1987 crash, the stock market and related derivatives moved so fast that participants were unable to react in a timely manner, which only exacerbated the market's volatility and caused concerns about the entire system's financial integrity.

After the 1987 crash, the newly formed President's Working Group on Financial Markets, consisting of the heads of the CFTC, Federal Reserve Board, SEC, and U.S. Treasury, recommended that all U.S. markets listing stocks and stock-related products halt trading for one hour upon a 250-point drop in the Dow (about 12%) and for two hours upon a 400-point drop (about 20%). The group also recommended that the point level be reviewed quarterly to reflect the current 12% and 20% parameters.

One year and one day after the 1987 crash, circuit breakers to that effect were established at the NYSE. The CME developed coordinated circuit breakers for futures and options based on movement in the S&P 500 Index, which also included an opening limit of 5 points up or down (later raised to 7 points) that would precipitate a 10-minute pause in trading and a 12-point, down-only, limit (equal to about 100 DJIA points), which would halt trading for 30 minutes and trigger the use of the *sidecar* for program trading at the NYSE. This limit was later raised to 15 points, and the time of the halt was reduced to 15 minutes. If the NYSE halted trading, the CME would halt as well, if the nearby S&P 500 futures contract were down 30 or 50 points (reflecting the two DJIA stopping points). Futures would not reopen until stocks representing at least 50% of market capitalization in the S&P 500 Index were open. The CME also decided that a 50-point movement in the S&P 500 to the upside would halt trading as well.

In 1996, the length of the trading halt at NYSE was reduced to 30 minutes for a 250-point drop and to one hour for a 400-point decline. In 1997, the trigger points were raised to 350 points and 550 points, which represented moves of about 5% and 8% at the time. Also in 1997, the CME limits were expanded to 45 points and 70 points, respectively.

It took 10 years from the 1987 crash for the circuit breakers to be tested for the first time at the NYSE. On October 27, 1997, both trigger points were hit, and the NYSE effectively closed trading for the day about 30 minutes earlier than normal due to hitting the second trigger point. Because of the bull market, the Dow's point losses on October 27 represented moves of about 4% and 7% and induced another re-evaluation of the circuit-breaker system. As a result, circuit breakers are now based on percentage moves in the Dow, rather than point moves, and are reset quarterly, with new limits in effect at the beginning of January, April, July, and October.

The first trigger, a downmove of 10%, causes a one-hour trading halt at the NYSE if it occurs before 2 P.M. (New York time) and a 30-minute halt if it happens between 2 P.M. and 2:30 P.M. A 10% drop triggers no trading halt if it occurs after 2:30 P.M. A 20% downmove stops trading for two hours if it occurs before 1 P.M., one hour if it happens between 1 P.M. and 2 P.M., and closes the exchange for the day if it occurs after 2 P.M. The NYSE closes for the day on a 30% downmove in the Dow, no matter what time it occurs. U.S. futures exchanges post the relative point moves that coordinate with the Dow's percent losses for their index products on their respective web sites.

In addition to the coordinated circuit breakers with the NYSE, the futures exchanges with stock index products also have in place two speed bumps that induce a 10-minute trading halt in futures at or below the limit offered price. These speed bumps are pegged to declines of 2.5% and 5%. At the CME and CBOT, overnight trading in all the indexes, including the S&P 500 and DJIA, have a 2.5% limit throughout the session. At the KCBT, the percentage moves in points for the Value Line Index and Internet Stock Index (ISDEX) are recalculated each day based on the previous day's close. Due to the volatility of Internet stocks, the first speed bump for ISDEX equals a 5% move.

Internationally, adoption of market circuit breakers has been mixed. No limits exist on daily price movement in Australian, Canadian, German, Italian, Spanish, Swedish, British, or European stock index futures or options. However, the underlying Spanish stock market halts trading after a 15% downmove. Meanwhile, all the Japanese stock index contracts use circuit breakers, as do the Hong Kong and Taiwan indexes that trade on SIMEX. In Europe, only the CAC 40 Index in France has a circuit breaker. (Details of these circuit breaker limits can be found in Appendix 2, "Stock Index Contract Specifications.")

DO WE NEED CIRCUIT BREAKERS?

The merit of circuit breakers remains debatable. Proponents point out that they may be useful because the trading halt allows participants time to gather new information and to assess their situation. Brokerage firms can check on customer funding as well as their own regulatory compliance status. Exchanges and their clearinghouses can look into the current financial conditions of their member firms and own organizations. In sum, circuit breakers are seen as a way to prevent panic selling.

Opponents of circuit breakers argue that they only postpone the inevitable and limit the flow of market information, which worsens the situation. In addition, they claim that the circuit breakers become magnets during volatile moves as participants rush to execute their orders before the anticipated trading halt.

In an opinion piece published in *The Wall Street Journal* shortly after the U.S. stock market circuit breakers were hit late in the trading day on October 27, 1997, Sydney Futures Exchange Chief Executive Les Hosking claimed that, "the circuit breakers nearly precipitated a global stock market collapse."[5] He argued that the "exaggerated" declines of 10% to 13% in the Hong Kong, German, French, and London stock markets the following day were largely due to "the complete absence of information about the real value of U.S. stocks—the direct result of the circuit breakers." In contrast, Hosking said that the markets in Australia remained open during the entire trading session that immediately followed the U.S. market close, and the Australian Share Price Index dropped 7%, a level that matched the Dow's decline at the final circuit breaker.

Collars and Sidecars

Another outgrowth of the 1987 market crash was the imposition of a market *collar* that restricted index arbitrage trading whenever the DJIA moved 50 points up or down from the previous close. Under such conditions, arbitrage sell orders for stocks in the S&P 500 Index can be executed only on an uptick while buy orders may be executed only on a downtick. Although several government agencies, brokerage firms, and futures exchanges complained in 1998 that the collar was unduly restrictive and perhaps unnecessary, the NYSE chose only to expand its collar trigger to a 2% move in the DJIA, rather than eliminate it entirely. However, the NYSE did eliminate the sidecar rule that routed program trading orders on the NYSE Superdot system to a separate blind file for five minutes before becoming eligible for execution whenever the S&P 500 futures market at the CME was down 12 points on the day.

UNDERSTANDING STOCK INDEX EXPIRATIONS

When stock index futures contracts were first listed, they followed the convention of other cash-settled products in that the final settlement price upon the contract's expiration was equal to that day's closing value of the cash index. However, due to the large participation of institutions and others who traded baskets of stock against various index offerings (futures, options on futures, and options on the cash index), the market closes on these common expiration days became wild affairs. In response to the triple-witching-hour phenomenon that occurred the third Friday of March, June, September, and December when futures, options on futures, and options on cash stock indexes expired simultaneously, most U.S. stock index contracts now settle to a special quotation based on the opening prices of component stocks on those third Fridays, the day after the contract's last trading day.

At the CME, for example, the S&P 500 and most other U.S. stock indexes settle on each quarterly expiration (March, June, September, and December) at a *special opening quotation* (SOQ) for the index. This SOQ likely will differ from the index's market open value that day, because the first quote released on any trading day almost always will be based on the preceding day's closing values for the component stocks, and then will move according to new prices generated as each stock in the index opens and continues trading. In contrast, the SOQ uses only the current day's opening values for each stock to determine the index value at which the futures contract settles. In indexes with a large number of stocks, components might not open until a hefty portion of the trading day has passed. As a result, the SOQ may not be within the range of index values quoted for that day's trade. If component stocks never open on the day the SOQ is calculated, the preceding day's closing value is inserted into the calculation.

Final settlement values for the Japanese stock indexes follow a similar procedure based on opening market values. Most other international indexes settle to a figure on the contract's last trading day that represents some sort of average closing value for the component stocks.

Cash settlement for a stock index futures contract means that the contract is settled in cash, not by an exchange of stocks in the index. The cash value of the index is determined by multiplying the index settlement level by the contract multiplier. If you hold your stock index futures position to expiration, your account will be credited or debited by the difference between the contract's final settlement value and the value of the contract (index level times multiplier) when you initiated the position. This same procedure is in effect when options expire in March, June, September, and December. Options that expire in other months will be exercised into the appropriate underlying futures position, not cash.

2

WHAT MAKES STOCK INDEX FUTURES TICK?

Unless you're the hero in a television show who gets tomorrow's newspaper today, you're just like everyone else in the world, from professional analysts to individual investors, who are trying to figure out the market's next move. Some people focus on market fundamentals, such as corporate earnings or interest rate levels, for guidance; others hone in on charts and other technical indicators; and some folks use a smattering of both methods when making trading decisions.

No way of analyzing the market is more right than another, just different. It is important to remember that whatever approach you find makes sense is the right one for you. Still, you should be aware of the factors for which the various analytical camps may be watching as their next trading signal, because even that knowledge may play into your own decision-making process. For example, a technical trader looking for an oversold signal might be more alert in anticipation of an important fundamental report coming out soon. A fundamentally oriented trader might wait for a technically oversold condition to develop before placing a buy order.

This chapter takes a look at the factors that stock index futures and options traders watch every day in the never-ending challenge of predicting what tomorrow may bring.

FUNDAMENTALS

Fundamental factors that affect stock index futures values are the same fundamental factors that affect the prices of stocks that make up an index. In short, anything that affects a company's capability to make money is a fundamental factor worth paying some attention. Generally, these factors are news about the economy, inflation, politics, the country's currency, and interest rates. This section focuses on reports (mainly from the federal government) that track the U.S. economy and are familiar to U.S. investors, but the same principles concerning their impact on stocks, the stock market, and stock indexes apply to similar information generated about other economies worldwide.

Company News

From a fundamental standpoint, nearly all the news you hear on radio or television or over the Internet is digested in terms of how it will affect corporate earnings, which are reported quarterly. Earnings increase when sales and profits are rising; they decline when sales are slow or when costs are rising.

Following quarterly earnings reports and the pre-report period in which companies provide a whiff of what's to come is an exercise in judging results versus expectations. If the news is better than expected, a stock's price may rally; if the news is worse than expected, prices are almost sure to take a hit. Either way, the price movement affects stock index levels.

On a company-by-company basis, news such as changes in management, potential merger or acquisition, or product market share updates may affect an individual stock's price, which will in turn affect the value of the stock index of which it is a component. How much it affects the index depends on the stock's weighting in the index. For example, IBM carries a weight of just 0.0006% in the Value Line Index but about 8% in the DJIA.

Economy

One thing the U.S. government does well is to capture and release raw data to the public on a regular reporting schedule. Over time, these statistics and their changes have formed a basis for evaluating current economic conditions. Generally, good economic news revolves around increases in demand and production, low inflation, and low interest rates. However, rising demand can turn into bad news if the market is concerned that the demand portends inflation, which in turn, might bring rising interest rates. Likewise, rising production without accompanying demand can signal a slowing economy.

Following are some of the reports released regularly that traders of both stocks and stock indexes watch. In the age of the Internet, these sensitive figures have sometimes seen their market influence come earlier than expected. In November 1998, for example, the Bureau of Labor Statistics mistakenly posted employment data on the Internet a day earlier than the report's scheduled release, sending the stock market lower as word of the news spread.

Manufacturing and Trade Inventories and Sales. Released by the U.S. Census Bureau (www.census.gov) on a two-month delayed basis, this report tracks monthly adjustments that have been made to keep production and sales in balance.

Construction Indicators. Given the American dream of owning one's own home, economic security and optimism are reflected in the housing starts, housing permits, and new single-family home sales' figures released monthly by the Census Bureau.

Employment. Typically released during the first week of each month, this report includes the preceding month's figures for the unemployment rate and non-farm payroll jobs. The Bureau of Labor Statistics (www.bls.gov) of the U.S. Department of Labor is the source for these reports.

Gross Domestic Product (GDP). A country's GDP is its broadest measure of economic health and represents the domestic production of goods and services. The Bureau of Economic Analysis (www.bea.doc.gov) figures U.S. GDP on a quarterly basis but releases estimates monthly starting one month after the end of a quarter; the final figure for any particular quarter comes at the end of the next quarter. (The United States used to track Gross National Product, (GNP) but switched in 1991 to more closely match international standards; GNP includes income from GDP as well as foreign income.)

Index of Leading Economic Indicators. This index, formerly distributed by the U.S. Department of Commerce, has been issued since 1996 by The Conference Board, a business research group (www.tcb-indicators.org). The index is the crystal ball of economic data because it is designed to foretell the future of the U.S. economy. Issued monthly, this report includes indicators that represent important components of the economy, including employment, manufacturing, and housing. Since 1968, this index has included the monthly average of the Standard & Poor's 500 Index as its only measure of U.S. stock prices.

Industrial Production. The Federal Reserve Board collects production data from a variety of government sources to produce a monthly estimate of industrial production for manufacturing, mining, and public utilities. The estimates are subject to revision based on the availability of data for the period in question; they are released in conjunction with capacity utilization figures (www.bog.frb.fed.us).

Manufacturers' Shipments, Inventories, and Orders. The data represented in these reports released by the Census Bureau are used as indicators of the outlook for the industrial sector of the economy. The figures are released with a one-month lag; a subset for durable goods' orders is released somewhat earlier than the full report.

Personal Income. The ability for individuals to make consumer purchases is reflected in this monthly report from the Bureau of Economic Analysis.

Purchasing Managers' Index. One of the few non-government reports that is important to the market, the Purchasing Managers' Index comes from the National Association of Purchasing Management (www.napm.org). At the time of release, the report reflects association members' survey responses that were gathered in the previous three weeks. The index compares the current situation to the one previous.

Retail Sales. How much money consumers are spending is revealed in this monthly report from the U.S. Commerce Department (www.doc.gov). The report includes sales of all types of consumer merchandise sold at the retail, not wholesale, level.

Inflation

Inflation is the bug-a-boo that socked it to the stock market in the 1970s, and its absence (beyond normal annual expectations) is credited as one of the underlying pillars of the bull market in the 1980s and 1990s. The problem with inflation is that it not only has the potential to decrease corporate profits (by both rising prices and reduced demand), but also invites an upward change in interest rates.

When the stock market is particularly sensitive to inflation and interest rates, it often takes its cues from the bond market, which is closely attuned to a variety of economic reports revealing the economy's health. Besides the following reports, which are considered inflation-sensitive, traders sometimes also look to the durable goods and retail sales figures for insights into inflationary tendencies.

Capacity Utilization. This measurement shows to what degree all available production capacity is being used and indicates the potential for further economic expansion. It is released monthly by the Federal Reserve Board.

Consumer Price Index (CPI). The CPI report is considered the best measure of inflation, with many cost-of-living increases tied to its annual changes. The costs of a predetermined group of goods and services are tabulated and reported monthly by the Bureau of Labor Statistics within the U.S. Department of Labor.

Producer Price Index. The Bureau of Labor Statistics also compiles an index related to prices received by the producers of goods. These price changes are a barometer of inflation's potential push on the consumer sector.

Interest Rates and Currency

Interest rate movement is often closely tied to the outlook for inflation because of the Federal Reserve Board's ability to make monetary policy to keep inflation in check. When it looks like inflation is rising and the Fed might raise interest rates, the stock market falters. Rising interest rates work against stock values on two fronts. First, they increase the expense of corporate borrowings. Second, they increase the attractiveness of competitive investments, such as Treasury bonds.

As a result, traders hang on every word of the Fed Chairman, looking for clues on the next move for interest rates. Here's why: After a quarter-point rate cut in late September 1998 that failed to jar the market from its depression, the Fed came back two weeks later with an unexpected quarter-point cut that lifted the DJIA 330 points for its third-largest point gain on record. Indeed, news about interest-rate cuts, either from remarks from Fed Chairman Alan Greenspan or actual rate cuts, were behind the top three gaining days (in points) for the Dow through the first quarter of 1999. (In three of the four largest daily point losses for the Dow through the same period, international economic woes have been blamed, not the Fed or news about interest rates.)

In essence, the value of a country's currency is often a reflection of domestic interest rates, which provide a return on holding the currency. For the stock market, currency values are important because they influence the amount of goods imported or exported from a particular country and, therefore, demand for those products.

International Trade. The U.S. Census Bureau and Bureau of Economic Analysis track international trade in goods and services with U.S.

trading partners on a monthly basis, releasing the data with about a six-week lag. The difference between U.S. imports and U.S. exports is the trade balance, which is considered a deficit if imports are greater than exports and a surplus if exports are greater than imports.

Politics

Political winds in any given country do not tend to affect individual stocks on a regular basis but do provide a backdrop for the general market environment. Certainly, a country's leadership, monetary and fiscal policies, and trade policies are important to the profitability prospects for individual companies. Thus, the potential for any major change in those factors gets thrown into the fundamental evaluation of companies and the stock market.

Look no further than the United States for an example of how politics can influence the stock market. Throughout 1998, the stock market reacted to news about the investigation of President Bill Clinton, which eventually led to his impeachment. Indeed, the DJIA twice dropped more than 200 points on news concerning the Monica Lewinsky scandal that appeared to be harmful to the President. Conversely, the Dow rallied a similar amount the day President Clinton's videotaped grand jury testimony was publicly released and deemed less damaging than anticipated.

Big-Picture Clues

Besides the wide variety of economic reports, which feed the stock and bond markets on an almost daily basis, a couple of other ways exist to get a feel for the stock market's overall health. First, try focusing on those stocks with the most influence on an index. Second, track the amount of money being invested in the market; in the United States, for example, statistics are reported monthly concerning the amount of money that is flowing into mutual funds.

In a market-capitalization index, which covers the majority of worldwide stock indexes, the stocks with the most outstanding shares trading at the highest prices will have the biggest influence on index movement. To get a quick handle on how the index is doing, therefore, keep your eyes open for news about the top 10 stocks in the index. (A snapshot of these top 10 stocks is provided for each stock index covered in Chapters 5, 6, and 7; remember that the percent weightings change as the price of the underlying stock changes or as adjustments are made to the number of shares used in the capitalization calculation.) In a price-weighted index, such as the DJIA, the highest priced stocks are weighted the heaviest and should command your attention, as should those whose prices are volatile.

U.S. stock analysts also pay attention to the amount of money that mutual funds are receiving to invest. The Investment Company Institute (www.ici.org) publishes monthly reports on how much money is flowing into or out of mutual funds. Stock mutual funds claimed more than 50% of all monies in mutual funds for the first time in 1997, and in February 1999, stood at 53% of the total $5.6 trillion, with taxable money market funds coming in second at 22%. The record net inflow for stock mutual funds was $28.5 billion in January 1998. Eight months later, when the market was within tenths of a percentage point of being officially called a bear market, investors made net withdrawals of $11.7 billion from stock funds. Conventional wisdom holds that as long stock fund inflows continue, mutual fund managers keep buying stocks.

Triple-Witching Effect

As the popularity of U.S. stock index futures products grew, traders began to notice what became known as the *triple-witching effect* which occurred on the third Friday of March, June, September, and December. Those four days marked the expiration of stock index futures, options on futures, and cash index options. As a result, the markets often experienced high volume and volatility as hedgers and arbitragers jockeyed to close out the stock index derivatives positions they held against an underlying basket of stocks.

To remove some of this triple-witching effect, most U.S. stock index futures and options on futures now expire on the day before the third Friday of those four months and settle to a value determined by the opening prices of stocks the following morning. Options for other contract months still expire on the third Friday of the month.

Still, a lot of trading activity often occurs on the last day of trading in futures and options, and the position close-outs tend to be mechanical in nature. As a result, stock index futures values may make unusual moves that correct themselves quickly after the quarterly expiration is over. During the bull market, these unusual moves have tended to be bullish.

TECHNICAL ANALYSIS

Too many fundamental factors to follow? Don't have time to be glued to CNBC or the Internet? *Technical analysis* may be the answer. The premise of technical analysis is that all known fundamentals are reflected in prices; that's because prices result from the buying and selling of those who take action on the fundamentals (and technical indicators, too).

Although not so often hailed as precipitating market moves as market fundamentals, technical analysis had its day in August 1998. On the morning of August 4, prominent technician Ralph Acampora of Prudential Securities switched his long-held bullish gears and said on CNBC that the DJIA could drop 20% from its highs. By the end of the trading day, the Dow had dropped 299 points (the third-largest point loss in history at the time) and triggered a bear market signal from the Dow Theory. By month's end, the Dow had lost another 1,000 points.

This section takes a look at some of the major areas of technical analysis that are particularly popular in the futures markets and may differ from technical methods traditionally used in evaluating the underlying stock market. For the U.S. stock market, most technical research has focused on the DJIA because it has recorded daily index levels since 1896. What's more, one of the venerable stock market analysis tools of all time—the Dow Theory—was developed specifically for use with the DJIA. Dozens, if not hundreds, of books explore various technical analysis methods in depth. In addition, technical analysis software packages can make examining ideas a breeze.

Charting Methods

Like a road map, various charting methods that plot the basic data of a stock market's open, high, low, and close can tell you where you've been. And, various ways to plot the map range from traditional to exotic. Whatever you choose, remember that you're on your own when it comes to mapping out where the road will lead next.

Bar Charts and Patterns. The traditional bar chart makes a single line that spans the day's range from high to low and places a tick to the right of the line for the day's close; a tick to the left of the line signifies the day's opening price. (Although bar charts are typically made based on daily prices, short-term traders might watch and track them in periods of hours, or even minutes.)

A technician staring at a freshly made bar chart is like a three-year-old staring at a white wall with new crayons in hand: The temptation to draw lines and pictures is irresistible. For the technician, a trendline is probably the first thing that demands to be drawn. A trendline can go up or down: An uptrend line is formed by connecting two low prices; a downtrend line connects two high prices.

The tendency for many market-watchers to draw trendlines using similar points makes them important price-making factors. The general rule of thumb is that prices must close above (*downtrend*) or below (*uptrend*) the line to consider it broken. Technicians often pay close attention to price behavior around a trendline to judge how prices broke the trendline (with vigor or just barely) to see whether the action might be a false breakout, with prices later getting back in step with the trend, normally in a day or two.

Trendlines on weekly or monthly charts carry more clout than those on daily charts, because prices have just one chance a week or month to react with the trendline. That's why weekly and monthly trendlines are particularly important to defining long-term trends. When these types of trendlines are broken, they can signify a major turn in market sentiment that colors how day-to-day trading should be handled.

Besides trendlines, long-term charts also reveal potential points of support in a price decline. Old lows are obvious areas of potential support that traders will target. But, when lows congregate around a certain level on the long-term charts, they convey an even stronger message of support.

Over the years, technicians have seen certain patterns repeat on their bar charts to the point that these pictures have their own names. For example, a flag or pennant on a price chart has a long flagpole of swiftly moving price action followed by a consolidation phase. A head-and-shoulders pattern marks an upward market extreme with two areas of similar resistance (the shoulders) interrupted by one last upmove (the head). A rounding bottom shows prices gently declining into and out of a market low, usually over a long period of time. Technicians seek many market patterns on their charts and divine future price movement from their formation based on their height, width, or other parameters.

Candlesticks and Gann. Two other ways to plot price charts make different demands on the basics of price ranges and the days on which they trade. Candlestick charts, used by the Japanese for hundreds of years, consider the most important price range of the day to be between the opening price and the closing price. This range is plotted as a box called the *body* of the candle while single lines extend from the body to reach the day's high and low prices. The patterns these candlesticks form go by standard, yet exotic-sounding names, such as doji, dark cloud cover, hanging man, and harami.

W.D. Gann, a legendary stock market trader early in the twentieth century, constructed his price charts based on the belief that time and price carry equal importance in analyzing a market. On a Gann chart for the stock market, for example, one square of time across the horizontal axis would equal one point of market movement on the vertical axis. In addition, Gann charts make no horizontal break for nontrading days, such as weekends or holidays.

Indicators

Market indicators, such as moving averages or oscillators, not only provide a different view of the market compared with price charts, but also generate specific buy or sell signals.

Moving averages are typically used to help identify a market's trend. A simple moving average is simply the average of a certain number of prices, typically the market's close. This average price is calculated and plotted on top of a regular bar chart. If current prices are above the moving average, the market is considered bullish; if prices are below the average, bearish. One of the most popular long-term simple moving averages is based on the last 200 days of market activity. Often, two or three moving averages of different lengths, for example, 4 (short), 9 (medium), and 18 (long) days, are combined, with their crossovers providing trading signals. Moving averages can be as varied as your imagination. The prices can be weighted; the number of days, weeks or months can change, and the combination of averages optimized.

Two other trend indicators are known by their acronyms, MACD and DMI. The *Moving Average Convergence-Divergence* indicator involves three exponential moving averages, with an emphasis on their own market direction as well as in comparison with underlying prices. The *Directional Movement Index* distills upward and downward price movement into a bullish/bearish index number between 0 and 100.

The *Relative Strength Index* (RSI) used in futures markets indicates a market's internal strength or weakness compared with a chosen number of days' history. Taken to an index number between 0 and 100, it tends to diverge from current price action at market turns. It should not be confused with the relative strength comparisons made in the stock market between an individual stock versus the market or between different market segments.

Finally, the *Stochastic* oscillator is another popular method of judging overbought and oversold conditions. The %K line, which measures closing prices in relationship to the daily price range, is smoothed as a moving average, called %D. The two lines can be used like a moving average and can be judged according to divergence/convergence with underlying prices.

Sentiment

In addition to technical-analysis methods that focus on price or momentum, ways exist for using data to interpret who is doing what in the market. In this area, the stock index futures markets have a leg up on the underlying stock market.

Stock index futures and options markets track both the day's volume as well as each contract month's open interest, or the number of outstanding contracts yet to be offset. Because no limit is placed on the number of futures or options contracts that can be created, open interest not only provides information about each contract month's liquidity, but also whether players are buying or selling. It is often plotted along with volume on daily price charts.

Although more complex ways of looking at volume and open interest exist, the traditional view holds that high volume and rising open interest is bullish if prices rose that day because it means new long positions were initiated. In contrast, high volume and rising open interest on a down day signifies newly opened short positions and is considered bearish.

You don't even have to guess who's doing what if you pay attention to the *Commitments of Traders* report released every two weeks by the Commodity Futures Trading Commission (www.cftc.gov). The data is generated daily by brokerage firms, who are required to report the status of open positions held at their firms, broadly broken down into reportable and non-reportable positions. A report for futures contracts is released every second Friday, with one that combines futures and options on futures released the following Monday. Previous reports are available to 1986 on the CFTC web site.

In order to keep tabs on those whose positions may threaten market integrity, a level of open positions is established for each market in the United States above which individual holders are identified to the government. These reportable positions are further broken down into commercial and noncommercial categories. Generally, the nonreportable positions are considered to be those held by small speculators, and the noncommercial reportable positions are thought to belong to managed futures funds.

Cycles and Elliott Wave

The idea that the stock market moves in broad cycles, or seasonals, from months to years to decades stems from research that has extended at least as far back as the start of the British stock market in the 1780s. (Some researchers have pieced together information to create a chart of prices that starts before the turn of the last millennium, or Y1K if it were to be identified in the current vernacular.)

Of the long-term stock market cycles, there is focus on 72 years, 60 years, and 55 years. The latter is presumed to be related to the Kondratieff economic cycle of 54 years identified by Russian economist Nikolai Kondratieff in the mid-1920s. From there is a jump to a midlength cycle of about 18 years, three of which would complete a 54-year cycle. Coming from the other direction, cycle analysts look at four-year cycles that tend to combine into the larger 18-year pattern. The four-year cycle is made up of smaller phases that tend to be a little less than two years. On an annual basis, evidence shows that stocks perform their worst from August through October and do their best from November through the following January.

Analysts also look at a four-year presidential cycle, in which the third year of a U.S. president's term supposedly is positive for the stock market. Another cyclic indicator looks to the last digit of a year for similar market behavior; for example, years ending in 7 typically are bearish for stocks. Finally, football fans can place their stock market and Super Bowl bets at the same time. The Super Bowl Predictor, which calls for a rise in the stock market if an original National Football League team wins the Super Bowl, was 28 for 32 through 1998.

The Elliott Wave Principle, first publicly outlined in 1939 by its creator Ralph N. Elliott, is founded on the similarities between nature and market behavior. The bullish pattern of three upwaves interrupted by two corrective waves is corrected in its entirety by a three-wave (down, up, down) pattern. A bearish pattern is the reverse, with three downwaves separated by two corrective upwaves or sideways patterns; the bear-market correction comes with a three-wave (up, down, up) pattern. These wave patterns repeat according to any time frame, from minutes to decades, often in similar mathematical relationships. The ability to program the extensive number of rules about applying the Elliott Wave Principle into computer software has broadened the reach of this somewhat esoteric market approach.

Dow Theory

Even though Charles Dow, inventor of the DJIA, never used the phrase *Dow Theory*, the analytical system credited to him stems from editorials he published in *The Wall Street Journal* from 1899 through 1902. The Dow Theory, as championed by *Journal* editor William Peter Hamilton from 1908 to 1929, held that Charles Dow focused on the interaction between the DJIA and the Dow Jones

Transportation Average. Specifically, the transports must confirm the direction of the industrials in order for the latter to continue its trend. Other considerations include trading volume, the move's duration, and the phase in which the signal occurred. Dow recognized the market moved within three orbits (long, medium, and short) and that a bull market went through three distinct phases before topping.

Hamilton's most famous market call concerning the Dow Theory came just days before the October 1929 stock market crash. Hamilton wrote an editorial, "A Turn in the Tide," in which he noted, "The twenty railroad stocks on Wednesday, October 23, confirmed a bearish indication given by the industrial two days before." He concluded, "Together the averages gave the signal for a bear market in stocks."[1]

3

STOCK INDEX PLAYER SHEET

In baseball, you can't tell the players without a scorecard, and the same holds true for stock index trading. Three main groups of players exist in stock index futures and options—individual investors, institutional investors, and professional traders. Obviously, all of them are participating in order to benefit in some way, but the motivations vary, and that's what we'll look at in this chapter.

Floor traders say there's nothing like the information they get from watching player interaction in the pits. They see which brokerage firms or brokers handle orders that can move the market and try to figure out what type of clients they represent. (Customers remain anonymous except to the firm through which they do business.) Is it fund business coming into the market? Small speculators? Institutions? Knowing who's doing what is an important piece of the floor trading puzzle.

Putting those pieces together is harder when you're not on the trading floor. However, electronic trading systems often show pending orders on either side of the market in an effort to bring transparency to users. For U.S. markets, the CFTC reports on percent holdings of different types of traders every two weeks in its *Commitments of Traders* report. It's not quite like being there, but the figures do provide a sense of who was in the market at the time and may provide insight into how those positions have changed when compared with market action since then.

INDIVIDUAL INVESTORS

It's probably fair to assume that most individuals trading stock index futures contracts are in it to score big, be part of the excitement, or experience the thrill of outguessing the market. If they're bullish, they take a long position. If they're bearish, they're short. If they're wrong, they're gone. These types of traders are motivated by volatility (the faster the market moves, the more potential for profit), the amount of initial margin required to trade a contract, and ease and quality of execution. They may trade on news or on technical signals.

Individual investors who are a bit more cautious may be drawn to the options on futures contracts. In options, they can eliminate the dreaded margin call by buying a call, or put, or reduce the amount of upfront money required by spreading two options.

The opposite of individuals who are speculating on the market's next move are those who use futures or options to hedge their stock portfolios or index mutual fund holdings. These participants may be selective in when they place a short position in futures or options in order to not lose any upside potential in their underlying holdings.

It is estimated that about 5 to 10% of all trading volume on U.S. futures exchanges originates with individual investors. It may be that this group of traders follows the trend toward day-trading that the securities industry has experienced as a result of an explosion in online brokers and easy accessibility to information on the Internet.

INSTITUTIONAL INVESTORS

Institutional investors, such as pension funds and mutual funds, use the stock index futures and options markets as one of many tools at their disposal to prudently manage their stock investments. Indeed, one of the biggest benefits of trading stock index products is that they allow these users to make subtle changes in strategy without disrupting the core stock portfolio.

Leaders in the futures and options industries were thrilled in 1997 when the short-short rule for mutual funds was repealed, which made it easier for mutual funds to use stock index derivatives. The short-short rule, enacted as part of the Internal Revenue Code in 1936, said that a mutual fund's entire gross income would be taxed if it earned more than 30% of that income from instruments held for less than 90 days. Because most derivatives trades tend to be held for less than 90 days, the short-short rule was an effective barrier to extensive use by mutual funds.

Here are some of the ways that institutional investors use stock index futures and options:

- **Asset Allocation.** Stock index futures and options make it easy for fund managers to adjust their stock asset allocation. They are quick, cheap, and easily reversible. Suppose that a manager had 50% of the fund's money in stocks and wanted to increase it to 60%. Instead of actually buying the stocks, the manager could establish a long position with stock index futures or options, liquidating some of the contracts or adding to them to further tweak the percentage exposure.

- **Sector Exposure.** Adjusting a portfolio's weight among certain market sectors, such as large-cap versus small-cap stocks, or even among countries or regions, is handled similarly to the asset allocation situation described previously. Based on a core physical portfolio, a manager can adjust exposure to certain market segments with stock index products. To increase exposure, a manager would establish a long position; to decrease exposure, a manager would establish a short position. If desired, the positions would be lifted when the actual stock adjustments were completed.

- **Hedging.** This strategy is the all-time classic use for futures markets. In a portfolio manager's world, it typically means establishing a short stock index futures or options position in expectation of a market downturn. The strategy enables the manager to keep the portfolio of stocks intact but protects the holdings from overall market losses. If the stock market declines, the short stock index position likely will be profitable and will offset some of the losses incurred by the portfolio.

- **Equitize Cash.** Equity fund managers use stock index futures as synthetic exposure to stocks when they equitize the cash in their portfolios resulting from the fund's regular cash holdings, dividend flow, or net inflows. In anticipation of cash inflows that eventually will be deployed directly into the stock market, managers who buy stock index products don't miss out on the market's interim gains. On the flip side, managers can use short positions in stock indexes to get ready for an unusually large redemption without taking the risk of moving too much money into cash and, thus, underperforming the index benchmark. Both of these tactics help eliminate the cash drag on a stock portfolio, which can occur when not all funds are exposed to an asset class.

- **Yield Enhancement.** A manager with a portfolio of stocks can attempt to boost its return by writing covered-call options on the appropriate stock index futures contract. The risk is that the option will be exercised, and the manager will be short the index futures contract at the option's strike price. The reward is complete retention of the premium taken in if the options are not exercised. This strategy is particularly attractive when the outlook is for a sideways market or one in which option volatilities appear to be too high.

- **Synthetic Indexing.** This approach is a substitute for indexing a portfolio to a particular stock index, a strategy that demands exact duplication of the index's holdings and weights. Instead, managers can buy stock index futures, which automatically reflect any changes in index components or weight changes, and still earn interest on the cash that would have been used to buy stocks.

PROFESSIONAL TRADERS

Professional traders are in the stock index markets for one reason: to make money. They seek to buy low and sell high, or sell high and buy low, it makes no difference to them which they do first. These traders have invested a lot of time and money into technology and talent to make sure that they're on the cutting edge.

Locals or Market-Makers

Whether these traders stand on a trading floor or sit in front of a computer screen, their job is to buy and sell quickly, making perhaps no more than the bid/ask spread on any particular trade. They can afford to do that because these traders typically are members of the exchange on which they trade, or have purchased trading rights there, which means that their out-of-pocket trading costs are miniscule in comparison to those of the average investor.

These scalpers, who tend to make the skinniest of profits on a trade, are the main providers of a market's highly sought-after liquidity because of their ability to take the other side of any trade that comes at them and then get rid of it like a hot potato if necessary. Trading by this group typically accounts for the bulk of trading volume on an exchange given that they open and close positions so quickly.

Arbitragers

Arbitragers make their living finding out-of-line relationships between stock index futures contracts and their underlying basket of stocks and making the trade that brings the relationship back into balance. These traders not only watch a contract's fair value like a hawk, they also are part of the group known as *program traders*, who execute entire baskets of stocks in a matter of seconds.

If a stock index futures contract value is greater than its calculated fair value, arbitragers sell futures and simultaneously buy the underlying basket of stocks. If the futures are less than fair value, they buy futures and sell stocks. In either case, the reward is an incremental return over simply buying and holding the stocks that is greater than the arbitrager's cost of money and transaction fees. (Arbitragers instead may either maintain an inventory of stocks that match the indexes they trade or execute smaller stock baskets with a high correlation to the underlying index.)

This sort of arbitrage took a lot of heat during the 1987 stock market crash on the presumption that it increased market volatility. As a result, the New York Stock Exchange imposed Rule 80-A, or collar rule, that limits arbitrage activity. The rule required arbitragers who wanted to trade stock baskets to wait for an uptick to sell or a downtick to buy once the DJIA had moved a certain amount during the day. The initial collar trigger was a 50-point move in the DJIA, which was not changed until 1998, to a 2% daily move in the Index.

The NYSE tracks the amount of program trading (and index arbitrage trading as a subset of that group) on a weekly basis. In 1997 and 1998, program trading accounted for at least 10% of the average daily volume each week and as much as 29%. Index arbitrage during the weeks of futures and option contract expirations ranged from roughly 18% to 33% of all program trading during those two years. During the week that June 1999 stock index futures and options expired, index arbitrage was nearly 17% of all program trading, which equaled about 25% of the average daily volume at the exchange.

Managed Futures Funds and Hedge Funds

Managers of futures funds are the institutional traders of the futures markets, holding portfolios of market positions rather than a portfolio of stocks. As of early 1999, these managed futures funds controlled about $35 billion in customer assets, which are deployed in futures markets around the world. Many managed funds use technically based trend-following systems, and their orders can congregate around certain points. As a result, fund trading can have a big impact over a short period of time and then vaporize.

Hedge funds, originally created because of their ability to short stock in a portfolio, have expanded their reach and are available in many different styles. Some of the most aggressive take outright speculative positions in the futures markets. It is estimated that hedge funds control perhaps 8 to 10 times as much in assets as managed futures funds but have a much broader plate from which to select investments.

4

WAYS TO USE STOCK INDEX FUTURES

There are as many ways to trade stock index futures as there are traders. However, there are some broad categories of how you can use stock index futures and options, depending on whether you trade to make a profit or consider them part of a do-it-yourself money-manager toolbox. And, of course, you might want to do both depending on the current market situation.

Ideas for specific trading strategies abound in magazines, books, and seminars and are far too numerous to examine in detail here. Instead, this chapter focuses on how using stock index futures markets may benefit you and your portfolio in the broad investment scheme.

SPECULATE

Taking a position based on your market outlook is the most common way of using stock index futures and options. Go long if you're bullish. Go short if you're bearish. It's as easy as that. Options add another dimension, especially if you're expecting the market to move sideways or to become volatile.

Bullish

Bullish strategies tend to pay off when the market rises. With futures, you buy a contract when you expect the market to go up. With options, you can buy a call option (payment of premium due in full up-front) or sell a put option (margined like a futures position). The long futures position and short put position both carry unlimited risk if the market declines. Buying a call option limits your risk to the amount of premium paid but detracts from potential profits by the same amount. In a hypothetical stock index contract with a value of 100 and a contract multiplier of $250, a 10-point move in the index would produce the following result, excluding commission costs:

Buy 1 futures	100
Sell 1 futures	110
Profit	10 index points x $250 = $2,500

Bearish

Bearish strategies tend to pay off when the market falls. With futures, you sell a contract when you expect the market to drop. With options, you can buy a put option or sell a call. A short futures or short call position carries unlimited risk if the market rises. Meanwhile, the long put position limits your risk to the amount of the premium paid but detracts from potential profits by the same amount.

Sell 1 futures	100
Buy 1 futures	90
Profit	10 index points x $250 = $2,500

Sideways

Writing, or selling, call or put options is just the tip of the iceberg when it comes to how you might design a strategy for a generally sideways market. A wide variety of option combinations can be constructed, which may exactly suit your expectations in terms of both market action and timing.

If you're looking for the market to remain stable, with a downward bias, you might write a call option and take in the premium as income. You keep the entire premium if the futures contract expires below your option's strike price. If, instead, you're looking for a stable environment with an upward bias, write a put option. You keep the entire premium if the futures contract expires above your option's strike price. In both these cases, remember that the exposure to potential loss is unlimited, just as in a futures contract, and that you are obligated to accept a futures contract at your option's strike price (short futures with a short call, long futures with a short put) if the option is exercised.

Volatile

Options are tailor-made for volatile market environments, and an option straddle enables you to take a position that should benefit from that condition. If you expect volatility to continue at high levels or to increase, a long straddle should do the trick. That trade involves buying a put and call at the same strike price, with the total premium, in points, paid initially determining how much the market must move (up or down) in order for the position to break even. Your risk is limited to the amount of total premium paid.

CAPITALIZE ON RELATIVE MOVEMENT

Instead of constantly reweighting a portfolio of stocks to reflect your opinion about the performance of one sector versus another, spreading stock indexes that represent those sectors is a quicker and cheaper way to reach the same goal. And, in some cases, you may be able to spread the indexes at a reduced margin rate versus an outright position in either leg.

Spreads

In futures trading of any sort, spreading one contract against another is a popular way to reduce both market risk and up-front margin requirements. It's safe to say that if an exchange offers a reduced spread margin between two stock index futures contracts, there is presumed to be reduced risk by holding opposite positions in two contracts as opposed to an outright position in just one. That's because the trade is based on how the price *relationship* between the two contracts behaves, not the outright movement. Whether exchanges establish spread margin breaks with products on other exchanges is up to each institution. Look to their web sites for current information.

For example, the Kansas City Board of Trade quotes spread margins (for its half of the spread trade) for several contracts that might be spread versus the broad-based Value Line Index, including the DJIA, S&P 500 Index, S&P 400 Index, NYSE Composite, and Russell 2000. The Mini Value Line adds a margin break for spreads against the E-mini S&P 500 Index.

At the Chicago Mercantile Exchange, you can spread the U.S. S&P 500 against Japan's Nikkei 225, because both contracts are listed on the same exchange. Likewise, spread rates are quoted among the several U.S. indexes listed at the CME.

Remember that the minimums set by exchanges are what their clearing members must maintain with the clearinghouse. It is very likely that your margin requirements will be higher than the exchange minimums. Ask your broker for the current rates at your firm. Also note that trading a spread will entail paying two commissions to your broker, one for each contract.

Initiating one of these spread positions enables you to capitalize on how you think one group of stocks will move compared with another. For example, if you thought small-cap stocks were going to make a comeback relative to large-cap stocks, you could buy the Russell 2000 Index contract and sell the Russell 1000. If you're looking for value-oriented stocks to gain, you could buy the S&P 500/BARRA Value Index and sell either the growth half of the S&P 500, the S&P 500/BARRA Growth Index, or the entire S&P 500.

A calendar, or time spread, may be used to capture the impact of a changing interest rate environment on stock index futures. Time to expiration is the important factor in this type of spread, and traders make decisions keyed on how interest rates may affect the most deferred contract month in the spread, because that contract month will have the most time to reflect the change. Therefore, traders would buy the deferred contract and sell the nearby contract if they expected rising interest rates; they would sell the deferred and buy the nearby if they expected rates to fall.

January Effect

One of the most widely studied seasonal effects in the stock market, the January Effect, has been easy to trade since the advent of stock index futures contracts. First, research that looked at stock prices from 1904 to 1974 showed that nearly 33% of any stock's average annual return came in January.[1] Second, small-cap U.S. stocks gain on large-cap U.S. stocks during January, even while both sets are making gains. This has occurred 78% of the time from 1925 through 1998.[2] Similar tendencies have been noted in the Canadian, U.K., Australian and Taiwan markets, although in Taiwan the effect begins at the end of the lunar new year.[3]

To capitalize on this tendency, stock index futures traders can buy an index that is sensitive to small-cap stocks, such as the Value Line or the Russell 2000, and sell an index weighted with large-cap components, such as the DJIA, S&P 500, the Russell 1000, or the NYSE Composite. Research by the Chicago Board of Trade found that the process of selling the DJIA, which tends to have a high average market capitalization for its component stocks, and buying an index whose stocks have a lower average market capitalization, even the S&P 500, also benefited from the seasonal tendency.[4]

A few explanations can be found for the phenomenon. First, individual investors have a tendency to sell losing stocks at year-end in order to offset gains in other holdings and, thus, reduce their potential tax liability. Because small-cap stocks tend to be riskier holdings than large-cap stocks, they are more prone to be the ones that show losses. In addition, individuals tend to buy stocks at the start of a new year after the holiday bustle has quieted, and they may be looking for bargains, such as the depressed small-cap stocks that came under pressure during the preceding month. Second, institutional portfolio managers may rebalance their portfolios at year-end; especially in a bull market, rebalancing may mean lightening the load of large-cap stocks and small-cap losers and then buying other small-cap issues later. Third, mutual fund managers also tend to sell their losers to minimize taxes as well as window dress the portfolio before its components are reported to shareholders. However, this type of tax-loss selling may be more prone to occur before October 31, the deadline for funds to distribute capital gains.

In the late 1990s, some buzz was beginning to be heard that the January Effect was turning into the December Effect as investors become increasingly aware of the January Effect and try to get a jump on it. Depending on the report, small-cap gains versus the large-cap stocks reached their maximum either during the second half of December or from mid-December to mid-January.

PROTECT VALUE OF STOCK PORTFOLIO OR MUTUAL FUND HOLDINGS

If you own a carefully assembled portfolio of stocks and/or mutual funds, stock index futures and options can help protect the value of your investments if the stock market declines. Assuming that you want to remain invested in the stock market, the advantage to using futures or options in this situation is that you don't need to sell the stocks or your mutual funds. This aspect of stock index futures trading may be especially important for those with retirement funds tied to stocks that would not have to be disturbed from a possibly aggressive growth structure.

The least risky way to handle this self-made insurance policy is to buy index puts on the stock index that most closely matches the character of your stock holdings. For example, if you hold only blue-chip U.S. stocks, you might use the DJIA options. If you own an S&P 500 Index mutual fund, puts on the S&P 500 or E-mini S&P 500 futures contracts would be most appropriate. Buying puts on a broad-based index might be considered a hedge against a portfolio of varied mutual funds. Buying puts limits your potential loss to the amount you paid in premium, which is figured by multiplying the option's price by the contract multiplier. A short futures position, with an upfront cost equal to your broker's initial margin requirement, is riskier because unlimited potential for loss exists if the market rises past your entry point.

For either long puts or short futures, start by comparing the value of your holdings to the contract value. In options, the contract value is figured by multiplying the strike price by the contract multiplier; in futures, the contract value is the contract month's index value multiplied by the contract multiplier. Then, decide how much of your portfolio you want to protect and how many options or futures contracts will cover that amount. For example, if your index is at 100 and has a $250 multiplier, each futures contract has a contract value of $25,000. If you had a portfolio worth $100,000, you could hedge all of it with four futures contracts or just 25% of it with a single contract. To use options requires figuring out how much an option moves in relation to the futures contract, a figure called delta. For example, an at-the-money option with a delta of 0.5 means you would need eight option contracts to do the job of four futures contracts. Don't forget to close out your futures or options position when you no longer are concerned about a market decline and don't want to protect the value of your stock holdings.

PUT ANTICIPATED FUNDS TO WORK IN THE MARKET

Here's the situation: You expect a bull market in stocks and know that the next time you'll have a big chunk of money to buy shares is months away, perhaps when you get your annual bonus at work. Instead of missing out on those potential gains in the stock market, you can take a long position in stock index futures that is fairly equal in value to the amount of investment funds you've earmarked. Once you've got the money in hand and made the stock purchases, you would close out the futures or options position. Of course, if the market falls, your futures or options position may lose money, but you then will be able to buy the cash market stocks at their current lower prices.

Going long futures essentially locks in the index value at which you became invested, even though the actual transactions have not yet been made. In futures industry lingo, this move is known as an *anticipatory hedge*, a strategy often used by institutions who expect a certain amount of funding at various times of the year and use futures or options to make the investment early.

REALLOCATE ASSETS

Just like pension and mutual fund managers, you, too, can use stock index futures to reallocate your investment assets, an approach that saves money versus buying and selling physical assets and doesn't undo all the time you spent in constructing your portfolio. Taking a long position in the index of your choice—buying futures, buying a call option, or selling a put option—increases your exposure to the stock market without disrupting your portfolio of stocks and bonds; in the institutional world, this is known as an *overlay*. Taking a short position—selling futures, buying puts, or selling calls—decreases your exposure to the stock market versus the other asset classes in your portfolio.

With a synthetic overlay, exiting the index futures or options position will bring your portfolio back to its initial weightings or asset allocations. If you decide to reweight your cash portfolio, you would exit the index futures or options position once you had completed the changes in your cash market or underlying portfolio.

DIVERSIFY STOCK HOLDINGS

The ease with which you can make a stock index futures or options trade in many different types of indexes around the world makes diversifying your stock holdings a breeze.

Sectors

If you want to emphasize or de-emphasize your investment in certain sectors of the market, you can look to indexes that are designed to represent a segment of the market—for example, futures and options trade on U.S. indexes that are geared toward blue-chip stocks, large-capitalized stocks, mid-cap stocks, small-cap stocks, value stocks, growth stocks, technology stocks, and Internet stocks. Diversification between large-cap and mid-cap stocks is available on the U.K. market, while a more subtle distinction in the Japanese market can be made between blue-chip and large-cap stocks.

Assuming you own a broad-based mutual fund or a portfolio of stocks that closely tracks the broad-based indexes, establishing a long position in a different type of stock index futures or options contract essentially increases your exposure to that segment of the market. A short position would let you de-emphasize that segment's influence on your portfolio.

Global

Most non-U.S. stock index contracts are designed to represent overall stock market movement in a country or region. Thus, you can gain exposure to a certain market by taking a long position in stock index futures or options. (The contract multiplier for most indexes is priced in the local currency, which also introduces currency risk for participants whose investment funds are not normally in that currency.) If you already are exposed to the global stock market, through a global mutual fund for example, you could increase or decrease your exposure to certain countries or regions with the appropriate stock index futures or options.

ENHANCE PORTFOLIO RETURN

You might already be familiar with the strategy of writing covered calls against individual stocks in your portfolio, in order to earn extra return. The same strategy can be used with stock indexes. Whether you own an individual stock, a stock index portfolio, or a long futures contract, writing a covered call is a way of saying that you would be willing to sell the underlying position at the option's strike price. The premium you take in by writing a call option is additional income beyond the profit you would expect to take if you sold the underlying position.

Selling a call option on a stock index futures contract would cover either a long futures position in the same index, a portfolio of stocks, or a mutual fund that tracks the futures index. An American-style option carries the risk that it could be exercised at any time until expiration. A European-style option can be exercised only on the contract's expiration day. Once again, the short option position carries unlimited risk just as a futures contract.

5

KNOW YOUR STOCK INDEX: NORTH AMERICA

Not all stock indexes are created equal. They represent varying numbers and types of stocks. They are calculated in different ways. They are targeted at a particular type of investor. That's why it is critical for you to understand how the index you are trading is designed and calculated. The design specifies which stocks are included in the index and how it may be categorized, for example, blue-chip or broad-based. How the index is calculated determines which stocks have the most influence in the index's movement.

Most indexes are capitalization-weighted, which means that the highest-priced stocks with the most outstanding shares will have the most influence on index movement. The S&P 500 Index is one of the best-known *market-cap* indexes. In this type of index, you can train your ears and eyes to focus on the most influential stocks in the index to get a feel for how the broader index is moving. Sometimes, the number used as the outstanding shares portion of the equation is adjusted to reflect only those shares that are freely available for trade, ignoring those shares held in solid hands, such as individuals who own the company. A modified-capitalization index seeks to limit the influence of the largest stocks in the index, which otherwise would dominate the entire index, and typically sets a limit on the percentage weight of the largest stock or a group of stocks.

A *price-weighted* index sums the prices of each stock in the index and equates the total to a designated index starting value through use of a divisor. In the United States, the DJIA and PSE Technology Index are price-weighted. The only other actively traded, price-weighted index is the Nikkei 225 Average of Japanese stocks. In these indexes, the stocks with the highest price are the most influential. Be aware that if a stock splits, its price is adjusted to maintain the same market capitalization with the new number of shares available, and it then will have less weight in a price-weighted index.

The third variation on index calculation is *equal-weighting*, which means that each stock's percentage weight in the index is equal, and all stocks have an equal influence on index movement. The Value Line Index at the KCBT is the lone example of this type of weighting scheme, which tends to dampen volatility.

Tables of the top ten influential stocks in each index, which accompany the indexes' descriptions, are snapshots of which stocks carried the most weight in the indexes on the date indicated. For indexes that are capitalization-weighted, the percentage is determined by a stock's number of market shares, used in determining its market influence, multiplied by price; for the price-weighted indexes, the percentage is determined by the stock's price.

This chapter and the next two chapters group indexes by region—North America, Asia/Pacific, and Europe—and by exposure to a market segment or country. If you're trading U.S. stock indexes, for example, you can choose from broad-based, large-cap, mid-cap, small-cap, technology, growth, value, or Internet indexes. Non-U.S. stock indexes typically are designed to provide exposure to the broad market. For Japanese stocks, you can choose your definition of market from three indexes (Nikkei 225, Nikkei 300, and TOPIX) trading on four exchanges in three countries. The Nikkei 225 and Nikkei 300 represent 225 and 300 stocks, respectively, while TOPIX covers more than 1,300 listings on the Tokyo Stock Exchange. The United Kingdom is the only other stock market with multiple offerings, with both a broad-based and mid-cap index trading in London.

The latest hotbed of activity is in developing indexes that represent the broad European markets or just those countries that are members of the *European Economic and Monetary Union* (EMU) and have adopted the euro as their common currency. Since mid-1998, more than a dozen European-oriented indexes have been developed and listed by exchanges in Europe and the United States.

U.S. BROAD-BASED STOCK INDEXES

Hundreds of stocks comprise a broad-based index, which is geared toward providing an overall picture of the stock market's health. The smallest U.S. broad-based index is the S&P 500, with 500 blue-chip stocks. The Value Line Index tracks about 1,600 stocks that are a cross-section of large-, mid-, and small-cap stocks that trade on the NYSE, Nasdaq, American Stock Exchange (AMEX), and in Canada. The NYSE Composite Index represents every common stock listed on the NYSE, a figure that equaled 3,114 at year-end 1998.

These three broad-based U.S. stock indexes—NYSE Composite, S&P 500, and Value Line—are listed on an equal number of U.S. futures exchanges. However, two to three listings are on each index, each with a different multiplier so that the contract value might appeal to different groups of users. For example, small versions of each index were introduced after the original contract was established to more closely match the portfolio size of individual investors.

NYSE Composite

The broadest of the broad stock indexes available for trading is the NYSE Composite, which represents every common stock traded on the NYSE. At the end of December 1998, 3,114 common stocks were listed on NYSE's total market capitalization equaled $10.9 trillion in four industry classifications (1,639 industrials, 1,136 financials, 287, utilities and 52 transportation).

The NYSE Composite also is the broadest in terms of its contract sizes, with three to choose from depending on the multiplier that best suits an investor. The Regular contract, launched on May 6, 1982, has a multiplier of $500 times the Index. The NYSE Large Composite Index contract, designed for institutional investors and launched in September 1997, has a multiplier of $1,000 while the NYSE Small Composite Index contract, launched in June 1998 for smaller traders and investors, uses a $250 multiplier.

Index at a Glance.

Index	NYSE Composite
Exchange	New York Board of Trade
Weighting	Capitalization
Ticker Symbol	YS (Small); YX (Regular); YL (Large)
Contract Value (Dec. 31, 1998)	595.81 x $250 = $148,952.50 (YS)
	595.81 x $500 = $279,905 (YX)
	595.81 x $1,000 = $595,810 (YL)
Clearinghouse	New York Clearing Corporation
Regulator	Commodity Futures Trading Commission
Web Site Information	www.nyce.com
	www.nyse.com

Understanding the Index. A capitalization-weighted index, the NYSE Composite is most affected by price movement in the largest stocks on the exchange. The 10 largest stocks in the index at year-end 1998 are shown in Table 5.1. These 10 stocks equaled 18.6% of the index weighting at year-end 1998. The latest listing of these top 10 stocks, including average daily volume, is available on the NYSE web site. A monthly chart of the NYSE Composite since 1980 is shown in Figure 5.1.

NYSE Composite Futures. The NYSE Composite was among the first stock index futures contracts to be listed, opening on May 6, 1982, at the New York Futures Exchange (NYFE), a subsidiary of the NYSE. The futures options contract opened less than a year later, on January 28, 1983. (An option on the cash index, with a $100 multiplier, trades at the Chicago Board Options Exchange.) The contract now is part of the offering at the New York Cotton Exchange, which acquired NYFE in 1993, and is now a division of the New York Board of Trade. The Regular contract multiplier is $500.

Until mid-1998, the NYSE Composite traded only from 9:30 A.M. to 4:15 P.M. in an open outcry session. As of June 26, 1998, the hours expanded to bring trading to nearly 20 hours a day during the business week. The exchange added a second open outcry session in New York that runs from 4:45 P.M. to 10 P.M. Monday through Thursday and 7 P.M. to 10 P.M. on Sunday. (During Daylight Savings Time, this session is extended one hour, ending at 11 P.M.) After a five-hour hiatus, open outcry trading starts once again in Dublin, Ireland, on the trading floor of FINEX, another NYCE subsidiary exchange. In

TABLE 5.1 Top 10 Stocks in NYSE Composite
(December 31, 1998)

Rank	Company	Market Capitalization (billion dollars)	Percent Weight
1	General Electric Company (GE)	379,045	3.5
2	The Coca-Cola Company (KO)	231,051	2.1
3	Merck & Co., Inc. (MRK)	219,172	2.0
4	Exxon Corporation (XON)	218,129	2.0
5	Wal-Mart Stores, Inc. (WMT)	187,308	1.7
6	International Business Machines Corp. (IBM)	181,089	1.6
7	Pfizer, Inc. (PFE)	173,019	1.6
8	Philip Morris Companies Inc. (MO)	150,119	1.4
9	Bristol-Myers Squibb Company (BMY)	146,204	1.4
10	AT&T Corp. (T)	136,825	1.3

Source: New York Stock Exchange

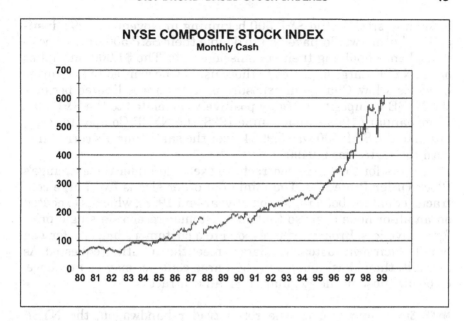

FIGURE 5.1 NYSE Composite Stock Index
Source: CRB-Bridge Information

Dublin, the hours are 8 A.M. to 2:15 P.M. (3 A.M. to 9:15 A.M. in New York). This move made the NYSE Composite the first U.S. index to trade in an open outcry forum on a foreign facility.

Since late 1997, volume and open interest figures for the NYSE Composite have been adjusted to reflect the addition of both the Large and Small contracts. From the day the Large contract was introduced until the Small contract was listed on June 26, 1998, volume for the Large contract was reported in terms of the Regular contract, or on a 2-for-1 basis. As of June 26, 1998, all volume figures in the NYSE Composite are reported in Small contract equivalents. Thus, each contract traded in the Regular Index counts for two contracts of volume while each Large contract traded counts for four contracts of volume.

NYSE Large. The NYSE Large Composite Index has the same contract specifications of the original contract, with the exception of the contract multiplier, which is $1,000 or double the original. The minimum tick of 0.05 points equals a minimum move of $50 per tick. There is no futures option contract for the Large.

The NYSE Large contract is aimed directly at institutional users. It opened in September 1997 and gained support early in its trading life because of the halving of the S&P 500 futures contract multiplier at the end of October 1997. In order to protect an equal amount of stock in the S&P 500 beginning in November 1997, institutional users would have had to double their S&P 500 futures positions, hence doubling their commission costs. The $1,000 multiplier of the NYSE Large appealed to those users who wanted to keep overhead costs low. Change in exposure protection was limited because the NYSE Composite is highly positively correlated to the S&P 500. From January 1996 through June 1998, the NYSE Composite correlation to the S&P 500 was 0.9924; over the same time, its correlation with the DJIA was 0.9490.

Orders for the Large contract are executed under the exchange's Block Order Procedure. The minimum order size is five Large contracts (equal to about $3 million at year-end 1998), which is executed on an all-or-none basis so that the customer receives a single price for all five lots. Brokers who respond to a customer's bid, or offer, can bundle their own customer orders to meet the quantity requested. As a result, the bid/ask quotes in the Large contract may be at, above, or below those in the Regular or Small contract.

NYSE Small. Jumping on the retail trader bandwagon, the NYSE Small contract opened on June 26, 1998. Its multiplier is half that of the original contract, or $250, with each tick worth $12.50. The Small contract trades beside the Regular and Large contracts during the same trading hours. No futures option contract is available for the Small.

NYSE Small contracts can be offset against either the Regular or the Large contract. Thus, two Small contracts can offset one Regular contract, although it takes four Small contracts to offset a single Large contract.

Calculating the Index. The NYSE Composite Index comprises every common stock traded on the NYSE, which at year-end 1998 equaled 3,114 stocks. The NYSE Composite is calculated and disseminated by the exchange every 15 seconds when the exchange is open for trading.

In figuring the Index value, the market value of each stock is determined by multiplying current price by the number of shares listed. Then, all individual market values are totaled, and the sum is divided by the *adjusted base market value*, the result of which is multiplied by 50, which was close to the average price of all NYSE-listed stocks on the base date of December 21, 1965. The NYSE Composite has been published by the NYSE since 1966.

Adjustments in the NYSE Composite Index are made for the following:

- New listings (including spin-offs where additional value is created)
- Delistings

- Acquisition of a previously unlisted company by a listed firm
- Quarterly dividend reinvestment plans or employee stock purchase plans

Adjustments are *not* made for the following:

- Mergers when there was no change in aggregate market value
- Spin-offs of listed companies when there was no change in aggregate market value
- Stock splits and stock dividends
- Shares reacquired by a corporation and held as treasury stock

Standard & Poor's 500

The S&P 500 Index is the benchmark used by portfolio managers around the world for judging their performance against the U.S. stock market, with about $700 billion linked to it in index funds. Introduced in 1957 by Standard & Poor's Corporation, a financial ratings, research, and news organization, the Index was designed to represent the market value of 500 leading companies in leading industries. Since 1968, the S&P 500 has been the only measure of stock market performance in the Index of Leading Economic Indicators.

Index at a Glance.

Index	S&P 500
Exchange	Chicago Mercantile Exchange
Weighting	Capitalization
Ticker Symbol	SP
Contract value (Dec. 31, 1998)	1229.23 x $250 = $307,307.50
Clearinghouse	CME Clearinghouse
Regulator	Commodity Futures Trading Commission
Web Site Information	www.cme.com
	www.spglobal.com
	www.advisorinsight.com

Understanding the Index. Due to its focus on leading companies in leading industries, the S&P 500 has evolved into an index of large-cap, blue-chip stocks. At the end of December 1998, the 500 stocks in the index had a total market value of $9.9 trillion, with individual market capitalizations of stocks ranging from $487 million to $346 billion. (The market value of all 3,382 companies listed on the NYSE at year-end 1998 was $10.9 trillion.)

Industrial stocks, numbering 380 at the end of December 1998, accounted for 76% of the companies in the S&P 500. Financial companies were the second-most represented, totaling 71, or 14%. Utilities came in third with 39 companies, or 8%, while transportation firms numbered 10 and equaled 2% of the index listings. Of the 500 companies in the index, 92%, or 458, were listed on the NYSE. Another 40 traded on the Nasdaq while just two were listed at the AMEX. Look to the Standard & Poor's web site for the latest list of stocks in the S&P 500 stock index.

The highest priced stocks with the most outstanding shares will have the greatest influence on movement of the S&P 500 Index because it is weighted by market capitalization, or price times shares outstanding. Thus, a glance at the largest stocks in the Index, according to capitalization, can provide a quick insight into the S&P 500's current situation. At the end of December 1998, the following stocks, shown in Table 5.2, were the 10 largest in market capitalization in the S&P 500 Index and equaled 20.74% of the index total market value. A monthly chart of the S&P 500 since 1980 is shown in Figure 5.2.

S&P 500 Futures. The S&P 500 futures contract dominates stock index trading in the United States, regularly accounting for about 90% of all contracts traded on U.S. futures exchanges. Launched at the CME in April 1982 when the S&P 500 Index was 117, the futures contract value originally was determined by multiplying the Index by $500; in this example, the contract value would have been $58,500. Fifteen years later, the S&P 500 Index equaled 900, and the futures multiplier was halved to $250 to make the contract value more palatable to a wider group of participants. Still, a single contract under those parameters had a contract value of $225,000.

Standard & Poor's Corporation leased exclusive trading rights in futures and options on futures to the CME beginning in 1980, which specified that the CME pay the company $200,000 annually plus fees based on volume for those exclusive rights.[1] (Exclusive rights to trade options on the cash index belong to the Chicago Board Options Exchange.)

The S&P 500 contract was an early winner in the race to list stock index futures in the early 1980s. For starters, its timing was impeccable as it opened for trading just four months before the greatest bull market of the century began in August 1982. Most importantly, however, it appealed to institutional users, such as pen-

TABLE 5.2 Top 10 Stocks in S&P 500 Index
(December 31, 1998)

Rank	Stock	Market Capitalization (million dollars)	Percent Weight
1	Microsoft Corp. (MSFT)	345,827	3.48
2	General Electric (GE)	334,442	3.36
3	Intel Corp. (INTC)	197,643	1.99
4	Wal-Mart Stores (WMT)	183,466	1.85
5	Exxon Corp. (XON)	177,784	1.79
6	Merck & Co. (MRK)	175,905	1.77
7	International Business Machines (IBM)	172,383	1.73
8	Coca-Cola Co. (KO)	164,854	1.66
9	Pfizer, Inc. (PFE)	162,792	1.64
10	Cisco Systems (CSCO)	146,555	1.47

Source: Standard & Poor's Corporation

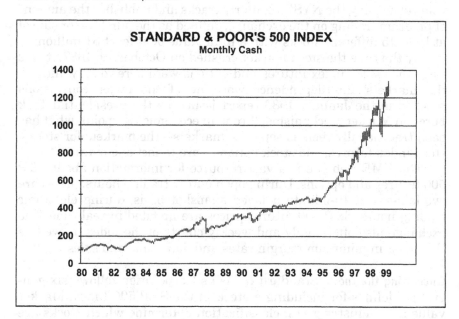

FIGURE 5.2   Standard & Poor's 500 Index
Source: CRB-Bridge Information

sion fund or mutual fund portfolio managers, whose performance was measured against that of the S&P 500 Index. These institutional players used the new instrument to establish a value for stock that had yet to be purchased in the underlying market, or to protect the entire portfolio against a market correction. In late 1998, about $700 billion was linked to the S&P 500 Index through index funds.

Portfolio insurance was the mid-1980s buzzword for the plan to establish a short position in stock index futures or options during a market decline in order to avoid disrupting the underlying portfolio of stocks. Many institutions used similar software designed to signal when to start selling, and when they all tried to execute the plan in October 1987 when the S&P 500 futures market was at a deep discount to the underlying index value, portfolio insurance earned a black eye. The big sell orders in the futures pit couldn't find immediate buyers and weighed even further on the index value, thus increasing the discount to cash and sending a negative signal as to the future value of stocks.

Other traders developed computer-assisted arbitrage programs that traded baskets of stocks against the futures contract when the values were out of line. This so-called form of *program trading* was controversial in the 1980s and cited as the source of excessive market volatility. Today, the NYSE regularly tracks and publishes the amount of program trading on the exchange, defined as the purchase or sale of at least 15 different stocks with a total value of at least $1 million.

By the time the stock market crashed on October 19, 1987, it was clear that stock index futures and options were here to stay. Indeed, the markets' interdependence was one of the major conclusions reached in the January 1988 report issued by the Presidential Task Force on Market Mechanisms, "From an economic viewpoint, what has been traditionally seen as separate markets—the markets for stocks, stock index futures, and stock options—are in fact one market."[2]

The CME web site is a vast resource for information about S&P 500 futures and options. During open outcry trading hours, prices are available on a 10-minute delayed snapshot basis; during electronic trading hours, S&P 500 futures prices are updated in real-time. The exchange also offers daily and weekly charts of the index as well as the latest in minimum margin rates and daily time and sales.

Calculating the Index Standard & Poor's Corporation follows six general guidelines for including a stock in the S&P 500 Index. Market value and industry group classification determine which stocks are the leaders in the field. A look at ownership of the outstanding shares ensures that companies in the index are not closely held ventures. Trading volume must be sufficient to ensure liquidity and efficient pricing. In order to keep turnover in the index low, Standard & Poor's analysts use fundamental analysis to determine whether the company is relatively stable. Finally, the stock of companies in emerging industries or new industry groups is screened regularly to see whether they meet the general guidelines for inclusion.

Standard & Poor's Corporation has sole responsibility in maintaining the S&P 500 Index and calculating the index value. Calculating the S&P 500 index requires multiplying each stock's price by the number of outstanding shares to obtain the stock's market value. All 500 market values are totaled and then compared to those of the base period (1941 to 1943 = 10) to derive the index value. S&P calculates the index continuously during the NYSE trading day and displays the values every 15 seconds. Modifications to the index due to stock splits or dividends, for example, are achieved through changing the index divisor, daily if necessary.

Stocks are removed from the index after merger, acquisition, leveraged buyout, or bankruptcy. Those that restructure are analyzed to determine whether they continue to meet the guidelines for inclusion. Also, a stock can be removed from the S&P 500 if it no longer is representative of its industry group. Announcements for changes in index stocks are made at 5:15 P.M., New York time, so as not to disrupt that day's official closing price for the stocks involved. In early 1999, the NYSE asked Standard & Poor's Corporation to consider adding/deleting stocks to the index as of the opening of trade rather than at the close.

E-mini S&P 500

The E-mini S&P 500 futures and options on futures contracts are based on the value of the S&P 500 stock index, just like the larger version of the contract trading at the CME. But, two main differences exist between the contracts, both of which are expressed in the term E-mini. First, the E-mini S&P 500 trades primarily on an electronic system. Second, the contract multiplier is $50, or just one-fifth the larger contract's size.

Index at a Glance.

Index	E-mini S&P 500
Exchange	Chicago Mercantile Exchange
Weighting	Capitalization
Ticker Symbol	ES
Contract Value (Dec. 31, 1998)	1229.12 x $50 = $61,461.50
Clearinghouse	CME Clearinghouse
Regulator	Commodity Futures Trading Commission
Web Site Information	www.cme.com
	www.spglobal.com
	www.advisorinsight.com

E-mini S&P 500 Futures. In mid-1997, launching a small, electronically traded version of a large, successful, open outcry contract was a daring move by the CME and one it would rather not have made. Indeed, plans to trade the E-mini gelled only because the exchange lost in its bid to gain trading rights to the DJIA, which were awarded to the CME's cross-town rival, the Chicago Board of Trade. To combat the Dow's appeal to individual investors, the CME decided to revamp its S&P 500 Index to target the retail trader. Not only did the CME create a smaller version of the S&P 500, but it also listed it for trading on a nearly 24-hour basis via its GLOBEX system, which until then had been used only for trading outside of open outcry hours. It was the first time in U.S. futures trading history that a contract traded simultaneously in both an electronic and open outcry platform. It also marked the futures industry's first use of a small-order routing and execution system.

Traders now could have access to the E-mini S&P 500 nearly every waking moment during the trading week. The only time the contract is closed is from 3:15 P.M. to 3:30 P.M., Monday through Thursday, and over the weekend from 3:15 P.M. Friday until 5:30 P.M. Sunday. Orders for both futures and options on futures of 30 contracts or less are matched, filled, and reported back to the customer by the GLOBEX trading system within seconds, which is a large part of the contract's appeal. In addition, the exchange posts real-time prices (including best bid, offer, and size of both) for the E-mini (as traded on GLOBEX, not in the pit) on the CME web site. Orders for more than 30 contracts are traded by open outcry during the S&P 500's regular trading hours of 8:30 A.M. to 3:15 P.M. and are filled on an all or none basis. That means brokers will fill the entire order at a single, specified price; no partial fills are allowed.

The E-mini was an instant success. Opening day volume on September 9, 1997, totaled 7,987 contracts, the best first-day volume of any currently traded CME product, including the S&P 500. By the turn of the year, it was called, "the fastest-growing index ever launched at the CME." Volume climbed steadily and averaged nearly 18,000 per day in 1998; open interest at the end of 1998 was about 9,600 contracts. After just 15 months of trading, the E-mini had become the third most actively traded futures contract at the CME, trailing only the larger version of the S&P 500 and eurodollars. It also was the third most active U.S. stock index contract in 1998, behind the S&P 500 futures contract and the option on the S&P 500 futures contract.

In September 1998, an enhanced GLOBEX trading platform was introduced, bringing several benefits to E-mini traders. The most liberating was expansion of the types of orders the system would accept, which on the original platform were restricted to limit orders.

On GLOBEX$_2$, traders can use stop limits, *one-cancels-other* (OCO), and *market-if-touched* (MIT) orders. Also, spread orders, which initially were limited to the last four weeks of trading in a contract, are now available all the time. For options, the new system allowed for an expansion in strike price ranges.

Value Line

The Value Line stock index is a broad-based index of U.S. and Canadian stocks created, maintained, and published by Value Line Publishing Inc., a subsidiary of Value Line Inc., a financial publisher, investment advisor, and provider of securities research data. A monthly chart of the Value Line Index since 1983 is shown in Figure 5.3.

Index at a Glance.

Index	Value Line
Exchange	Kansas City Board of Trade
Weighting	Equal
Ticker Symbol	VL
Contract Value (Dec. 31, 1998)	437.15 x $250 = $109,287.50
Clearinghouse	Kansas City Board of Trade Clearing Corporation
Regulator	Commodity Futures Trading Commission
Web Site Information	www.kcbt.com

Understanding the Index. The Value Line Arithmetic Index is an equal-weighted offering of approximately 1,600 large-, mid-, and small-cap stocks traded on the NYSE, Nasdaq, AMEX, and in Canada. Equal weighting de-emphasizes the importance of blue-chip stocks as price movement in each stock is given equal weight in calculating index change. As an example, International Business Machines (IBM) is included in the Value Line, S&P 500, and DJIA, but its influence on index movement ranges widely. In the Value Line, with its equal-weighting approach, IBM's weight equals just 1/1,600 stocks, or 0.0006%, the same percentage weight as every other stock in the index. In the S&P 500, IBM was weighted at 1.73% at the end of December 1998, and it carried a weight of 8.29% of the DJIA on December 31, 1998.

As of September 1998, the Value Line Index represented 1,587 companies in 96 industries, including 75% on the NYSE, 20% on

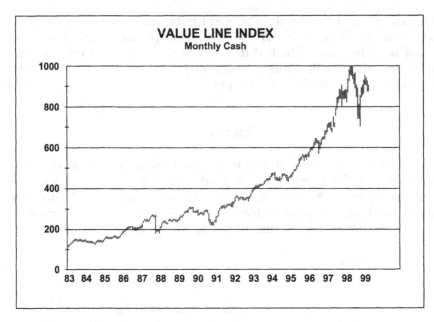

FIGURE 5.3   Value Line Index
Source: CRB-Bridge Information

Nasdaq, 3% on the AMEX and 2% at the Toronto Stock Exchange. Virtually all the stocks in both the S&P 500 and the DJIA are included in the Value Line Index. The *Value Line Investment Survey* includes the most current list of stocks in the index.

Value Line Futures. Futures on the Value Line Index were the first to be launched in the world, opening for trading on February 24, 1982, at the KCBT. The exchange, which had been offering futures contracts as risk-management tools to the agricultural community since 1876, had come up with the idea of extending that concept to stock ownership in 1977 and spent four years convincing regulators that it was a good one. The Johnson/Shad accord (or Shad/Johnson accord depending on your preference), reached December 1981, resolved the jurisdictional issues over stock index futures contracts that had surfaced between the CFTC and the SEC. In addition, the Federal Reserve Board wanted the authority to establish margin requirements for stock index futures contracts. It backed off when the KCBT announced it would raise the minimum margin to $6,500 from its initial proposal of $4,000.[3]

The KCBT offers on-line simulated trading for all its products, including Value Line and the Mini Value Line, at its web site. The site also provides 10-minute delayed snapshot futures quotes as well as daily stock index technical indicators.

Value Line futures had the jump on the rest of the world's stock index offerings but never was able to capitalize on its early lead. Average daily volume did not break 3,000 contracts until a year after the contract's launch and peaked at 6,087 in December 1985. Meanwhile, the S&P 500 futures contract averaged nearly 3,500 contracts per day in its opening month, April 1982, and by year-end was approaching 25,000 per day.

The Value Line futures contract trades on the March quarterly expiration cycle and has had a multiplier of $250 since June 1, 1998; a $500 multiplier had been in place since the contract's inception. It trades by open outcry from 8:30 A.M. to 3:15 P.M., Monday through Friday. There is no options contract on the original Value Line futures contract, although an option on futures traded very briefly at the Chicago Board of Trade in 1983. (See the "Futures" section of the "U.S. Large-, Mid-, and Small-Cap Indexes" discussion later in this chapter regarding the DJIA and the Chicago Board of Trade's attempt to gain a stock index contract for further details.)

On May 17, 1985, the Value Line trading pit was transformed into a stage for the annual remote broadcast of the financial television program "Wall Street Week." Host Louis Rukeyser noted that the KCBT was the birthplace of stock index futures and called the Value Line "the broadest, the most volatile, and in many ways, the most exciting index futures contract."

Mini Value Line Futures. The Mini Value Line futures contract at the KCBT is the exchange's most popular stock index offering. With a multiplier of $100, it was the first index tailored to individual investors. Futures on the Mini opened on July 19, 1983, 17 months after the Value Line stock index futures contract debut; options on the Mini were not listed until July 1, 1992. Still, the Mini did not generate enough volume to be listed daily in *The Wall Street Journal* until September 3, 1997, more than 14 years after it opened.

Contract specifications for the Mini mirror those of the larger Value Line contract with the exception of the multiplier ($100 versus $250) and tick value ($5 versus $12.50). Position limits equal 5,000 contracts net long or short in all months combined, including Mini futures and options on futures, figured on a delta-equivalent basis.

To celebrate the 15th anniversary of the Mini's contract launch, the KCBT ran a trading contest in conjunction with *Technical Analysis of Stock and Commodities* magazine for individual investors. Participants were required to open a $10,000 trading account to trade the Mini from September 1 through December 31, 1998. However, volume figures for the Mini Value Line did not rise significantly during those four months. For the year, Mini Value Line volume in futures and options was slightly less than half the year-earlier level.

Index at a Glance.

Index	Mini Value Line
Exchange	Kansas City Board of Trade
Weighting	Equal
Ticker Symbol	MV
Contract Value (Dec. 31, 1998)	437.15 x $100 = $43,715
Clearinghouse	Kansas City Board of Trade Clearing Corporation
Regulator	Commodity Futures Trading Commission
Web Site Information	www.kcbt.com

Calculating the Index. The Value Line Index level is figured by multiplying the average price change of the stocks in the Index by the Value Line's closing value for the previous day. The average price change is determined by summing each individual stock's price change (current price divided by yesterday's close) and dividing by the total number of stocks. The arithmetic formula has been used to figure the underlying Index value for the futures contract since March 9, 1988. Until then, the futures contract was based on the geometrically averaged Value Line Composite Index, which dates to 1961. The switch was made primarily because the arithmetic average outperformed the geometric average by about 5.5% annually.

Stock splits or dividends are reflected by adjusting the previous day's closing price downward in the same ratio so that price is equalized. New additions to the index are ignored on their first day of trading so that the first closing price can be used to establish the next day's percentage change. All additions and deletions to the index are made on a monthly basis, after the current monthly option expires at the KCBT.

U.S. LARGE-, MID-, AND SMALL-CAP INDEXES

Whether a company is large, medium, or small, there's an index to fit them all. Investors and analysts like to separate U.S. stocks by market capitalization, or a company's value as determined by multiplying its share price times the number of shares outstanding. Large-capitalization stocks include the biggest, most widely recognized companies in the country. Medium-sized companies in terms of capitalization generally are considered growth stocks, with more volatility than the large-caps but less than the small-caps. Companies with the smallest capitalization, usually issued by a young company, often attract attention from investors because of their volatility.

In the futures trading arena are active stock index futures and options contracts for each type of market-capitalization sector. The DJIA tracks U.S. blue-chip stocks, joining the trading arena just in 1997 with futures and options at the CBOT. Another large-cap index joined the mix in 1999 when the NYBOT listed the Russell 1000. The mid- and small-cap offerings are listed at the CME. The S&P MidCap 400 joined the standard-bearer S&P 500 Index at the CME in 1992. A year later, the CME listed the Russell 2000, the industry's benchmark for small-cap stocks.

Dow Jones Industrial Average

The DJIA is arguably the best-known stock measure in the world. First published on May 26, 1896, by Dow Jones & Company, it had tallied nearly 60 years of stock market history before another U.S. stock market index was developed. That longevity accounts for its continued popularity today as a preferred measure of the market with individuals, institutions, and news organizations. A monthly chart of the DJIA is shown in Figure 5.4.

Index at a Glance.

Index	DJIA
Exchange	Chicago Board of Trade
Weighting	Price
Ticker Symbol	DJ
Contract Value (Dec. 31, 1998)	9181.43 x $10 = $91,814.30
Clearinghouse	Board of Trade Clearing Corporation
Regulator	Commodity Futures Trading Commission
Web Site Information	www.cbot.com averages.dowjones.com

Understanding the Index. The DJIA is an index of 30 of the largest, most liquid blue-chip U.S. stocks, a number that has held steady since

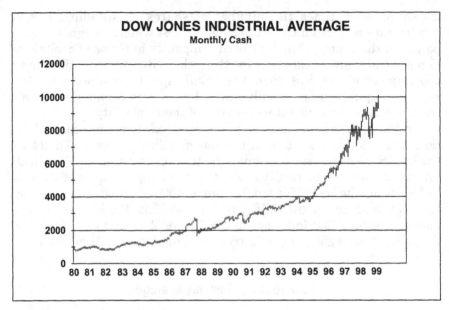

FIGURE 5.4   Dow Jones Industrial Average
Source: CRB-Bridge Information

1928. When the index was first introduced, it contained 12 stocks, a figure that was expanded to 20 in 1916. General Electric is the only stock in the current index that also was in the original configuration. Today, editors of *The Wall Street Journal*, who maintain and update the Index, take a very broad view of what constitutes an industrial company in today's technology and service-oriented economy.

Total market value of DJIA stocks at year-end 1998 was more than $2.4 trillion, representing about 23% of the total market value of all NYSE common stocks and about 19% of market value of all U.S. common stocks. Also, the 30 DJIA stocks typically account for close to 10% of total trading volume at the NYSE (14% on a dollar-volume basis), even though they represent just over 1% of the total number of listings.

The DJIA is price-weighted, which means that stocks with the highest price will have the most influence on the index (see Table 5.3). Other characteristics to watch for include the following: (1) volatile stocks with large price swings; (2) a change in the index components, which may alter the hierarchy of influence; and (3) a stock split, which will decrease the stock's influence on the index.

The Dow Jones web site has a plethora of information about the Dow indexes. Go there to find the latest top 10 lists for the DJIA's largest one-day moves, both up and down, in points and percentage. For inquiring minds, the site enables you to search its database by

TABLE 5.3 Top 10 Stocks in DJIA
(December 31, 1998)

Rank	Company	Price per Share (dollars)	Percent Weight
1	International Business Machines (IBM)	184.7500	8.29
2	Merck & Co. (MRK)	147.6875	6.63
3	United Technologies Corp. (UTX)	108.7500	4.88
4	J.P. Morgan & Co. (JPM)	105.0625	4.71
5	American Express Co. (AXP)	102.2500	4.59
6	General Electric Co. (GE)	102.0625	4.58
7	Procter & Gamble Co. (PG)	91.3125	4.10
8	Johnson & Johnson (JNJ)	83.8750	3.76
9	Chevron Corp. (CHV)	82.9375	3.72
10	Wal-Mart Stores Inc. (WMT)	81.4375	3.65

Source: Dow Jones & Company

date from May 26, 1896, and find the DJIA's high, low, and close for the date as well as the stocks in the index at the time.

DJIA Futures. Not even a Land Rover could have helped the Chicago Board of Trade (CBOT) maneuver the rocky road it took to list futures and options on the DJIA. The exchange tried and failed to list the contract in 1982, and 15 years passed before Dow Jones & Company agreed to license the DJIA to the exchange.

With stock index futures development fever at a peak in the early 1980s, the CBOT set its sights on the best-known index in the world—the DJIA. However, the index's publisher, Dow Jones & Company, was repulsed by the thought of a futures contract on its venerable index due to past scandals in futures trading and because of the perception that futures trading was little more than gambling.[4] Reportedly, the company turned down an offer of $2 million annually to use the name, made on behalf of the CBOT by Richard Sandor, who chaired the exchange's financial instruments committee and who was the major force behind development of the exchange's interest rate product complex, including U.S. Treasury bonds, in the 1970s.[5]

Plan B went into effect at the CBOT. The exchange developed and submitted to the CFTC contract specifications for the *Chicago Board of Trade Stock Market Portfolio Index,* which duplicated the stocks in the DJIA and their weighting. Already behind other exchanges who were readying their stock index futures contracts, the CBOT submitted the contract for approval on February 26, 1982, two days after the world's first stock index futures contract began trading. The CFTC approved the contract on May 13 that year, amid a legal battle between the exchange and Dow Jones that had gone to court in both Illinois and New York. The contract never traded.

Just days after submitting the contract proposal to the CFTC, the CBOT filed suit asking a Circuit Court judge in Chicago to determine whether the exchange was infringing on Dow Jones' rights and to let it proceed with trading if the contract was approved by the CFTC.[6] Dow Jones filed suit in New York District Court on March 31, 1982, claiming the exchange was violating federal copyright and trademark law as well as common law property interest.[7] A Dow Jones attorney called the battle "the most significant litigation in (Dow Jones') 100-year history."[8]

Although Cook County Circuit Court Judge James C. Murray ruled in early June 1982 to allow the CBOT to list its recently approved stock index futures contract, he also issued a stay allowing Dow Jones to seek an appeal as the CBOT was ready to start trading immediately. A week later, an Illinois appellate court indefinitely blocked the CBOT from trading the indexes and ruled against the exchange in August 1982. In January 1983, the Illinois Supreme Court agreed to hear the CBOT's appeal on April 5, 1983, ultimately deciding late that year that the exchange could not list the look-alike contract. The CBOT's DJIA dream was dead. While waiting for the legal dust to settle, the CBOT pulled out Plans C, D, E, and F.

- CBOT linked with the KCBT to trade options on Value Line futures on the CBOT trading floor beginning on March 4, 1983.[9] Trading had a lackluster start, with just 58 contracts exchanging hands on opening day; clearing problems prevented all but two of them from making it through as a matched, cleared trade.[10] Trading in Value Line options at the CBOT was dead within three months, when the KCBT board voted in May 1983 to go to liquidation only in the options starting on May 23. The total number of Value Line options contracts that changed hands was 168. Value Line options have never traded on the KCBT floor.

- It explored listing a futures contract on the Chicago Board Options Exchange (CBOE) 100 Index (renamed the S&P 100 Index in June 1983). However, the CBOT and its offspring CBOE could come to no agreement in early 1983.[11] Later, in 1988 and 1989, the CBOT traded futures on the CBOE 250 stock index.

- The CBOT's original stock index futures contract submission in February 1980, known as the *Industry Composite Portfolio,* of 50 stocks was approved in July 1983 but never traded.

■ Finally, in October 1983, the CBOT signed a licensing agreement with AMEX to list the Major Market Index, (MMI) a 20-stock, blue-chip index designed to mimic the DJIA (and included 15 of its stocks and had a 98% correlation) that began trading at AMEX in April 1983. It submitted contract specifications to the CFTC on October 21, 1983, and they were approved for trading in June 1984, more than two years after the first stock index futures contract began trading. (The MMI traded at the CBOT until 1993, when the CME won the licensing rights. The CME delisted the contract in February 1999.)

Just in case the CBOT did get the go-ahead to trade the DJIA look-alike contract in the early 1980s, the Chicago Mercantile Exchange was preparing to compete. It filed with the CFTC for a Dow-like contract in 1983 because it wanted "to trade a Dow 30 contract under the CME banner," according to then CME Executive Vice President (later President) William J. Brodsky. With a year of stock index futures trading under its belt, the CME already had become the industry leader. "We are the premier stock index futures market. The Dow is a very significant index and we'd like to trade it," Brodsky told *Futures* Magazine. "We think we'd do very well trading it, or we wouldn't have filed for it."[12]

By the mid-1990s, stock index futures trading had gained respectability in the eyes of Dow Jones & Company. John A. Prestbo, markets editor of *The Wall Street Journal*, said in a June 6, 1997, article in his newspaper that ". . . by 1995, the company became convinced that since 1982, experience with such products and safeguards designed by the exchanges made the time right to consider licensing indexes."[13]

Staff members at both the CBOT and its cross-town rival, the CME, burned the midnight oil in preparing their bids for the DJIA license to trade futures and options on futures as the submission deadline approached in the spring of 1997. But, the CBOT had taken steps over the previous two years it felt were critical to obtaining the license. First, it had spent two years and $182 million for a new trading facility, which opened in February 1997, that could accommodate what was hoped to be a complex of Dow Jones products in the same room as the mighty U.S. Treasury bond pit. Ultimately, the CBOT spent $8 million to build a state-of-the-art trading pit for DJIA futures and options. CBOT President Tom Donovan said in a press conference on the DJIA contract's one-year anniversary in October 1998 that the new trading floor was critical in the decision-making process. "We would not have won the Dow Jones contract if we had not built the new trading facility," he said.

The CBOT filed with the CFTC in September 1997 to trade futures on both the Dow Jones Transportation Average and the Dow

Jones Utilities Average. However, a stipulation of the Johnson/Shad agreement maintains that the SEC has veto power over the CFTC in approving which futures contracts are listed. The CFTC terminated the review in December that year following the SEC's rejection on grounds that the indexes were narrow in scope and could invite market manipulation.[14] Meanwhile, one of the coauthors of the agreement, former CFTC Chairman Philip McBride Johnson, said in early 1999 that the accord had outlived its usefulness.[15] The CBOT, after its appeal to the SEC was rejected, was continuing the appeal process in early 1999 in order to list the contracts.

Second, the exchange had worked with the Board of Trade Clearing Corp. (BOTCC), which would clear the DJIA trades. The BOTCC had an unblemished record in terms of defaults since its inception in the 1920s, to gain the world's only triple-A credit rating for a clearinghouse from S&P Corp. The rating designation came in April 1997, just weeks before the licenses were awarded. In addition, BOTCC obtained a $100 million default insurance policy. Third, the CBOT pledged to devote a significant portion of its marketing budget (some observers estimated it at $15 to $20 million) to promote the Dow Indexes.[16]

Enthusiasm at the CBOT, expressed in the value of memberships, was high when the exchange was awarded the DJIA license on June 5, 1997. A seat on the Index, Debt, and Energy Market (IDEM) division of the CBOT more than doubled in price that day, rising to $138,000 from $65,000 as 13 seats traded hands.[17] Exchange records show the IDEM seat price peaked at $143,000 on September 15, 1997, three weeks before DJIA futures opened for trading on October 6, 1997. A year later, an IDEM was valued at $28,000, a victim of both deflated enthusiasm about the DJIA and the threat of electronic trading, which had brought a full membership at the exchange to half its value in the span of 12 months.

Expectations were high for the DJIA contract, considering its well-known name among both individual and institutional investors. CBOT Senior Vice President of Market and Product Development Patrick Catania, who had been the exchange's chief negotiator with Dow Jones, told a reporter a week before the contract launch date that he'd like to see a daily volume of 20,000 to 30,000 contracts in the DJIA contracts in its first two weeks, a level equal to that achieved by the MMI before the stock market crash in 1987.[18]

In reality, average daily volume peaked in the contract's first month of trading at 19,572 contracts (futures and options on futures); in 1998, average daily volume ranged, on a monthly basis, between roughly 12,000 and 19,000 contracts, averaging 15,131 contracts for the year. Monthly volume at the CBOT for the DJIA products surpassed that of the CBOE, which listed European-style

DJIA cash options at one-tenth the contract value of the CBOT's offering, in 6 out of 12 months in 1998.

Still, the results were by no means shabby. The DJIA contracts at the CBOT had the most successful first year of any contract launched at the exchange. A total of more than 3 million Dow contracts had traded by August 21, 1988, a level that the 30-year Treasury bond did not reach until three years after it opened. And, the DJIA futures contract was the fourth most actively traded among U.S. stock indexes in 1998, trailing the S&P 500 futures and options contracts and futures on the E-mini S&P 500. To encourage even more awareness and use of the futures and options on futures contracts, the CBOT decided in March 1999 to provide free, real-time quotes on its web site for a certain period of time.

In February 1998, the CBOT also obtained the license from Dow Jones & Company to list the Dow futures and options on futures contracts during non-U.S. trading hours. On April 2, 1998, the two Dow contracts began trading on the CBOT's electronic system, Project A. In mid-1999, there was a one-hour session starting at 3:30 p.m. (Chicago time) on Monday through Thursday a second session on Sunday through Thursday that ran from 6:05 P.M. to 5 A.M the next morning, and a third session for futures only from 5:35 A.M. to 7:05 P.M., Monday through Friday. The CBOT intended to move to side-by-side trading in late 1999, with a Project A session running from 5:35 A.M. to 3:15 P.M., overlapping the open outcry session from 8 A.M. to 3:15 P.M.

Calculating the Index. When Charles Dow first calculated the DJIA in 1896, he did what any reasonable person would do with only paper, pencil, and math skills—he added the closing prices of the 12 stocks in the index and divided by 12 to get an average price (40.94 on May 26, 1896).

By 1928, when the number of components in the index reached 30, the editors began using a special divisor rather than just the number of stocks in the index in order to avoid distortions due to stock splits or changes in the index make-up. On October 1 of that year, the divisor was 16.02.

Today, the DJIA is the sum of each component stock's closing price at its home exchange (as opposed to the composite closing value), divided by the current divisor. In early 1999, the NYSE was the *home exchange* to all stocks in the DJIA. With the DJIA trading in the 10,000 area in 1999, the divisor has now extended eight places beyond the decimal point. Dow Jones calculates the index on a real-time basis with every trade that occurs in the component stocks and distributes the information every few seconds; the DJIA is not calculated when the NYSE is closed.

The component stocks in the DJIA are relatively stable because Dow Jones & Company believes that stability of composition enhances trust in the average. For example, the only change in index components from 1993 to 1998 occurred in March 1997, when four stocks were replaced. The most common reason to change a stock is a change in the company, such as an acquisition. All stocks are reviewed whenever one stock is changed.

Russell 1000

The Russell 1000 Index tracks the largest 1,000 stocks in the broader Russell 3000 Index, which tracks only U.S. companies. At the June 30, 1998, reconstitution, the Russell 1000 stocks represented about 89% of the total market capitalization of the broader index, which in turn represents nearly 98% of the investable U.S. equities market. The average market capitalization of these large-cap stocks was $9.9 billion; the smallest stock's market capitalization was just $2 million larger than the largest stock's capitalization in the Russell 2000 Index. A monthly chart of the Russell 1000 since 1988 is shown in Figure 5.5.

Index at a Glance.

Index	Russell 1000
Exchange	New York Board of Trade
Weighting	Capitalization
Ticker Symbol	R (Regular) RQ (Large)
Contract Value (Dec. 31, 1998)	642.87 x $500 = $321,435 (R) 642.87 x $1,000 = $642,870 (RQ)
Clearinghouse	New York Clearing Corporation
Regulator	Commodity Futures Trading Commission
Web Site Information	www.nybot.com www.russell.com/indexes www.russell1000futures.com

Understanding the Index. Because the Russell 1000 stocks are a subset of the Russell 3000 Index, you need to understand the criteria stocks must meet to be part of the larger index. All companies listed on a U.S. exchange or on the over-the-counter market are considered for inclusion in the Russell 3000 if they meet the following requirements: (1) the stock is trading at $1 or more on May 31; (2) the company offers common stock shares; (3) the company is domiciled in the United States and its territories; (4) the stock is trading on May 31; and (5) the Frank Russell Company has access to information

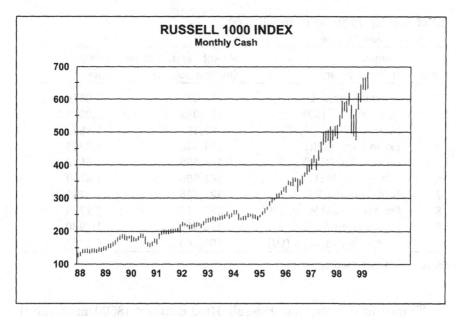

FIGURE 5.5   Russell 1000 Index
Source: CRB-Bridge Information

needed to determine eligibility by May 31. The following types of stock are excluded from the Russell 3000: preferred and convertible preferred stock; participating preferred stock; redeemable shares; warrants and rights; trust receipts; royalty trusts; limited liability companies; OTC Bulletin Board and pink-sheet stocks; closed-end mutual funds; limited partnerships; and foreign stocks. As a special exception, Berkshire Hathaway also is excluded. Once the field of potential stocks is assembled, they are ranked by total market capitalization. The top 3,000 make up the Russell 3000 Index; the largest 1,000 of that group become members of the Russell 1000 Index.

The Frank Russell Company estimates that more than $600 billion is benchmarked or indexed to its 18-member family of Russell indexes, including $56 billion in the Russell 1000 at year-end 1998. The 10 largest stocks in the Russell 1000 Index at its annual reconstitution of June 30, 1998 are shown in Table 5.4.

Russell 1000 Futures. NYBOT launched futures and options on futures contracts based on the Russell 1000 Index in March 1999. Similar to its strategy with the NYSE Composite Index, the NYBOT offers two contract sizes, one with a $500 multiplier and another with a $1,000 multiplier. Another similarity is that the Russell 1000 trades in open outcry during two sessions daily in New York and a third in Dublin, Ireland, for a total of more than 18 hours.

TABLE 5.4 Top 10 Stocks in Russell 1000
(June 30, 1998)

Rank	Company (million dollars)	Market Capitalization (million dollars)	Percent Weight
1	General Electric Co. (GE)	296,073	3.0878
2	Coca-Cola Co. (KO)	195,083	2.0345
3	Microsoft Corp. (MSFT)	187,198	1.9523
4	Exxon Corp. (XON)	174,640	1.8213
5	Merck & Co. (MRK)	159,866	1.6672
6	Pfizer Inc. (PFE)	141,906	1.4799
7	Intel Corp. (INTC)	125,716	1.3111
8	Procter & Gamble Co. (PG)	122,113	1.2735
9	Bristol Myers Squibb (BMY)	114,397	1.1930
10	Lucent Technologies (LU)	109,140	1.1382

Source: Frank Russell Company

Trades in the Regular Russell 1000 contract ($500 multiplier) can be done in any size. However, block order trades may be done with a minimum of 30 contracts. The Large contract ($1,000 multiplier) is aimed at institutional investors because the minimum trade size is five contracts; at year-end 1998 values, that would equal about $3 million. In the three minutes following execution of a five-lot order, the initiator may add contracts for execution in any amount. Block trades in the Large contract must be done in 15-contract minimums. Options are available only on the Regular contract.

Introduction of the Russell 1000 Index was aimed squarely at institutional portfolio managers who already are benchmarked to the index and who may have been using S&P 500 futures and options as a hedging tool, or a combination of the S&P 500 and the S&P 400 instruments. For them, direct availability of the Russell 1000 may reduce tracking error.

Calculating the Index. Stocks that make the cut for the Russell 1000 are determined by total market capitalization, but each one's *weighting* in the index is figured on available market capitalization, which is calculated by multiplying the stock's price by the number of shares available for trading. These available shares are determined by excluding those held by other listed companies, private investor holdings of 10% or more, and the company's employee stock ownership plans that amount to more than 10% of shares outstanding. Thus, it is the stocks with the most tradeable outstanding shares at the highest price that will hold the most influence on Index movement.

Based on data as of May 31 each year, the Russell 1000 Index is reconstituted and rebalanced each June 30. Stocks are removed from the index due to merger, acquisition, or other corporate activity, for example, a move to the pink sheets or OTC Bulletin Board. These stocks are not replaced until the next reconstitution. For example, Chrysler Corp. was removed from the index when it merged with Daimler, but DaimlerChrysler was not included afterward because it was not a U.S. company. However, if the acquiring company in a merger or acquisition is also a member of the index, the stock's capitalization moves to the acquiring stock. Thus, there would be no impact on the index total capitalization. Spin-off companies of index members are added to the index only if they are as large as the smallest security in the index.

The index was rebalanced quarterly from 1979 to 1986 and semiannually from 1987 to June 30, 1989. When a stock leaves the index before the annual rebalancing period, the weights of the remaining stocks are adjusted via the divisor so that the index maintains its continuity.

To determine the index level, each stock's price is multiplied by its available shares. These individual sums are then totaled and related to the base period market value of 130 on December 31, 1986, through a divisor. Bridge Information Systems calculates the index every 15 seconds and distributes it to data vendors.

S&P MidCap 400

The S&P MidCap 400 is a capitalization-weighted index of 400 U.S. stocks representing companies whose capitalization is in the middle range of all firms. Launched in June 1991, it has become the benchmark for mid-cap stocks in the United States, with $20 billion indexed to it in 1998. None of the stocks in the S&P 500 can be in the S&P MidCap 400 and vice versa. A monthly chart of the S&P MidCap 400 since 1981 is shown in Figure 5.6.

Understanding the Index. A market-capitalization index, the S&P MidCap 400 will be most influenced by high-priced stocks and those with the most shares outstanding. At the end of December 1998, the stocks in Table 5.5 were the 10 largest in market capitalization in the S&P MidCap 400 Index and equaled 15.83% of the Index total market value.

As of December 1998, the market value of companies in the S&P MidCap 400 ranged from $142 million to $29.7 billion, with a median value of $1.8 billion. Nearly 75% of the stocks traded on the NYSE, with about 25% on Nasdaq and 2% on AMEX. Of the 400 companies, 311 were industrials from eight sectors: basic materials,

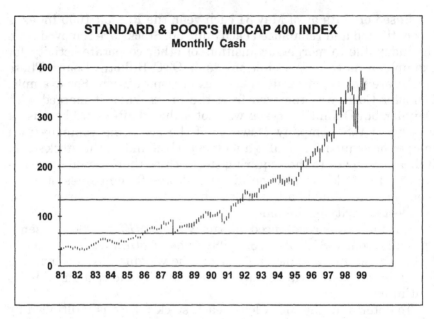

FIGURE 5.6   Standard & Poor's MidCap 400 Index
Source: CRB-Bridge Information

Index at a Glance.

Index	S&P MidCap 400
Exchange	Chicago Mercantile Exchange
Weighting	Capitalization
Ticker Symbol	MD
Contract Value (Dec. 31, 1998)	392.31 x $500 = $196,155
Clearinghouse	CME Clearinghouse
Regulator	Commodity Futures Trading Commission
Web Site Information	www.cme.com www.spglobal.com www.advisorinsight.com

capital goods, communications services, consumer cyclicals, consumer staples, energy, health care, and technology. Utility companies accounted for 43 of the total, financial companies totaled 35; and transportation firms totaled 11.

TABLE 5.5 Top 10 Stocks in Standard & Poor's MidCap 400
(December 31, 1998)

Rank	Stock	Market Capitalization (million dollars)	Percent Weight
1	America Online (AOL)	73,303	7.52
2	Compuware Corp. (CPWR)	14,356	1.47
3	AFLAC Inc. (AFL)	11,672	1.20
4	Office Depot (ODP)	9,077	0.93
5	Network Associates Inc. (NETA)	8,615	0.88
6	Crestar Financial Corp. (CF)	8,117	0.83
7	McKesson Corp. (MCK)	7,849	0.81
8	Cintas Corporation (CTAS)	7,398	0.76
9	Harley-Davidson (HDI)	7,239	0.74
10	Linear Technology Corp. (LLTC)	6,733	0.69

Source: Standard & Poor's Corporation

S&P MidCap 400 Futures. Trading in futures and options on futures for the S&P MidCap 400 began in February 1992 at the CME. The second successful U.S. stock index the exchange introduced, it opened for trade in a pit next to the flagship S&P 500. The S&P MidCap 400 is similar in design to the S&P 500, with two exceptions: (1) Its multiplier remained at $500 when the S&P 500 contract went with a $250 multiplier in late 1997; and (2) the speculative position limit is 5,000 contracts, just one-fourth the maximum in the S&P 500. From 1993 to 1998, volume in the CME's S&P MidCap 400 products has totaled between 230,000 and 310,000 contracts annually (about 900 to 1,200 on a daily basis), with most of that in the futures contract.

Calculating the Index. Standard & Poor's Corporation has sole responsibility for maintaining the S&P MidCap 400 index and calculating the Index value. It has leased exclusive trading rights in futures and options on futures to the CME. No stock in the S&P MidCap 400 can be in any other stock index from Standard & Poor's Corporation.

Calculating the S&P 400 Index requires multiplying each stock's price by the number of outstanding shares to obtain the stock's market value. All 400 market values are totaled and then compared to those of the base period, which equaled 100 on December 31, 1990, to derive the index value. S&P calculates the index continuously during the NYSE trading day. Modifications to the index due to stock splits or dividends, for example, are achieved through changing the index divisor, daily if necessary.

Stocks are removed from the index after merger, acquisition, leveraged buyout, or bankruptcy. Announcements for changes in index stocks are made at 5:15 P.M., New York time, so as not to disrupt that day's official closing price for the stocks involved. Those companies that restructure are analyzed to determine whether they continue to meet the guidelines for inclusion. When a stock is removed from the S&P MidCap 400 on grounds of lack of representation, it typically has become too large to be considered a mid-cap company. These stocks often find their way into the S&P 500 stock index.

Standard & Poor's Corporation follows six general guidelines for including a stock in the S&P MidCap 400 Index. Market value and industry group classification determine which stocks are the leaders in the field. A look at ownership of the outstanding shares ensures that companies in the Index are not closely held ventures, although the requirements are not as stringent as those for stocks in the S&P 500 Index. Trading volume must be sufficient to ensure liquidity and efficient pricing. In order to keep turnover in the index low, S&P analysts use fundamental analysis to determine whether the company is relatively stable. Finally, the stock of companies in emerging industries or new industry groups are screened regularly to see whether they meet the general guidelines for inclusion.

Russell 2000

The Russell 2000 Index was developed in 1983 by the Frank Russell Company to measure the market for small-cap stocks of U.S. companies; the index was calculated back to 1979. It has become the benchmark for small-cap investment, and as of year-end 1998 the index had $15 billion passively invested in it. Russell, an institutional investment consultancy in Tacoma, Washington, developed the index (along with the companion Russell 3000 and Russell 1000) to better reflect the investment styles of institutional investors who increasingly had been focusing on stocks based on their capitalization. The Russell 2000 measures the performance of the 2,000 smallest companies in the broader Russell 3000 Index, which represents about 98% of the investable U.S. equity market. A monthly chart of the Russell 2000 since 1980 is shown in Figure 5.7.

Understanding the Index. Because the Russell 2000 stocks are a subset of the Russell 3000 Index, you need to understand the criteria stocks must meet to be part of the larger index. All companies listed on a U.S. exchange or on the over-the-counter market are considered for inclusion in the Russell 3000 if they meet the following requirements: (1) The stock is trading at $1 or more on May 31; (2) the company offers common stock shares; (3) the company is domiciled in the

Index at a Glance.

Index	Russell 2000
Exchange	Chicago Mercantile Exchange
Weighting	Capitalization
Ticker Symbol	RL
Contract Value (Dec. 31, 1998)	421.96 x $500 = $210,980
Clearinghouse	CME Clearinghouse
Regulator	Commodity Futures Trading Commission
Web Site Information	www.cme.com www.russell.com/indexes

United States and its territories; (4) the stock is trading on May 31; and (5) the Frank Russell Company has access to information needed to determine eligibility by May 31. The following types of stock are excluded from the Russell 3000: preferred and convertible preferred stock; participating preferred stock; redeemable shares; warrants and rights; trust receipts; royalty trusts; limited liability

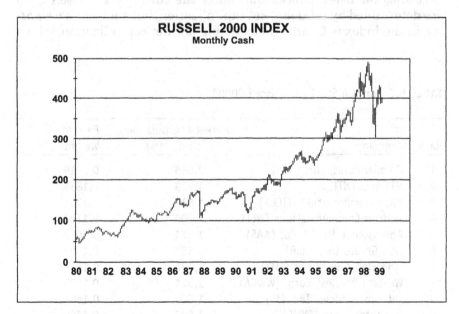

FIGURE 5.7 Russell 2000 Index
Source: CRB-Bridge Information

companies; OTC Bulletin Board and pink-sheet stocks; closed-end mutual funds; limited partnerships; and foreign stocks. As a special exception, Berkshire Hathaway also is excluded. Once the field of potential stocks is assembled, they are ranked by total market capitalization. The top 3,000 make up the Russell 3000 Index; the smallest 2,000 of that group become members of the Russell 2000 Index.

The stocks in Table 5.6 were the highest weighted in the Russell 2000 Index at the June 30, 1998 reconstitution.

Russell 2000 Futures. A futures contract on the Russell 2000 Index was first launched on September 10, 1987 by the NYFE, which had shown success in listing the NYSE Composite Index starting in 1982. However, trading in the Russell 2000 apparently fell victim to fallout from the October 1987 market crash just five weeks later, with volume of 5,644 contracts in 1987 and 32 in 1988.

Futures trading met with success in 1993 after the CME listed the Russell 2000 on February 4. Annual volume has risen steadily, about doubling the year-earlier mark in both 1996 and 1997 and rising more than 50% in 1998.

Another small-cap contract, the Wilshire Small Cap Index, made a fleeting appearance at the CBT in 1993 but failed to record more than 1,700 in trading volume that year.

Calculating the Index. Stocks that make the cut for the Russell 2000 are determined by total market capitalization, but each one's *weighting* in the index is figured on available market capitalization, which

TABLE 5.6 Top Ten Stocks in Russell 2000
(June 30, 1998)

Rank	Company	Market Capitalization (million dollars)	Percent Weight
1	Premier Parks, Inc. (PKS)	2,086	0.2219
2	NTL Inc. (NTLI)	1,728	0.1838
3	ICG Communications (ICGX)	1,633	0.1738
4	Winstar Communications (WCII)	1,600	0.1702
5	Amerisource Health Co. (AAS)	1,571	0.1672
6	HSB Group, Inc. (HSB)	1,558	0.1657
7	Fingerhut Companies (FHT)	1,536	0.1634
8	Western Wireless Corp. (WWCA)	1,511	0.1608
9	Interim Services, Inc. (IS)	1,509	0.1605
10	Symantec Corp. (SYMC)	1,503	0.1599

Source: Frank Russell Company

is calculated by multiplying the stock's price by the number of shares available for trading. These available shares are determined by excluding those held by other listed companies, private investor holdings of 10% or more, and the company's employee stock ownership plans that amount to more than 10% of shares outstanding. Thus, it is the stocks with the most tradeable outstanding shares at the highest price that will hold the most influence on index movement.

Based on data as of May 31 each year, the Russell 2000 Index is reconstituted and rebalanced each June 30. Stocks are removed from the index due to merger, acquisition, or other corporate activity, for example, a move to the pink sheets or the OTC Bulletin Board. These stocks are not replaced until the next reconstitution. However, if the acquiring company in a merger or acquisition is also a member of the index, the stock's capitalization moves to the acquiring stock. Thus, no impact is felt on the index total capitalization. Spin-off companies of index members are added to the index only if they are as large as the smallest security in the index.

The index was rebalanced quarterly from 1979 to 1986 and semi-annually from 1987 to June 30, 1989. When a stock leaves the index before the annual rebalancing period, the weights of the remaining stocks are adjusted via the divisor so that the index maintains its continuity.

To determine the index level, each stock's price is multiplied by its available shares. These individual sums are then totaled and related to the base period market value of 135 on December 31, 1986, through a divisor.

U.S. STYLE AND SECTOR INDEXES

Stock index contracts in the United States successfully expanded to encompass investment styles beyond market capitalization as well as individual market sectors in the mid-1990s. Within the span of six months, four new contracts opened that enabled investors to trade indexes based on growth, value, and technology stocks. The S&P 500/BARRA Growth Index and the S&P 500/BARRA Value Index opened for trade at the CME on Nov. 6, 1995. The CME listed the Nasdaq-100 Index, dominated by technology stocks, on April 10, 1996. The New York Cotton Exchange (now known as the New York Board of Trade) followed closely with an April 23, 1996 launch of the PSE Technology Index.

In 1999, the CME listed a smaller, electronically traded version of the Nasdaq-100 contract, the E-mini Nasdaq-100. Also that year, the KCBT launched ISDEX futures and options on futures contracts, based on the Internet Stock Index from internet.com LLC.

S&P 500/BARRA Growth Index;
S&P 500/BARRA Value Index

Following academic research into what causes differences in equity mutual fund returns, S&P Corporation joined forces with BARRA, a leading provider of analytical models, software, consulting, investment data, and money management services, to develop two new indexes that split the S&P 500 Index into either growth or value issues. Combined, the components of these two new indexes matched the components of the S&P 500 Index.

Index at a Glance.

Index	S&P 500/BARRA Growth
Exchange	Chicago Mercantile Exchange
Weighting	Capitalization
Ticker Symbol	SG
Contract Value (Dec. 31, 1998)	697.27 x $250 = $174,317.50
Clearinghouse	CME Clearinghouse
Regulator	Commodity Futures Trading Commission
Web Site Information	www.cme.com
	www.spglobal.com
	www.advisorinsight.com
	www.barra.com

Index at a Glance.

Index	S&P 500/BARRA Value
Exchange	Chicago Mercantile Exchange
Weighting	Capitalization
Ticker Symbol	SU
Contract Value (Dec. 31, 1998)	551.55 x $250 = $137,887.50
Clearinghouse	CME Clearinghouse
Regulator	Commodity Futures Trading Commission
Web Site Information	www.cme.com
	www.spglobal.com
	www.advisorinsight.com
	www.barra.com

Understanding the Indexes. Nobel Laureate William F. Sharpe researched the performance of growth and value stocks as well as those defined by their capitalization in 1990; the two S&P/BARRA Indexes were an outgrowth of that study. Two other academicians, Eugene Fama and Kenneth French, determined that book-to-price ratios were more important than market capitalization in understanding cross-sectional return variability.

Although no clear definition of growth versus value stock exists, members of these two S&P 500/BARRA indexes are determined solely on the stock's book-to-price ratio, a stable measure that results in indexes with fairly low turnover. The two Indexes are designed to be equal in market capitalization. As a result, more stocks are in the Value Index because those companies tend to have lower market capitalization and higher book-to-price ratios than the growth stocks. Financial services dominated the Value Index as of year-end 1998, accounting for 26% of the index weight; energy, telecommunications, and technology stocks accounted for another 33% of the stock weightings. In the Growth Index at year-end 1998, technology issues dominated at 27% of the weighting; health care stocks were the second-most prevalent group at 20% while consumer noncyclical stocks equaled 18% of the Index weightings.

Although the indexes were initially constructed in 1992, their history extends to December 31, 1974, when each base value was set to equal 35. Figure 5.8 and Figure 5.9 show weekly values since 1996 of the S&P 500/BARRA Growth Index and the S&P 500/BARRA Value Index, respectively. The 10 largest stocks in the Growth Index and the Value Index as of year-end 1998 are shown in Table 5.7 and Table 5.8, respectively.

S&P 500/BARRA Growth and S&P 500/BARRA Value Futures. Futures and options on futures for the S&P 500/BARRA Growth Index and Value Index opened on November 6, 1995. Trading interest in futures is relatively small but has grown steadily each year. Options trading for each contract reached its peak in 1996 and fell to virtually nothing by 1998.

Like the S&P 500 futures contract, the Growth and Value Indexes have a multiplier of $250, which eases the ability to construct spread trades across all three markets. Indeed, a long position in both the Growth and Value Indexes is considered nearly equal to a long position in the S&P 500. Holdings of these two contracts are considered part of the S&P 500 futures position limit of 20,000 contracts, net long or short.

Calculating the Indexes. The S&P 500/BARRA Growth and Value Indexes are rebalanced every January 1 and July 1, based on closing

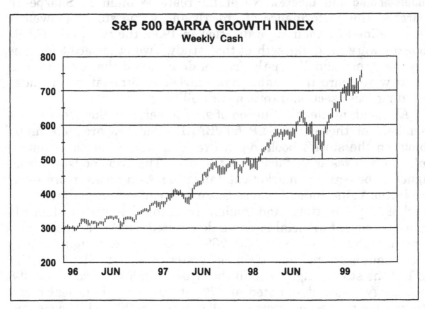

FIGURE 5.8 S&P 500/BARRA Growth Index
Source: CRB-Bridge Information

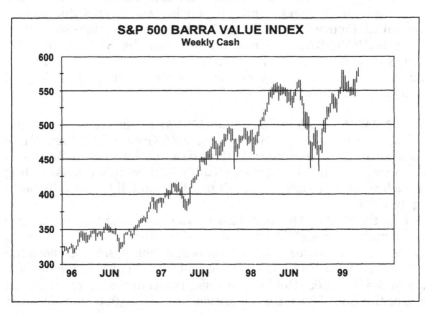

FIGURE 5.9 S&P 500/BARRA Value Index
Source: CRB-Bridge Information

TABLE 5.7 Top Ten Stocks in S&P 500/BARRA Growth Index
(December 31, 1998)

Rank	Company	Market Capitalization (million dollars)	Percent Weight
1	Microsoft Corp. (MSFT)	345,827	6.21
2	General Electric (GE)	334,442	6.01
3	Intel Corp. (INTC)	197,644	3.55
4	Wal-Mart Stores (WMT)	183,467	3.30
5	Merck & Co. (MRK)	175,905	3.16
6	International Business Machines (IBM)	172,383	3.10
7	Coca-Cola Company (KO)	164,854	2.96
8	Pfizer, Inc. (PFE)	162,792	2.92
9	Cisco Systems (CSCO)	146,555	2.63
10	Lucent Technologies (LU)	144,648	2.60

Source: Standard & Poor's Corporation

TABLE 5.8 Top 10 Stocks in S&P 500/BARRA Value Index
(December 31, 1998)

Rank	Company	Market Capitalization (million dollars)	Percent Weight
1	Exxon Corp. (XON)	177,784	4.06
2	AT&T Corp. (T)	135,927	3.11
3	MCI WorldCom (WCOM)	131,548	3.01
4	Citigroup Inc. (C)	112,462	2.57
5	BankAmerica Corp. (BAC)	104,056	2.38
6	Royal Dutch Petroleum (RD)	102,658	2.35
7	BellSouth (BLS)	97,535	2.23
8	Fannie Mae (FNM)	76,731	1.75
9	Time Warner Inc. (TWX)	76,149	1.74
10	COMPAQ Computer (CPQ)	71,294	1.63

Source: Standard & Poor's Corporation

trade data on the last trading day of November and May, respectively. This rebalancing brings the indexes to their ideal levels of approximately 50% capitalization in each. However, the indexes are adjusted monthly to accommodate changes in the S&P 500 Index.

Calculation of the indexes is handled similarly to that of the S&P 500 Index. Each stock's price is multiplied by the number of outstanding shares to obtain the stock's market value. For each index, all market values are totaled and then compared to those of the base period (December 31, 1974 = 35) to derive the index value, with a divisor handling any disruptions due to stock splits or dividends, for example.

Nasdaq-100

The Nasdaq-100 comprises the top 100 nonfinancial stocks (both domestic and foreign) listed on The Nasdaq Stock Market, an electronic marketplace created in 1971 by the National Association of Securities Dealers, Inc.

Index at a Glance.

Index	Nasdaq-100
Exchange	Chicago Mercantile Exchange
Weighting	Modified Capitalization
Ticker Symbol	ND ($100 multiplier)
	NQ ($20 multiplier)
Contract Value	1836.01 x $100 = $183,601 (ND)
(Dec. 31, 1998)	1836.01 x $20 = $36,720.20 (NQ)
Clearinghouse	CME Clearinghouse
Regulator	Commodity Futures Trading Commission
Web Site Information	www.cme.com
	www.nasd.com
	www.nasdaqtrader.com
	www.nasdaq-amex.com

Understanding the Index. Stocks eligible to be included in the Nasdaq-100 must be among the largest based on market capitalization (price times available shares outstanding), be listed on Nasdaq or another major exchange for at least two years (one year if the stocks are in the top 25% of the index), and show an average daily volume of 100,000 shares. A foreign stock must have a minimum U.S. market value of $4 billion, trade at least 200,000 shares a day, and be eligible for listed-options trading.

Stocks in major industry groups are included in the Nasdaq-100, including computer hardware and software, telecommunications, retail/wholesale trade, and biotechnology. Two of the computer issues, Microsoft Corporation and Intel Corporation, accounted for nearly 40% of the index weighting as of August 29, 1997; the 10 largest stocks in the index accounted for 60% of the index weighting. As of December 21, 1998, the index became a modified-capitalization offering in order to reduce the overwhelming influence of these top stocks. As a result, at year-end 1998, Microsoft and Intel equaled less than 23% of the entire index weight, and the 10 largest stocks were 47% of the index's total weight. At year-end 1998, the 100 stocks in the Index had a total market value of $1.5 trillion. The 10 most heavily weighted stocks in the index at year-end 1998 are listed in Table 5.9.

The index was created on February 1, 1985, with a base value of 250. By the end of 1993, the Nasdaq-100 had nearly reached the 800 level and was halved on January 3, 1994. A monthly chart of the Nasdaq-100 since 1987 is shown in Figure 5.10.

Nasdaq-100 Futures. Trading in Nasdaq-100 futures and options opened at the CME on April 6, 1996. Increasing interest in the technology sector propelled trading volume in the contracts to hit more than 400,000 in their first year. Volume more than doubled in 1997 and surpassed 1 million in 1998. The Nasdaq-100 is the second-most popular index at the CME, behind the S&P 500 Index.

The quarterly expiration settlement for the Nasdaq-100 is figured a bit differently than most U.S. stock indexes, which settle to a special opening quotation based on the opening price of all stocks in the index on the third Friday of the contract month. For the Nasdaq-100, the settlement price is determined from a volume-weighted average of each stock's prices in the opening five minutes of trade.

TABLE 5.9 Top Ten Stocks in Nasdaq-100 Index
(December 31, 1998)

Rank	Company	Market Value (million dollars)	Percent Weight
1	Microsoft Corporation (MSFT)	223,569	14.46
2	Intel Corporation (INTC)	130,159	8.42
3	Cisco Systems, Inc. (CSCO)	98,352	6.36
4	MCI WorldCom, Inc. (WCOM)	88,888	5.75
5	Dell Computer Corp. (DELL)	64,483	4.17
6	Oracle Corporation (ORCL)	32,828	2.12
7	Sun Microsystems, Inc. (SUNW)	26,628	1.72
8	Amgen Inc. (AMGN)	23,299	1.50
9	Tele-Communications, Inc. (TCOMA)	22,441	1.45
10	Amazon.com, Inc. (AMZN)	21,140	1.36

Source: Chicago Mercantile Exchange

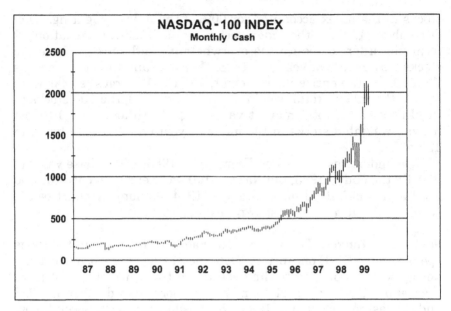

FIGURE 5.10   Nasdaq-100 Index
Source: CRB-Bridge Information

Based on its success with the E-mini S&P 500 contract, the CME listed an E-mini version of the Nasdaq-100 on June 21, 1999. The multiplier of $20 for the E-mini is one-fifth the size of the original contract; the contract trades on the GLOBEX$_2$ system virtually 24 hours per day. Like the E-mini S&P 500, large orders for 30 or more E-mini Nasdaq-100 contracts trade via open outcry on an all-or-none basis when pit trading is available. Opening day volume for the E-mini Nasdaq-100 totaled 2,136 contracts, equal to 24% of that day's trade in the regular-sized Nasdaq-100 futures contract.

An early attempt to trade futures on the Nasdaq-100 failed at the Chicago Board of Trade, which listed the contract on October 25, 1985. In a battle for an over-the-counter market index, the CME listed the S&P OTC 250 (SPOC) futures on the same day. The two exchanges spent an estimated $6 million in marketing the indexes, but neither survived the slowdown in volume that occurred during the year-end holidays. By mid-January 1986, average daily volume in each market was less than 100 contracts.[19]

Calculating the Index. In December 1998, the Nasdaq-100 Index became a modified-capitalization index in order to enhance diversification of the underlying index and its representation of the overall market for Nasdaq stocks. Before the change, the top five stocks in the index accounted for more than 60% of the index weight; after the change, those stocks equaled just 40% of the index weight.

The modified-capitalization weighting scheme for the Nasdaq-100 limits the weight of any single stock to 24% of the index. It also limits the combined weight of all securities with individual weightings of at least 4.5% to no more than 48% of the total market value of the index. Readjustments to the index are reviewed quarterly but made only if the 24% and 48% thresholds are violated.

The Nasdaq-100 Index level equals the current market value of component stocks multiplied by 125 and then divided by the stocks' market value of the adjusted base period. The adjusted base period market value is determined by multiplying the current market value after adjustments times the preceding base period market value and then dividing that result by the current market value before adjustments.

The adjustments relate to capitalization changes due to stock additions and deletions as well as changes to the depository receipt multiplier for component securities other than stock splits or stock dividends; no adjustments are made for cash dividends. Thus, the index reflects only the effects of price changes in the stocks resulting from market action.

The Nasdaq-100 is influenced most by the component stocks that have the highest market value. The market value of an Index security is equal to the security's price multiplied by a *depository receipt multiplier*, which is the figure used instead of shares outstanding to determine a stock's market value for weighting purposes in the index.

PSE Technology

The PSE Technology Index (or PSE Tech 100) broadly represents the technology sector, with 100 technology stocks across 15 industries that are traded on the NYSE, Nasdaq, and the AMEX. It is the oldest of several technology indexes traded on U.S. securities options exchanges, with daily history that has been maintained by the Pacific Exchange since 1983.

Understanding the Index. The base value for the PSE Technology Index was established on December 31, 1982, equal to 100. However, the index was split in September 1995, bringing the base value to 50. In 1997, the mutual fund rating service, Morningstar, Inc., began using the PSE Tech 100 as the performance benchmark for technology mutual funds.

Index at a Glance.

Index	PSE Technology
Exchange	New York Board of Trade
Weighting	Price
Ticker Symbol	TK
Contract Value (Dec. 31, 1998)	449.21 x $100 = $44,921
Clearinghouse	New York Clearing Corporation
Regulator	Commodity Futures Trading Commission
Web Site Information	www.nyce.com
	www.pacificex.com

The industries represented in the PSE Tech 100 include the following:

- Biotechnology
- CAD/CAM
- Computer software products
- Data communications
- Data storage and processing equipment
- Electronic equipment
- Information processing services
- Medical technology
- Micro computer manufacturing
- Mini and mainframe computer manufacturing
- Office automation equipment manufacturing
- Semiconductor capital equipment manufacturing
- Semiconductor manufacturing
- Test, analysis, and instrumentation equipment
- Large diversified computer manufacturing

A price-weighted index, the PSE Tech 100 responds most to the biggest dollar moves in its component stocks. Thus, the highest priced stocks typically will have the most influence on index movement. However, volatile price movement also can be key to changes in the Index value. The 10 most heavily weighted stocks in the index at year-end 1998 are shown in Table 5.10.

TABLE 5.10 Top 10 Stocks in PSE Technology 100
(December 31, 1998)

Rank	Company	Price (dollars per share)	Percent Weight
1	Yahoo!, Inc. (YHOO)	236.94	4.73
2	International Business Machines (IBM)	184.38	3.68
3	America Online (AOL)	155.13	3.19
4	Microsoft Corp. (MSFT)	138.69	2.77
5	Immunex Corp. (IMNX)	125.81	2.51
6	Intel Corp. (INTC)	118.56	2.36
7	Xerox Corp. (XRX)	118.00	2.35
8	Lucent Technologies (LU)	109.94	2.19
9	Amgen Inc. (AMGN)	104.56	2.09
10	Perkin-Elmer (PKN)	97.56	1.95

Source: Pacific Exchange

PSE Technology Futures. The Pacific Exchange (formerly the Pacific Stock Exchange), traded options on the cash Index from 1984 to 1987. However, according to the exchange, the options were delisted due to lack of market interest and the absence of a suitable hedging instrument for traders to use in neutralizing their risk. The PSE Tech 100 was relisted for trading at the Pacific Exchange on September 18, 1995. Futures and options on futures followed shortly, opening at the New York Futures Exchange on April 26, 1996.

Volume in both the futures and options on futures contracts have grown steadily since their introduction. In contrast to trading in most index products, however, the options on futures contracts attract more trading volume than the futures contracts. This is mainly due to the presence of three major options market makers in the pit who hedge their proprietary technology stock portfolios with the PSE Tech 100 options.

To stimulate individual investor interest in the PSE Tech 100, the New York Board of Trade cut the contract multiplier to $100 beginning with the December 1998 listing; the multiplier on prior contracts was $500.

Calculating the Index. The PSE Technology Index is price-weighted, so the prices of all component stocks are added and then divided by a divisor. The divisor is adjusted for stock splits and stock dividends that equal at least 10% of an issue's market value. A weekly chart of the PSE Technology Index is shown in Figure 5.11.

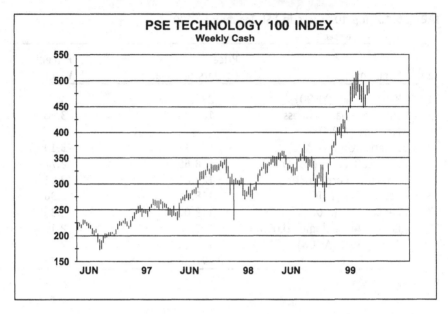

FIGURE 5.11   PSE Technology 100
Source: CRB-Bridge Information

Internet Stock Index

The Internet Stock Index (ISDEX) was one of the first stock indexes to represent publicly traded Internet companies, defined as companies that exist because of the Internet and derive at least 51% of revenues from the Internet. It began calculation in April 1996 with the debut of *The Internet Stock Report*, a twice-daily market update on the internet.com web site.

As of February 1999, internet.com LLC determined that 89 stocks met the 51% revenue criteria and could be considered for inclusion in ISDEX. These 89 stocks had a total market capitalization of $400 billion. ISDEX represents 50 of these stocks, and their capitalization at the time was $380 billion, or 95% of the Internet stock universe.

Understanding the Index. No minimum market capitalization, trading volume, or shares-outstanding requirements exist for inclusion in ISDEX. However, internet.com LLC does consider market share leadership (measured by revenues) and the company's diversity according to the ISDEX subsectors. The seven subsectors and an example of an ISDEX component include the following: e-commerce/e-tailer (Amazon.com); software (Netscape Communications Corp.); hardware

Index at a Glance.

Index	Internet Stock Index (ISDEX)
Exchange	Kansas City Board of Trade
Weighting	Modified capitalization
Ticker Symbol	IS
Contract Value (Dec. 31, 1998)	302.13 x $100 = $30,213
Clearinghouse	Kansas City Board of Trade Clearing Corporation
Regulator	Commodity Futures Trading Commission
Web Site Information	www.kcbt.com www.isdex.com

(Cisco); security (Checkpoint Software); content (Yahoo!); high-speed services (@Home Corp.); and access (America Online).

ISDEX Futures. The contract applications for both futures and options on futures for the ISDEX were submitted to CFTC in December 1998, and opened for trading on June 1, 1999. The ISDEX contracts trade in the exchange's open outcry pit along with the Value Line and Mini Value Line stock indexes. Daily price limits are calculated on a percentage basis per the previous trading day's closing value.

Calculating the Index. The ISDEX is calculated as a modified-capitalization index that limits the percent weight of any single stock to 10% of the total market capitalization of all 50 component stocks. A stock's market value is determined by multiplying its price by its outstanding number of shares by its percent weight in the index. The current values for all component stocks are summed and divided by the previous day's comparable figure; that result is multiplied by the previous day's index level to determine the current index value (see Figure 5.12).

Individual stock weights in the index are reviewed and adjusted on at least a quarterly basis. When any stock's weight exceeds 15% of the total capitalization of all 50 stocks in the index, its weight will be adjusted so it again meets the 10% cap requirement.

The ISDEX is reviewed quarterly to adjust for stocks that best represent Internet diversity. If a merger, acquisition, or other significant action makes it necessary to replace a stock in between these quarterly reviews, internet.com LLC will determine the replacement.

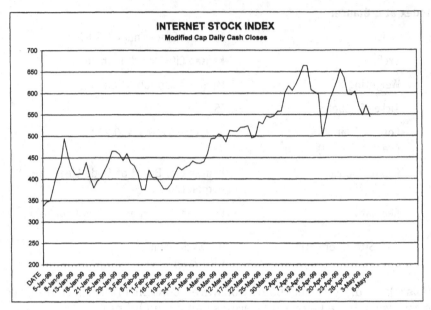

FIGURE 5.12   Internet Stock Index
Source: Kansas City Board of Trade

TABLE 5.11 Top 10 Stocks in Internet Stock Index
(April 1, 1999)

Rank	Company	Modified Market Capitalization (million dollars)	Percent Weight
1	Amazon.com, Inc. (AMZN)	23,232	10.00
2	America Online (AOL)	23,232	10.00
3	Cisco Systems, Inc. (CSCO)	23,232	10.00
4	Yahoo!, Inc. (YHOO)	23,232	10.00
5	@Home Corp. (ATHM)	18,536	7.98
6	eBay (EBAY)	17,751	7.64
7	CMG Information (CMGI)	9,383	4.04
8	Excite (XCIT)	7,536	3.24
9	E*Trade (EGRP)	6,706	2.89
10	Broadcom (BRCM)	6,173	2.66

Source: Kansas City Board of Trade

What's more, if a new category emerges between the quarterly reviews, a stock from that category may be added immediately upon its initial public offering. Look to either the KCBT or ISDEX web site for the latest list of ISDEX stocks.

Prior to April 1, 1999, the ISDEX was calculated as an equal-weighted index, in which each stock was weighted at 2% of the index value. When it switched to a modified market-capitalization weighting scheme, four stocks each were at the 10% weight limit, and the top 10 stocks were nearly 70% of the entire index's weight (see Table 5.11.).

CANADA

Stock index trading in Canada was undergoing massive change in 1999, with both a switch to a new set of indexes as well as a potential change in trading venue. After developing and trading derivative products on three Canadian stock market measures beginning in 1984, the Toronto Stock Exchange (TSE) agreed with Standard & Poor's Corporation in late 1998 to develop the first of a family of indexes for the Canadian stock market, the S&P/TSE 60. In March 1999, the stock exchanges in Canada proposed sweeping changes to the country's trading structure, which was expected would move all derivative-product trading to the Montreal Exchange by mid-2000 (pending regulatory approval).

The TSE, Canada's largest equities market with more than 1,300 listed companies and 90% of the country's equity trading business, developed three indexes to represent the Canadian stock market. The TSE 300 Composite Index, developed in 1977 and often quoted by the news media, covers the broad market. The Toronto 35 Index was started in 1987 as a derivatives trading vehicle that mirrored the broader TSE 300. In 1993, the TSE 100 Index was designed as a benchmark for institutional portfolios of Canadian stocks. The S&P/TSE 60 is designed as a large-cap investable index that eventually will replace the Toronto 35 and TSE 100 Indexes.

The S&P/TSE 60, TSE 100, and the Toronto 35 Indexes all include stocks that are part of the TSE 300 Composite. For a stock to be included in the TSE 300, the company must be a Canadian corporation and listed on the Toronto Stock Exchange. Also, the stock must be (1) listed for at least 12 months (six months if it is a large stock that meets certain market value requirements); (2) trade a minimum of 100,000 shares and 100 transactions in the last year; and (3) have a trading value in the last year of at least C$1 million. Stocks in the TSE 300 are ranked according to their float quoted market value (QMV), which adjusts the company's quoted market value so that only liquid, tradable shares are represented. The adjusted, or float, shares are determined by removing from consideration those held by any individual or group of shareholders that exceeds 20% of the total outstanding shares.

The TSE 300 is reviewed annually, with changes in its makeup effective with the opening of trade on the day the February index options and futures contracts expire, generally the third Friday of the month. Share weights of the component stocks are adjusted quarterly to reflect changes in capitalization such as dividends, conversions, employee stock options plans, small treasury issues, share buybacks, and private placements. As a result of the development partnership established in 1998, S&P Corporation will take over the day-to-day calculation of the TSE 300 Index. However, as with the other S&P/TSE indexes, administrative decisions will be determined jointly by the exchange and S&P.

The TSE 300 futures contract was developed in 1984 to represent the Canadian stock market but was hard for investors to duplicate due to many stocks that presented size or liquidity problems. Thus, there was a significant performance difference between institutional portfolios and the index. The U.S. Commodity Futures Trading Commission provided a no-action letter for the TSE 300 contract in April 1984. A spot-month TSE 300 futures contract was listed in 1985 that attracted the lion's share of volume in 1986 and 1987 but eventually died out in 1992.

Three years after the TSE 300 contract began trading, the TSE sought to solve the replication problem by introducing the Toronto 35 Index, which was designed to track the TSE 300 Composite, but with much fewer and very liquid stocks. However, the institutional community was not entirely satisfied with the Toronto 35 Index because it was too narrow, set a weighting cap on some stocks, and didn't track the broad market as well as was expected. The TSE 100, designed in 1993, set out to become the institutional benchmark, but remains a distant second to the Toronto 35 when it comes to trading volume in both futures and options.

Toronto 35

The Toronto 35 Index was developed in 1987 specifically to become an exchange-traded product that mirrored the broader TSE 300 Composite Index. Indeed, every major industry group with a weighting of at least 5% of the TSE 300 must be represented in the Toronto 35 Index. With the exception of real estate, the Toronto 35 Index represents all sectors of the TSE 300 and boasts a 97% correlation with the larger index.

Understanding the Index. To determine the component stocks in the Toronto 35, stocks are first ranked according to their float QMV. Then, each stock must rank within the top 125 of the TSE 300 over the last 12 months in the following categories: (1) volume traded;

(2) value traded; and (3) total transactions executed. The weight given each stock in the Toronto 35 is based mainly on the float QMV relative to the other stocks, but never exceeds 10% (initially) for an individual issue so that no single stock can dominate the index value. (The percentage weights may change throughout the year according to market action but are initially established just once a year.)

Index at a Glance.

Index	Toronto 35
Exchange	Toronto Futures Exchange
Weighting	Modified capitalization
Ticker Symbol	TXF
Contract Value (Dec. 31, 1998)	351.96 x C$500 = C$175,980
Clearinghouse	Canadian Derivatives Clearing Corporation
Regulator	Ontario Securities Commission
Web Site Information	www.tse.com

Stocks in the Toronto 35 are reviewed monthly to make sure that their float QMV is within the top 200 stocks of the TSE 300. If not, the stock is replaced at the opening of the next month's futures and options expiry. All the stocks are reviewed annually to ensure that they meet all the requirements for inclusion in the Toronto 35 Index. Every five years, a review determines whether the stocks in the index remain both liquid and representative of their industry. At year-end 1998, the stocks shown in Table 5.12 were the most heavily weighted in the Toronto 35 Index. At that date, the closing basket-weighted QMV value of all stocks in the index equaled about $2 million.

Toronto 35 Futures. Of the investable indexes trading at TSE, the most volume occurs in the Toronto 35 futures and cash option contracts. Index futures are listed by the *Toronto Futures Exchange* (TFE), a separate entity sponsored by the TSE, while options on the cash indexes are traded on the stock exchange.

Futures and options trading on the Toronto 35 Index opened on May 27, 1987. The U.S. Commodity Futures Trading Commission approved the Index for trading by U.S. investors on October 6, 1988; options trading was approved the U.S. Securities and Exchange Commission for only some states.

Calculating the Index. The Toronto 35 Index value is determined by multiplying the stock price by the number of shares, as determined by the share-weighting scheme, and dividing by a divisor that keeps

TABLE 5.12 Top 10 Stocks in Toronto 35
(December 31, 1998)

Rank	Company	Basket-Weighted QMV (Canadian dollars)	Percent Weight
1	BCE Inc. (BCE)	231,400	11.53
2	Northern Telecom (NTL)	153,200	7.63
3	Royal Bank (RY)	114,825	5.72
4	Toronto-Dominion Bank (TD)	96,840	4.82
5	Canadian Imperial Bank (CM)	95,000	4.73
6	Imasco Ltd. (IMS)	91,560	4.56
7	Bombardier CI B (BBD.B)	88,000	4.38
8	The Seagram Co. (VO)	87,375	4.35
9	Bank of Montreal (BMO)	86,380	4.30
10	Canadian Pacific Ltd. (CP)	86,250	4.30

Source: Toronto Stock Exchange

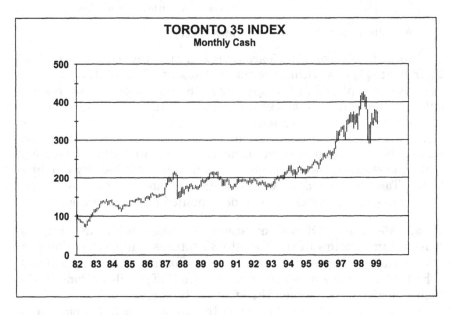

FIGURE 5.13 Toronto 35 Index
Source: CRB-Bridge Information

the index in relation to its starting value of 100 in January 1982 (see Figure 5.13). The divisor also is adjusted for the following: (1) reorganizations or spin-offs; (2) dividends and rights or cash distributions that are at least 4% of the underlying stock's price; (3) stock splits that create separate share classes; (4) bankruptcy that requires removal from the index; and (5) any other situation that causes a stock to be added or removed to the index, or when constituent shares in the index are adjusted.

TSE 100

The TSE 100 Index was designed to become the benchmark for institutional investment in Canadian stocks. It includes the top 100 stocks in the broader TSE 300, based on float QMV and liquidity, a list that is examined monthly. An annual review of stocks in the index is based on information from the last trading day in February, with changes effective at the opening of the March futures and options contracts expiration. Four sectors are represented in the TSE 100 with 1998 weightings: resource (18%), consumer (13%), industrial (25%), and interest-sensitive (44%).

Understanding the Index. To be included in the TSE 100 Index, a company's stock must be either (1) in the top 100 stocks of the TSE 300 Composite based on float QMV and in the top 150 in terms of aggregated trading value (on the TSE and Montreal Stock Exchange combined) or (2) within the top 50 stocks based on float QMV. Stocks in the TSE 100 represent 58% of Canadian listed companies and 35% of all companies listed in Canada.

Even though the TSE 100 was not designed to track the TSE 300 Composite Index, its tracking error to the larger index is lower than that of the Toronto 35 Index, which was specifically designed to mirror the broad index. Based on daily data from January 1982 through December 1998, the TSE 100 had a 99.5% correlation with the TSE

Index at a Glance.

Index	TSE 100
Exchange	Toronto Futures Exchange
Weighting	Capitalization
Ticker Symbol	TOF
Contract Value (Dec. 31, 1998)	397.26 x C$500 = C$198,630
Clearinghouse	Canadian Derivatives Clearing Corporation
Regulator	Ontario Securities Commission
Web Site Information	www.tse.com

TABLE 5.13 Top 10 Stocks in TSE 100
(December 31, 1998)

Rank	Company	Float QMV (million Canadian dollars)	Percent Weight
1	BCE Inc. (BCE)	37,002	8.08
2	Northern Telecom (59%) (NTL)	30,108	6.57
3	Royal Bank of Canada (RY)	23,638	5.16
4	Bank of Nova Scotia (BNS)	16,599	3.62
5	Bank of Montreal (BMO)	16,305	3.56
6	Seagram Co. Ltd. (70%) (VO)	16,140	3.52
7	Toronto-Dominion Bank (TD)	15,981	3.49
8	Canadian Imperial Bank of Commerce (CM)	15,761	3.44
9	Barrick Gold (ABX)	11,212	2.45
10	Bombardier Inc. CL B (BBD.B)	11,077	2.42

Source: Toronto Stock Exchange

300. The 10 largest stocks in the TSE 100 at year-end 1998 are shown in Table 5.13. Note that two of the stocks have percentage qualifiers that represent the control block for each and the percentage of outstanding shares excluded from the float QMV. For example, the 70% noted for Seagram's mostly represents the holdings of the Bronfman family.

TSE 100 Futures. The TSE 100 index was first publicly disseminated on October 1, 1993, but trading in the futures and cash option contracts did not begin until May 20, 1994. The CFTC approved the TSE 100 for trading by U.S. investors in some states on April 14, 1994. Trading in TSE 100 options dwindled to less than 100 contracts for 1997 and died out in 1998.

Calculating the Index. The TSE 100 index is calculated similarly to the TSE 300 Composite Index. The TSE 100 Index value is determined by multiplying the stock price by the float shares and dividing by a divisor that keeps the index in relation to its starting value of 250 on August 31, 1993 (see Figure 5.14). The divisor also is adjusted for the following: (1) reorganizations or spin-offs; (2) dividends and rights or cash distributions that are at least 4% of the underlying stock's price; (3) stock splits that create separate share classes; (4) bankruptcy that requires removal from the index; and (5) any other situation that causes a stock to be added or removed to the index, or when constituent shares in the index are adjusted.

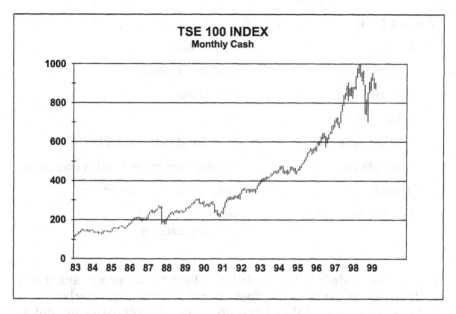

FIGURE 5.14 TSE 100 Index
Source: CRB-Bridge Information

S&P/TSE 60

In late 1998, the Toronto Stock Exchange and S&P Corporation announced they would be developing a new large-capitalization stock index. The new S&P/TSE 60 tracks 60 large-cap stocks that are members of the broad TSE 300 index, represents 71% of the broader index's market capitalization and has a correlation of 98% to the TSE 300. Futures and cash options on the TSE 35 and TSE 100 indexes eventually will be phased out in favor of similar products on the S&P/TSE 60. Stocks in the index represent all 11 subgroups of the TSE 300, including basic materials, capital goods, communications services, consumer cyclical, consumer staples, energy, financials, health care, technology, transportation, and utilities.

Understanding the Index. Stocks are selected for the index based on their size, liquidity, and sector leadership. Size is determined by ranking stocks according to market capitalization. However, only the number of available shares for investment are multiplied by price to determine a stock's market value. Float adjustments are made for cross holdings, government holdings, strategic partners, and other control groups that hold 20% or more of the stock. Stocks also are evaluated on the basis of liquidity, defined as the stock's 12-month

Index at a Glance.

Index	S&P/Canada 60
Exchange	Montreal Exchange
Weighting	Capitalization
Ticker Symbol	SXF
Contract Value (Dec. 31, 1998)	375.98 x C$250 = C$93,995
Clearinghouse	Canadian Derivatives Clearing Corporation
Regulator	Quebec Securities Commission
Web Site Information	www.me.org www.spglobal.com

dollar value traded. Value traded and float turnover are evaluated monthly. Adjustments to the float shares are made quarterly.

Finally, the financial and operating condition of each company is analyzed in order to include stable companies in the index and to reduce turnover. This feature distinguishes the S&P/TSE 60 from the TSE 300, TSE 100, and Toronto 35 indexes, which looked mainly to market capitalization and trading volume as qualifiers for inclusion. As of year-end 1998, the stocks shown in Table 5.14 were the 10 most influential in the S&P/TSE 60.

TABLE 5.14 Top 10 Stocks in S&P/TSE 60
(December 31, 1998)

Rank	Company	Float QMV (million Canadian dollars)	Percent Weight
1	BCE Inc. (BCE)	37,002	9.56
2	Northern Telecom Ltd. (NTL)	30,108	7.78
3	Royal Bank of Canada (RY)	23,638	6.11
4	The Bank of Nova Scotia (BNS)	16,600	4.29
5	Bank of Montreal (BMO)	16,305	4.21
6	The Seagram Company Ltd. (VO)	16,140	4.17
7	The Toronto-Dominion Bank (TD)	15,981	4.13
8	Canadian Imperial Bank of Commerce (CM)	15,761	4.07
9	Barrick Gold Corporation (ABX)	11,212	2.90
10	Bombardier Inc. CL 'B' SV (BBD.B)	11,077	2.86

Source: Standard & Poor's Corporation

S&P/Canada 60 Futures. The S&P/Canada 60 index, based on the S&P/TSE 60, was launched on September 7, 1999 at the Montreal Exchange. As a result, no further contract months will be listed for trading in the Toronto 35 and TSE 100 Indexes after the December 1999 expiration.

Under the proposed restructuring of the Canadian stock exchanges, derivatives products were scheduled to move to the Montreal Exchange. Stock index products trading at TSE will remain in Toronto.

Officials expected that they would seek no-action letters from both CFTC and the SEC on the new S&P/TSE 60 futures and options contracts.

Calculating the Index. The S&P/TSE 60 index is capitalization-weighted, but the number of shares used to determine a company's market value represents only those available for investment. If owners of a particular stock control more than 20% of the entire pool of stock, those shares will not be included in the available amount used to weight the stock in the index. These *investable weight factors* are reviewed and updated quarterly following expiration of the futures and options contracts. However, any change that causes a member stock's weight in the index to change by more than 0.05% will be implemented immediately.

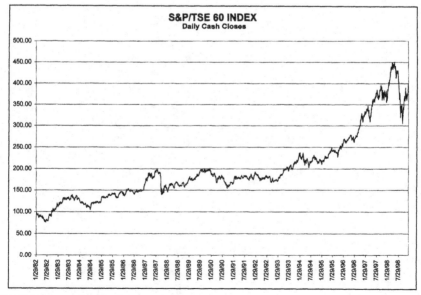

FIGURE 5.15   S&P/TSE 60 Index

Source: Standard and Poor's

A seven-person Index Policy Committee of representatives from S&P Corporation and the TSE meets at least monthly to discuss the index make-up. Additions to the index generally are made only when a stock has been deleted from the index, most typically due to its acquisition by another company. However, a stock also may be deleted from the index for bankruptcy, corporate restructuring, or a lack of representation in its industry group. The Index Policy Committee maintains a confidential pool of potential replacement stocks. Changes to the index make-up will be made after the daily close of trading, typically three days in advance of the corporate change.

Calculation of the index began on December 31, 1998, with an opening value of 374.51, and has been reconstructed to January 29, 1982, when the index had an approximate value of 89 (see Figure 5.15). S&P Corporation calculates the index in real-time and distributes it every 15 seconds.

6

KNOW YOUR STOCK INDEX: ASIA/PACIFIC

Development of stock index futures products in the Asian-Pacific region was not far behind that in the United States. The All Ordinaries Share Price Index was listed in Australia in 1983, just one year after the first U.S. index began trading. Three years later, the Nikkei 225 Average contract began trading in Singapore.

The Sydney Futures Exchange (SFE) announced in December 1998 that it would work with Dow Jones Indexes to develop a set of stock indexes to represent the entire region, known as the Dow Jones Asia Pacific Extra Liquid Series (Dow Jones AP/ELS). Regional, country and sector-specific indexes will be part of the group and trade exclusively at SFE. The first of these indexes, based on 35 Austalian stocks, opened for futures trading on September 13, 1999.

AUSTRALIA

The Australian stock market is the 10th largest in the world, with market capitalization of $312 billion in 1997, according to the World Bank. Although the Australian Stock Exchange has developed several stock indexes, the only one with a listed derivative product is the All Ordinaries Index.

All Ordinaries Share Price Index

The All Ordinaries Share Price Index is the Australian stock market's benchmark. The index comprises the largest stocks listed on the Australian Stock Exchange and totaled 254 companies out of the 1,222 listed in early 1999. The companies in the index at year-end 1998 represented nearly 90% of the market's total capitalization.

Index at a Glance.

Index	All Ordinaries Share Price Index
Exchange	Sydney Futures Exchange
Weighting	Capitalization
Ticker symbol	AO SA on SYCOM
Contract Value (Dec. 31, 1998)	2813.4 x A$25 = A$70,335
Clearinghouse	Sydney Futures Exchange Clearing House
Regulator	Australian Securities Commission
Web Site Information	www.sfe.com.au www.asx.com.au

Understanding the Index. A capitalization-weighted index, the All Ords is most influenced by the highest priced stocks with the highest number of shares outstanding, adjusted for a market liquidity factor. At year-end 1998, the 10 largest stocks in the index by capitalization accounted for about 45% of the total weighting (see Table 6.1).

The All Ords Index is made up of two subindexes, the All Ordinaries Resources Index and the All Industrials Index. In turn, each of these indexes reflects composite industry or sector indexes. In mid-1998, the industrials accounted for about 70% of the total market value. In 1980, when the All Ords was first devised, industrials were just 43% of the market.

All Ordinaries Share Price Futures. Futures on the All Ordinaries Share Price Index (SPI) were the first stock index contract to be listed outside the United States. The SPI contract was launched in February 1983, just a year after stock index futures were introduced in the United States. Options on the futures contract followed in 1985. The two contracts were approved by the CFTC for trading by U.S. investors on September 5, 1991. The big jump in volume and open interest noticeable in 1993 was due to a reduction in the contract multiplier, to A$25 from A$100 on October 11 that year.

TABLE 6.1 Top 10 Stocks in All Ordinaries Share Price Index
(December 31, 1998)

Rank	Company	Market Capitalization (million Australian dollars)	Percent Weight
1	News Corporation (NCP)	39,133	8.24
2	National Australia Bank (NAB)	35,628	7.51
3	Telstra Corporation (TLS)	32,686	6.89
4	Broken Hill (BHP)	24,964	5.26
5	Commonwealth Bank (CBA)	21,654	4.56
6	Westpac Banking Corp. (WBC)	20,565	4.33
7	Australia and New Zealand Bank (ANZ)	16,456	3.47
8	Rio Tinto Limited (RIO)	11,669	2.40
9	AMP Limited (AMP)	22,235 (50%)	2.34
10	Lend Lease Corp. (LLC)	11,038	2.33

Source: Australian Stock Exchange

Unlike American stock index contracts, no daily limit is placed on index movement for the SPI. Thus, participants have confidence that they will always have access to the market. In late October 1997, when the U.S. stock market plummeted, the SPI fell a record 89 points during trading on the overnight screen system at SFE, known as SYCOM. Trading volume in SPI futures hit a record 3.2 million in 1997 and broke that record a year later when volume hit 3.7 million.

On a daily basis, SPI settles to the midpoint of the closing bid and ask futures quotations, rounded up. A contract's final settlement price upon expiration is the closing quotation of the All Ordinaries Index as provided by the Australian Stock Exchange on the following business day.

The SFE plans to close its floor-trading facility and move all trading in its futures and options products to the screen in October 1999. Decisions on the SPI ticker symbol and trading hours were to be decided in mid-1999.

Calculating the Index. The index was developed by the Australian Stock Exchange and had an opening base value of 500 on December 31, 1979 (see Figure 6.1). The All Ordinaries replaced two indexes from the Sydney and Melbourne markets, which had been calculated from 1958 and 1960, respectively. A record of monthly market movement in Australia was calculated retrospectively, dating to 1875.

Companies in the index must meet a minimum market capitalization figure and post adequate trading volume on the stock exchange. The minimum market capitalization equals a level that is

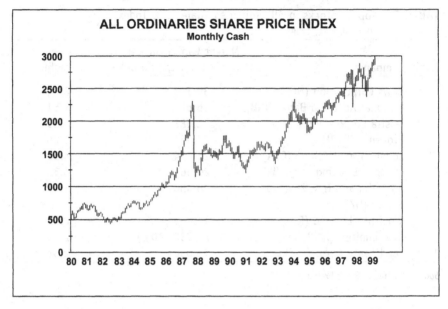

FIGURE 6.1   All Ordinaries Share Price Index
Source: CRB-Bridge Information

10% above 0.02% of all domestic equities listed on the Australian Stock Exchange; that level must be maintained for six consecutive months (three months if a new issue).

The market capitalization measure is multiplied by a liquidity factor for purposes of weighting each stock in the All Ordinaries Index. This liquidity factor is determined by comparing the liquidity of each stock in the index to the liquidity of market as a whole. Liquidity for an individual stock is found on a daily basis by dividing the volume of shares traded by the total number of shares; then a monthly median value is determined based on the daily values. Liquidity for the market as a whole also is calculated on a daily basis but is weighted by market capitalization. For example, the company AMP Limited would have ranked fifth in Table 6.1 if 100% of its total capitalization of A$22.2 billion had been used to determine its weighting in the index. With only 50% of its capitalization going into the market value formula, the company slipped to ninth in terms of its index weighting.

The index is calculated by dividing the current market capitalization of stocks in the index by their market capitalization at the start of the day, which has been adjusted for any overnight changes such as delistings, additions, new issues, and capital reconstructions. Then that result is multiplied by the previous day's closing index value to determine the current index value.

HONG KONG

The Hong Kong stock market is the second largest in Asia in terms of market capitalization. At the end of September 1998, 674 companies were listed on the Stock Exchange of Hong Kong (SEHK), with total market capitalization of US$275.7 billion.

The Hang Seng Index, published by the SEHK and listed as both a futures and option contract at the Hong Kong Futures Exchange (HKFE), has a long history of serving as the market's proxy. In late 1998, a challenger arose in the MSCI Hong Kong⁺ Index, developed by Morgan Stanley Capital International, which opened for trade in futures at the Singapore International Monetary Exchange (SIMEX) in Singapore.

The HKFE and SEHK responded to the challenge quickly. The first salvo came from SEHK, which warned its data vendors that to supply real-time information to those who use it to develop a competing product would violate their contract with the exchange. Then the HKFE decided to expand its trading hours to match those of SIMEX, waive commissions and fees in December 1998, and cut the margin retention rate held by the exchange to 1.2% from 1.8%, effective January 1999.[1]

Hang Seng Index

The Hang Seng Index (HSI) of blue-chip stocks has been distributed since November 24, 1969, and is the most widely quoted and followed index of issues on the SEHK. It is a market-capitalization-weighted index of 33 stocks, representing about 70% of the stock market's total capitalization, which at year-end 1998 stood at HK$2,662 billion.

Index at a Glance.

Index	Hang Seng
Exchange	Hong Kong Futures Exchange
Weighting	Capitalization
Ticker Symbol	HSI
Contract Value (Dec. 31, 1998)	10048.58 x HK$50 = HK$502,429
Clearinghouse	HKFE Clearing Corporation Limited
Regulator	Securities and Futures Commission
Web Site Information	www.hkfe.com
	www.hsiservices.com

Understanding the Index. The HSI is considered the benchmark for investment in Hong Kong stocks and closely tracks the broader All Ordinaries Index at the SEHK. HSI Services Ltd., a wholly owned subsidiary of Hang Seng Bank and a member of the HSBC Group, compiles, computes, and disseminates the index. The index dates to July 31, 1964 when its base was set at 100.

The stocks in the HSI are grouped under one of four subindexes that were developed in 1985: Commerce and Industry, 19.23% weighting in HSI; Finance, 34.96% weighting; Properties, 17.15% weighting; and Utilities, 28.64% weighting. Note that although the index represents 33 stocks, just two—HSBC Holdings and Hutchison Whampoa—accounted for 35% of the weighting at year-end 1998 (see Table 6.2). A current list of constituent stocks and weekly weighting updates are available at the HSI Services web site.

Hang Seng Futures. The Hang Seng futures contract is the flagship product at HKFE, accounting for about 80% to 90% of daily trading volume. It opened for trading on May 6, 1986, and was approved for U.S. investors by the CFTC on June 1, 1994. The cash option index contract opened on March 5, 1993; SEC approved the option for U.S. distribution on December 14, 1995.

Acceptance of the Hang Seng Index as a derivatives product was nearly immediate. Trading volume in Hang Seng futures reached more than 3 million contracts in its second year of trading, 1987, but

TABLE 6.2 Top 10 Stocks in Hang Seng Index
(December 31, 1998)

Rank	Company	Market Capitalization (million HK dollars)	Percent Weight
1	HSBC Holdings plc	521,015	25.05
2	Hutchison Whampoa	212,358	10.21
3	Hong Kong Telecommunications Ltd.	162,024	7.79
4	China Telecom(Hong Kong) Ltd.	157,864	7.59
5	SHK Properties	135,193	6.50
6	Hang Seng Bank Ltd.	132,490	6.37
7	Cheung Kong (Holdings) Ltd.	128,122	6.16
8	CLP Holdings	94,635	4.55
9	Henderson Land Development Co. Ltd.	69,052	3.32
10	Hong Kong Electric Holdings Ltd.	47422	2.28

Source: Hong Kong Futures Exchange

due to market-related problems, it did not reach that level again until 1994. During the October 1987 market crash, the SEHK closed for four days, waiting for the market to settle down; in accordance with a rule at the time, the HKFE also was dark for four days. When the market reopened on October 26, 1987, the prospect of a broker default highlighted the weaknesses in the exchange's structure and risk-management operations. The HKFE was reorganized according to reform measures recommended by a government-sponsored committee of market professionals, and HKFE shareholders approved a new constitution in 1989.

In 1997, the Hang Seng Index was once again in the spotlight as the Asian financial crisis relating to the Hong Kong dollar value sent the index down more than 30% in October and November. Daily volume in the HSI reached a record 83,445 contracts on October 23 that year; options volatility reached an unprecedented 90.8% on October 28.

Hong Kong's Financial Services Bureau reviewed the late 1997 market situation and gave a clean bill of health to the HKFE, recommending only continued refinements to some rules and margin levels. The report also recommended moving futures and options trading to the electronic platform, introduction of futures trading on the broader Hang Seng 100 Index, and cross-margining between futures and stock positions. Futures and the cash options on the Hang Seng currently trade via open outcry but will be moving to the HKFE's electronic platform, the Automated Trading System (ATS), by year-end 1999. The Hang Seng 100 products moved to the screen on September 18, 1998. The report also found no evidence of market manipulation in the late 1997 market period.

In 1998, the Hong Kong government intervened in the stock market to the tune of HK$118 billion, as part of a plan to support the Hong Kong dollar. During that same month, August, open interest in both the futures and options contracts increased by about 50%, and the HKFE imposed increased margin requirements and reporting rules on large position holders. Indeed, part of the increase in trading that month was due to direct government purchase of futures and options contracts, reported at 48,000 contracts.[2]

In early 1999, the Hong Kong government announced it planned to merge the stock exchange and the futures exchange into a single entity—The Hong Kong Exchanges and Clearing, Ltd.—no later than September 30, 2000.[3] As part of the move, the government said it would demutualize the exchanges and list the new entity as a publicly held company.[4] The news came on the heels of a similar announcement in November 1998 from the Singapore government that the Stock Exchange of Singapore and the Singapore International Monetary Exchange would merge into a publicly owned company by January 2002.[5]

Calculating the Index. To be eligible for inclusion in the Hang Seng Index, a company must meet the following criteria:

1. Be in the top 90% of total market capitalization, in a 12-month average, of all ordinary shares listed on the SEHK

2. Have total volume over the last two years within the top 90% of SEHK stocks

3. Be listed for two years

4. Not be a foreign company, as defined by SEHK

Final selection of companies for the index is based on market capitalization, representation of subindexes, and the company's financial performance. HSI Services reviews the component stocks semiannually.

To determine the index level, the total market capitalization of all 33 stocks is divided by the preceding day's total market capitalization for all 33 stocks. This figure is multiplied by the preceding day's closing index value to determine the new index value. A monthly chart of the Hang Seng Index since 1987 is shown in Figure 6.2.

Final settlement for both the futures and options contracts is determined by taking the average of index values taken every five minutes during the last trading day and rounding down to the nearest whole number.

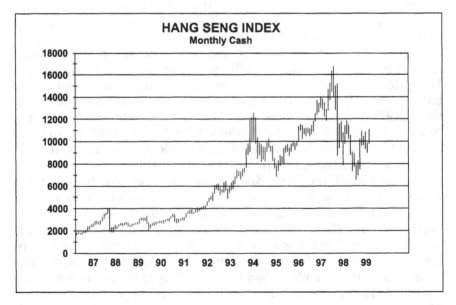

FIGURE 6.2   Hang Seng Index
Source: CRB-Bridge Information

MSCI Hong Kong+

The MSCI Hong Kong+ Index, created by Morgan Stanley Capital International, is a newcomer to the field of products on the Hong Kong market. Introduced in late 1998, it differs from the more established MSCI Hong Kong Index because it includes HSBC Holdings in its list of component stocks. The company, whose stock is easily the most widely traded on the SEHK, was excluded from the older index because it already was part of Morgan Stanley's index on stocks in the United Kingdom. However, because the MSCI Hong Kong+ Index seeks to be a proxy for the Hong Kong stock market, which can underlie derivatives products, it includes the entire market capitalization of HSBC in its calculation.

Index at a Glance.

Index	MSCI Hong Kong+
Exchange	Singapore International Monetary Exchange (SIMEX)
Weighting	Capitalization
Ticker Symbol	HK
Contract Value (Dec. 31, 1998)	7166.04 x US$5 = US$35,830.20
Clearinghouse	SIMEX Clearing House
Regulator	Monetary Authority of Singapore
Web Site Information	www.simex.com.sg www.msci.com

Understanding the Index. Like the Hang Seng Index, the MSCI Hong Kong+ is capitalization-weighted. The index represents 35 stocks with capitalization that equals about 68% of the Hong Kong market. It has a daily correlation of 99.995% with the Hang Seng Index. Twenty stocks in the MSCI Hong Kong+ match those in the Hang Seng Index, including the top 10 by capitalization. The top two or three stocks typically equal more than 50% of the total index weight (see Table 6.3).

The index is split into 15 sectors, the most dominant being banking, 38.56% of the total weighting; real estate, 19.79%; multi-industry, 15.63%; and telecommunications, 11.25%.

MSCI Hong Kong+ Futures. SIMEX initially listed futures on the original MSCI Hong Kong+ Index on March 31, 1993, and the CFTC

TABLE 6.3 Top 10 Stocks in MSCI Hong Kong⁺
(October 26, 1998)

Rank	Company	Market Capitalization (billion HK dollars)	Percent Weight
1	HSBC Holdings	480.8	29.48
2	Hutchison Whampoa	200.6	12.30
3	Hong Kong Telecom	183.4	11.25
4	Hang Seng Bank	125.7	7.71
5	Cheung Kong Holdings	116.6	7.15
6	Sun Hung Kai Properties	110.2	6.76
7	CLP Holdings	103.6	6.35
8	Swire Pacific (A)	50.6	3.10
9	Hong Kong and China Gas Co.	46.0	2.82
10	New World Development	34.6	2.12

Source: SIMEX

granted the contract a no-action letter making it eligible for U.S. investors on June 1, 1994. The futures contract traded more than 80,000 in 1993 but just 317 in 1994, the year that Hang Seng Index futures at the HKFE became available to U.S. investors. SIMEX delisted the contract on August 28, 1997. The MSCI Hong Kong⁺ Index futures contract is considered approved by the CFTC on the basis of the original contract's OK. The multiplier of the newer futures contract is in U.S. dollars rather than Hong Kong dollars. Orders of 100 lots or more may be entered as an all or none order to be executed at a single price.

Calculating the Index. The MSCI Hong Kong⁺ Index is calculated by dividing the sum of current total market capitalization of stocks (adjusted for changes such as stock splits, stock dividends, and rights issues) in the index by the previous sum of total market capitalization and multiplying that result by the preceding index level. The index adjusts for capital changes, such as rights offerings and stock splits, but does not include dividends in its calculation. Although the index is calculated several ways with differing currencies and policies toward dividends, the futures contract is based on the local currency (Hong Kong dollar) index without dividends. The base was set at 100 on December 31, 1969, with the index calculated monthly through 1985 and daily since 1986. A program to calculate the MSCI Hong Kong⁺ Index on a real-time basis is available at the Morgan Stanley Capital International web site.

The index strives to cover at least 60% of the Hong Kong market's total capitalization and to replicate its composition by industry.

Large-, medium, and small-cap stocks are represented in the index, but those with a limited availability of free-trading shares are avoided. Stocks may be deleted when they have been suspended from trading for a prolonged period, upon merger, or on rebalancing. The stocks in the index are reviewed quarterly, with changes announced at least two weeks in advance.

JAPAN

The Japanese stock market is second only to the United States in size, touting market capitalization of $3.1 trillion in 1997 versus U.S. market capitalization of $8.5 trillion. Nearly 2,500 stocks are listed on Japan's domestic exchanges. Listed stocks are assigned to either the first section or the second section. First-section listings are large stocks with good liquidity; second-section listings are for newer companies. The major Japanese stock indexes are based on first-section stocks.

Japanese stocks are traded on eight exchanges throughout the country, but two typically account for more than 90% of total annual volume. The Tokyo Stock Exchange (TSE) is the dominant securities exchange in Japan, with 75% to 85% of total annual volume. The Osaka Securities Exchange (OSE) is the second largest exchange in Japan, typically claiming 10% to 20% of the country's total volume; OSE also lists futures and cash options on two of Japan's stock market measures, the Nikkei 225 and Nikkei 300 Indexes. The TSE lists futures and cash options on the Tokyo Price Index (TOPIX). Japanese stock index contracts also are traded in Singapore and the United States.

The first stock index futures contract in Japan was the Osaka Stock Futures 50 (OSF 50), introduced in June 1987. The OSF 50 called for physical delivery of the underlying shares of stock and traded actively only through 1988; it was delisted in 1992. Its demise was linked to a change in Japanese securities law in 1988 that allowed cash settlement for stock index futures and options contracts; the OSE started trading Nikkei 225 futures in September 1988.

Nikkei 225 Averages

The Nikkei Stock Average is to Japan what the DJIA is to the United States—a price-weighted average of stock prices with a long history and a well-known name among the general public. Three exchanges in as many countries trade futures on the Nikkei 225, including the CME in the United States, the OSE in Japan, and SIMEX in Singapore. The 225 stocks in the average are listed on the first tier of the TSE.

Index at a Glance.

Index	Nikkei 225
Exchange	Chicago Mercantile Exchange
Weighting	Price
Ticker Symbol	NK
Contract Value (Dec. 31, 1998)	13842 x $5 = $69,210
Clearinghouse	CME Clearing House
Regulator	Commodity Futures Trading Commission
Web Site Information	www.cme.com www.nikkei.co.jp

Index	Nikkei 225
Exchange	Osaka Stock Exchange
Weighting	Price
Ticker Symbol	None
Contract Value (Dec. 31, 1998)	13842 x ¥1,000 = ¥13,842,000 ($121,948)
Clearinghouse	OSE Clearing Administration Department
Regulator	Ministry of Finance Financial Supervision Agency
Web Site Information	www.ose.or.jp www.nikkei.co.jp

Index	Nikkei 225
Exchange	Singapore International Monetary Exchange
Weighting	Price
Ticker Symbol	NK
Contract Value (Dec. 31, 1998)	13842 x ¥500 = ¥6,921,000 ($61,043)
Clearinghouse	SIMEX Clearing House
Regulator	Monetary Authority of Singapore
Web Site Information	www.simex.com.sg www.nikkei.co.jp

Understanding the Index. The Nikkei Stock Average is Japan's longest-running stock index, first introduced by the TSE in September 1950 as the TSE Adjusted Stock Price Average. It was retroactively calculated to May 16, 1949, the day Japanese stock markets reopened after being closed for about two years due to World War II troubles, the so-called "Blank Period of Exchange Markets in Japan." Twenty years later, business news publisher Nihon Keizai Shimbun, Inc. (Nikkei) took up the challenge of calculating and distributing the stock average. Today, the index represents 225 actively traded stocks on the first tier of the TSE across 36 sectors.

In late 1968, the TSE announced it had developed a new market-capitalization-weighted index, the Tokyo Stock Price Index (TOPIX), and would discontinue calculation of its Adjusted Stock Price Average, effective July 1, 1970. The move was based on the exchange's belief that the price-weighted index was: (1) confusing to investors who might think the average represented real prices; (2) was overly influenced by high-priced stocks of small companies; and (3) was not changing the list of component stocks enough to accurately reflect the current market makeup and serve as an appropriate market measure.

Despite the TSE's misgivings about its original index, the measure's long history and familiarity enticed the current publisher to take over its distribution. A Nikkei subsidiary, Nihon Short-wave Broadcasting Co. began calculating and announcing the former Adjusted Stock Price Average as the NSB 225 Adjusted Average on July 1, 1971. The index has had several names over the years including: (1) TSE Adjusted Stock Price Average, 1950 to 1970; (2) NSB 225 Adjusted Average, 1971 to 1975; (3) Nikkei Dow-Jones Stock Price Average, 1975 to 1985; and (4) Nikkei Stock Average, 1985 to present. The index is commonly known as the Nikkei 225 because of the number of stocks included in the calculation. A monthly chart of the Nikkei 225 since 1982 is shown in Figure 6.3.

Nikkei 225 Futures. Futures contracts on the Nikkei 225 trade on three exchanges—the CME, OSE, and SIMEX—and U.S. investors may trade all of them. Trading volume has been the highest at Osaka since it appeared on the scene in 1988; futures trading there has been more popular than cash options every year but 1989. However, trading figures are healthy at all three exchanges. The multiplier for the CME contract is in dollars, while the other two contracts are priced in yen.

According to OSE, members accounted for 55% of Nikkei 225 futures trading volume in 1997, and the second-highest group was foreign investors, at 25%. In Nikkei 225 cash options, the members' share was 59% that year; foreign investors came in at 19%; and individuals were 9% of the total trade.

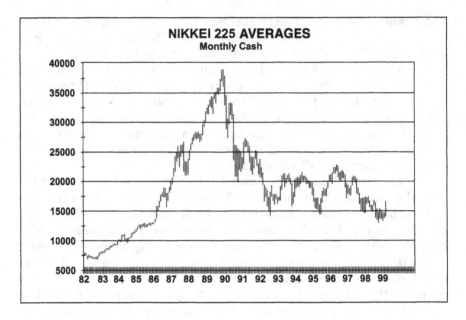

FIGURE 6.3   Nikkei 225 Averages
Source: CRB-Bridge Information

Futures trading is handled electronically at OSE, with open out-cry the method of choice in Chicago. In Singapore, the Nikkei 225 trades in both an open outcry and electronic session. During the open outcry session in Singapore, traders can place all-or-none (AON) orders for a minimum of 300 Nikkei 225 futures contracts. The AON designation means that the entire order will be filled at the same price.

The CME first obtained licensing rights to the Nikkei 225 in 1985 but did not list the contract until 1990. No mutual offset exists between the CME and SIMEX contracts because they have noncompatible multipliers and currencies. At both Singapore and Chicago, the futures market also offers single-priced calendar spreads in the Nikkei 225.

Calculating the Index. From the start, the Nikkei Average calculation method has been based on the model developed by Dow Jones & Co. to calculate its DJIA. At first, like the original DJIA, the Nikkei Average was a simple average calculated by dividing the sum of all the stock prices by the number of stocks in the index. Later, the TSE adopted the divisor method used by Dow Jones & Co., so that non-market events, such as stock splits, would not affect the index level.

The divisor is adjusted for dividends, stock splits, capital decreases, stock buybacks by the company, and component replacements.

Since 1991, the stocks in the Nikkei Average has been reviewed annually to ensure that they are representative of the Japanese stock market and are highly liquid. Indeed, all stocks in the TSE first section are sorted annually by a combination measure of trading volume and price fluctuation over the last 10 years, with the top 50% constituting the high liquidity group, from which any replacement stocks are chosen. The 10 highest-capitalized stocks in the Nikkei 225 at year-end 1998 are shown in Table 6.4.

Stocks may be deleted from the index for the following reasons: (1) bankruptcy; (2) merger or acquisition; (3) delisting or a move to the Seiri-Post or Kanri-Post categories; and (4) a move to the second section of the TSE. Stocks may also be removed if they show low liquidity, but deletions based on this criteria are limited to 3% of the component stocks, or six out of 225. When stocks need to be added to the index, the selection is based on an ideal number of components from each industry that should be included in the average, based on the proportion of stocks each industry has in the high-liquidity group. The first stocks to be chosen as replacements are those from under-represented industries, with individual stock choices made on the basis of liquidity. These replacement stocks must have been listed on the TSE first section for at least three years or have more than 60 million shares outstanding, based on a 50-yen par value.

TABLE 6.4 Top 10 Stocks for Nikkei 225
(ranked by market capitalization, December 31, 1998)

Rank	Company	Market Capitalization (billion yen)	Price (yen)
1	Nippon Telegraph & Telephone Corp.	13,875	872,000
2	Toyota Motor Corp.	11,601	3,070
3	The Bank of Tokyo-Mitsubishi, Ltd.	5,470	1,170
4	Matsushita Electric Ind. Co., Ltd.	4,159	1,999
5	Takeda Chemical Ind., Ltd.	3,868	4,350
6	The Tokyo Electric Power Co., Inc.	3,775	2,790
7	The Sumitomo Bank, Ltd.	3,643	1,160
8	Honda Motor Co., Ltd.	3,615	3,710
9	Sony Corp.	3,378	8,230
10	Fujitsu Ltd.	2,824	1,505

Source: Chicago Mercantile Exchange

Nikkei 300

The Nikkei 300, a broad capitalization-weighted index, was developed to compete with the older TOPIX measure as Japan's institutional investment benchmark. Both indexes have an institutional following, much like that enjoyed by S&P's 500 Index, which tends to get the institutional nod in the United States. The Nikkei 300 Index is based on 300 stocks from the first section of the Tokyo market. A weekly chart of the Nikkei 300 is shown in Figure 6.4.

Index at a Glance.

Index	Nikkei 300
Exchange	Osaka Securities Exchange (OSE)
Weighting	Capitalization
Ticker Symbol	None
Contract Value (Dec. 31, 1998)	216.89 x ¥10,000 = ¥2,168,900
Clearinghouse	OSE Clearing Administration Department
Regulator	Ministry of Finance Financial Supervision Agency
Web Site Information	www.ose.or.jp
Index	Nikkei 300
Exchange	Singapore Monetary Exchange Limited (SIMEX)
Weighting	Capitalization
Ticker Symbol	N3
Contract Value (Dec. 31, 1998)	216.89 x ¥10,000 = ¥2,168,900
Clearinghouse	SIMEX Clearing House
Regulator	Monetary Authority of Singapore
Web Site Information	www.simex.com.sg

Understanding the Index. The Nikkei 300 was designed to represent the broad Japanese stock market (more than 1,300 listings at the TSE) with a smaller number of stocks. It seeks to be well-balanced in terms of industry-sector representation as well as liquidity. At year-end 1998, the market value of the 10 largest stocks in the Nikkei 300 (see Table 6.5) equaled 28.85% of all 300 stocks combined.

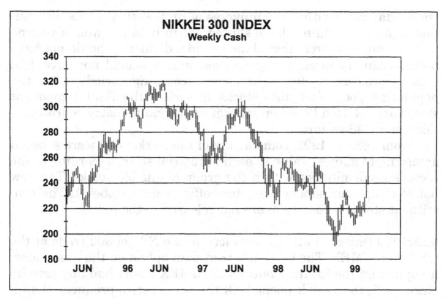

FIGURE 6.4 Nikkei 300 Index
Source: CRB-Bridge Information

TABLE 6.5 Top 10 Stocks in Nikkei 300
(December 31, 1998)

Rank	Company	Market Value* (billion yen)	Percent Weight
1	Nippon Telegraph & Telephone	13,875	7.01
2	Toyota Motor	11,601	5.86
3	The Bank of Tokyo-Mitsubishi	5,470	2.76
4	Matsushita Electric Industrial	4,159	2.10
5	Takeda Chemical Industries	3,868	1.95
6	Seven-Eleven Japan	3,790	1.91
7	The Tokyo Electric Power	3,774	1.91
8	The Sumitomo Bank	3,643	1.84
9	Honda Motor	3,615	1.83
10	Sony Corp.	3,378	1.71

*Price multiplied by all types of shares, including common stock, preferred shares and shares owned by the Japanese government.
Source: Nihon Keizai Shimbun, America Inc.

Constituent stocks for the Nikkei 300 are selected annually in September, with the changes effective in early October. To be eligible for inclusion in the Nikkei 300, the stocks must not have a conspicuously low volume, volume-to-outstanding shares ratio or low traded-day ratio within the universe of first-section stocks. In addition, a stock should not have shifted abruptly in its ratio of volume to outstanding shares, should have paid a dividend, should not have posted ordinary losses for some time, and/or should not have debt that exceeds assets for consecutive accounting periods. After the population pool of eligible stocks is sorted, the final component stocks are selected based on market value and industry representation among 36 sectors.

From 1982 to 1993, components of the Nikkei 300 were selected according to market value in each industrial sector according to the sector's predominance within the group of eligible stocks. The new list of component stocks went into effect each October 1. The constituent stocks before 1992 are not released to the public.

Nikkei 300 Futures. Futures contracts on the Nikkei 300 trade at the OSE and SIMEX. The OSE also trades an option on the cash index; an option on the futures contract at SIMEX hasn't had any activity since 1995, the year it opened. Of the three active products, the futures contract at OSE is the most liquid, trading at least 10 times more than the one at SIMEX from 1995 to 1998. According to OSE, 60% of the futures volume in 1997 was attributable to foreign customers, with exchange members tallying 34% of the annual volume. In contrast, foreign customers were only 3% of volume in Nikkei 300 options at OSE in 1997. Trust banks were the largest customer group, with 23% of the total volume, followed by individuals with 14%; members traded 53% of the total options volume.

Both futures contracts have received no-action letters from the CFTC and are available to U.S. customers. SIMEX hosts an electronic trading session for the Nikkei 300 from 3 P.M. to 7 P.M., after the floor trading session is closed. Interestingly, the SIMEX contract specifications call for final settlement of the futures contract to match the final settlement price used for Nikkei 300 futures at the OSE.

Calculating the Index. To calculate the Nikkei 300 Index, the market value (price times outstanding shares, excluding those owned by the government) of each stock is summed and divided by the total market value on the base date, otherwise known as the *divisor*; this result is multiplied by 100 to reach the current index value. The divisor is adjusted for stock additions/deletions as well as changes in the number of shares available for each stock, such as what occurs when a stock splits or a company merges with another.

The Nikkei 300 was set equal to 100 on October 1, 1982. Daily market values were made until January 31, 1994, when the index began being calculated once per minute.

Tokyo Stock Price Index

The TOPIX was the first benchmark for institutional investors in the Japanese stock market because it was developed in 1968. A market-capitalization index, it is closely correlated to other measures of Japanese stock market performance.

Index at a Glance.

Index	TOPIX
Exchange	Tokyo Stock Exchange (TSE)
Weighting	Capitalization
Ticker Symbol	HTPX
Contract Value (Dec. 31, 1998)	1086.99 x ¥10,000 = ¥10,869,900
Clearinghouse	Japan Securities Clearing Corporation
Regulator	Ministry of Finance Financial Supervision Agency
Web Site Information	www.tse.or.jp

Understanding the Index. TOPIX avoids the dilemma of how best to construct an index so that it *represents* the entire market by just including every common stock in the first section of the TSE, a figure that equals more than 90% of all publicly traded equities in Japan. In late 1998, more than 1,300 stocks were represented in TOPIX. The index was first distributed on July 1, 1969, with market index levels calculated to January 4, 1968, when the Index base was established at 100 (see Figure 6.5).

Through December 1998, the index's biggest daily percentage gain was 9.54% on October 2, 1990, the day Japan's Ministry of Finance announced emergency measures to support the market. In points, the biggest daily gain was on October 21, 1987, the day following the worldwide market crash. On the downside, both the biggest percentage and point declines were on October 20, 1987, at 14.62% and 307.27 points, respectively.

Three sectors account for about 40% of the index's total market value: banks, 16% at year-end 1997; electrical appliances, 15%; and transportation equipment, 11%. A capitalization-weighted index, the stocks with the most outstanding shares at the highest price have the most influence on index movement. At year-end 1998, the top 10 stocks in market capitalization included some very familiar names as shown in Table 6.6.

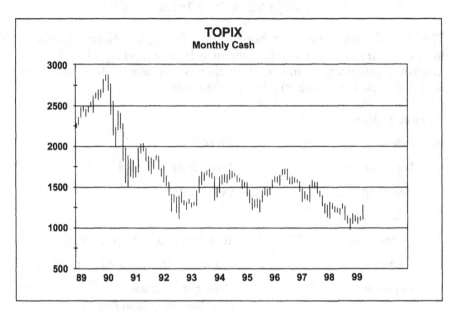

FIGURE 6.5 Tokyo Stock Price Index
Source: CRB-Bridge Information

TABLE 6.6 Top 10 Stocks in TOPIX
(December 31, 1998)

Rank	Company	Market Capitalization (billion yen)	Percent Weight
1	Toyota Motor	11,600	4.33
2	NTT Mobile Communications Network	8,905	3.33
3	Nippon Telegraph and Telephone	5,674	2.12
4	The Bank of Tokyo-Mitsubishi	5,470	2.04
5	Matsushita Electric Industrial	4,158	1.55
6	Takeda Chemical Industries	3,868	1.44
7	Seven-Eleven Japan	3,785	1.41
8	Tokyo Electric Power	3,774	1.41
9	The Sumitomo Bank	3,643	1.36
10	Honda Motor	3,615	1.35

Source: Tokyo Stock Exchange

TOPIX Futures. Futures trading in TOPIX began on September 3, 1988, the same day the OSE began trading the Nikkei 225, and exactly two years after SIMEX introduced the first futures contract on a Japanese stock index. TOPIX futures were approved by the CFTC for trade by U.S. customers in January 1992. TOPIX cash options were introduced in October 1989 but are not available to U.S. citizens because they have yet to be granted a no-action letter from the SEC.

Stock index trading got a relatively late start in Japan because laws that defined the contracts as securities and allowed for cash settlement of the index were not passed until 1988. The legal OK followed extensive study by both the TSE and the Japanese government. Indeed, the Ministry of Finance's advisory body, the Securities and Exchange Council, reported in May 1987 that "early introduction of a stock index futures contract, *et al* in this country is necessary."[6] In 1995, investment trusts were allowed to use stock index futures.

Like the derivatives markets in Osaka, TOPIX futures and options trade on an electronic system, called Computer-assisted Order Routing and Execution System for Futures (CORES-F) at TSE. Orders are filled with a priority to price and time entered. Unlike trading in the United States, customer accounts are not marked-to-the-market daily. Instead, the daily mark-to-the market adjustments are made at the member-firm level.

In 1997, the investor profile in TOPIX futures showed two primary users, securities companies at 53% of the volume and foreigners at 30% of the volume. Banks and investment trusts accounted for 16% of the annual volume. Individual investors did not trade enough to register even a 0.1% share of volume.

The CBOT introduced a dollar-denominated TOPIX futures contract in 1990, but it traded only 230 contracts that year.

Calculating the Index. The TOPIX value is determined by dividing the current market value (outstanding shares times share price) of all the stocks in the index by the *base market value,* the aggregate market value on the base date; that result is then multiplied by 100 and reduced to a decimal figure to the nearest one hundredth. The base market value is adjusted for several reasons:

- New listing
- Stock moving to first section from second section or vice versa
- Delisting
- Rights offering
- Public offering

- Private placement

- Merger

- Exercise of stock subscription warrant

- Conversion of convertible bond or preferred stock into common stock

- Purchase and retirement of company's own stocks

However, the base market value is not adjusted for any corporate decision that does not change the company's market capitalization, for example, a stock split. The TSE calculates and publishes the TOPIX level every minute.

S&P/TOPIX 150

In June 1999, the TSE and Standard & Poor's Corporation announced they had jointly developed a new index, the S&P/TOPIX 150, that would be calculated on a real-time basis beginning in July 1999. The index includes 150 highly liquid securities from each major sector of the Tokyo market, representing about 70% of the Japanese market's total value. No further details were available about futures or options products on the index at its announcement.

TAIWAN

The Taiwan stock market is among the most volatile of the emerging markets. Annual turnover velocity of domestic shares, computed as the market's total volume as a proportion of the total number of shares listed, is more than 200%. Access to the underlying stock market is difficult for non-Taiwanese investors due to restrictions on foreign investment.

Three futures exchanges around the globe have introduced a stock index contract on the Taiwan stock market, but only one has survived—the MSCI Taiwan Index at SIMEX, which was listed on January 9, 1997. CME sought to compete with SIMEX by listing the Dow Jones Taiwan Stock Index on January 8, 1997, but it traded less than 9,000 contracts in its first year and none after that. A third offering from the HKFE, the HKFE Taiwan Index, opened on May 26, 1998, but traded less than 100 contracts for the year.

MSCI Taiwan

The MSCI Taiwan Index tracks 77 stocks listed on the Taiwan Stock Exchange and aims to represent 60% of the entire market's value.

Index at a Glance.

Index	MSCI Taiwan
Exchange	Singapore International Monetary Exchange (SIMEX)
Weighting	Capitalization
Ticker Symbol	TW
Contract Value (Dec. 31, 1998)	257.427 x US$100 = US$25,742.70
Clearinghouse	SIMEX Clearing House
Regulator	Monetary Authority of Singapore
Web Site Information	www.simex.com.sg www.msci.com

Understanding the Index. The MSCI Taiwan Index has a base date value of 100 set on January 1, 1988, and is calculated without dividends (see Figure 6.6). The finance, capital equipment, and materials sectors each typically account for 20% to 30% of the index total weight. The 10 largest stocks in the index at year-end 1998 are shown in Table 6.7.

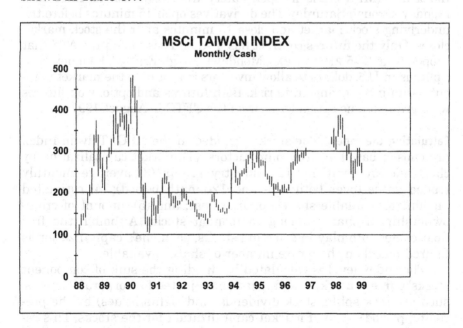

FIGURE 6.6 MSCI Taiwan Index
Source: CRB-Bridge Information

TABLE 6.7 Top 10 Stocks in MSCI Taiwan Index
(December 31, 1998)

Rank	Company	Market Capitalization (million U.S. dollars)	Percent Weight
1	Cathay Life Insurance	13,530	10.86
2	Taiwan Semiconductor Manufacturing	13,327	10.70
3	United Microelectronics	6,854	5.50
4	China Development Corp.	6,457	5.18
5	Nan Ya Plastic	5,210	4.18
6	China Steel Corp. (common)	4,936	3.96
7	Hua Nan Commercial Bank	4,554	3.66
8	First Commercial Bank	4,396	3.53
9	Formosa Plastic	4,112	3.30
10	Chang Hwa Commercial Bank	3,669	2.95

Source: Morgan Stanley Capital International

MSCI Taiwan Futures. Futures and options on futures on the MSCI Taiwan Index at SIMEX trade in open outcry from 8:45 A.M. to 12:15 P.M., Monday through Saturday. The derivatives open 15 minutes before the underlying stock market and close 15 minutes after the stock market closes. Only the futures contract has a second session on the ATS that is open from 2:45 P.M. to 7 P.M., Monday through Friday. The index multiplier is in U.S. dollars to allow investors exposure to the market without assuming exchange-rate risk. Both futures and options on futures were granted a no-action letter from the CFTC in August 1997.

Calculating the Index. The stocks included in the MSCI Taiwan Index are chosen based on five main factors: (1) market capitalization by class and by company; (2) industry group; (3) average monthly traded value (over both a 6- and 12-month period); (4) estimated amount of available shares, or free float; and (5) amount of cross-ownership of shares among component stocks. Although the free float comes into play in selecting stocks, each one's capitalization is figured based on the entire number of shares available.

The index level is calculated by dividing the sum of component stocks' current market capitalization (adjusted for corporate actions, such as stock splits, stock dividends, and rights issues) by the preceding period's sum of market capitalization for the stocks. This result is multiplied by the preceding period's index level to determine the new index value.

Changes to the index components can occur for both structural and market-driven reasons. Industry restructurings generally occur every 18 to 24 months but can take effect only on a quarterly basis, at the end of February, May, August and November. These changes are announced about two weeks in advance. Market-driven changes, resulting from actions such as a newly privatized company, bankruptcy, merger or acquisition, or spin-offs, take effect immediately.

7

KNOW YOUR STOCK INDEX: EUROPE

It's easy to see why development of stock indexes in Europe is on the upswing. Combining individual countries into a larger unit results in total stock market capitalization that is in a league with the world's largest marketplaces, the United States and Japan. In 1997, stock market capitalization of 16 European countries equaled $5 trillion, which would have made it second only to the United States at $8.5 trillion and displaced Japan, at $3.1 trillion, to the number 3 spot.

An even smaller group, just those countries that switched to the euro in 1999, had a total stock market capitalization in 1997 of $2.4 trillion. That amount would put the group third on the world rankings and move Europe's largest market, the United Kingdom at $1.7 trillion, to fourth.

Unlike the United States and Japan, which have had broad market measures in place for decades, the variety of currencies in Europe has dampened development of such an index.

Developing and trading a stock index that represented the European stock markets was first tackled in the early 1990s but became a hotbed of activity late in the decade when several European countries switched to a single currency, the euro, as part of the European Economic and Monetary Union (EMU). Now, the four biggest names in index development are duking it out with their versions of European stock indexes.

EUROPE

The oldest European stock index is the FTSE Eurotop 100, under the management of FTSE International, first listed in 1991 in Amsterdam. Futures and options on this Index also trade at LIFFE, NYMEX, and AMEX. The euro-denominated futures contract at LIFFE was awaiting CFTC approval in early 1999 as was the euro-denominated options contract from the Amsterdam Exchanges (AEX) at the SEC.

FTSE International, LIFFE, and AEX extended the range of products offered in 1999 by announcing that the exchanges would list new contracts for the FTSE Eurotop 300 and a subset of that index, the FTSE Eurobloc 100, on May 25, 1999. The FTSE Eurotop 300 covers the top 300 companies listed on the major European stock exchanges and accounts for about 80% of the total market capitalization of European stock markets. The FTSE Eurobloc 100 includes only the largest stocks in the FTSE Eurotop 300 that are from EMU countries. As with the FTSE Eurotop 100, LIFFE would list the futures contract while AEX would list the cash options. Both exchanges intend to ask the CFTC and SEC for no-action letters on these indexes.

In addition, LIFFE said it would list on the same date futures and options on an index called FTSE Eurotop 300 Ex-U.K., which excludes any U.K. stocks from its makeup. At LIFFE, all three futures contracts are traded on the LIFFE CONNECT electronic trading platform; options trading started in open-outcry format and was intended to switch later to the electronic system.

The narrowest index of any Euroland offering, FTSE EStars, opened for futures and options trading at LIFFE and AEX on June 29, 1999 in its bid to become the preferred market measure for euro-denominated stock markets. The index includes just 29 blue-chip stocks in five stock markets.

The Dow Jones STOXX 50 and Dow Jones EURO STOXX 50 were listed at both Marches des Options Negociables de Paris (MONEP) and Eurex in June 1998. As of early 1999, the futures contract listed by MONEP was awaiting a no-action letter from the CFTC; the cash option contracts at MONEP received no-action letters from the SEC in 1998. Neither the futures or options contracts listed at Eurex are approved for U.S. investors. The Dow Jones STOXX 50 contract represents 50 blue-chip European stocks; the Dow Jones EURO STOXX 50 tracks 50 top stocks in EMU countries. MONEP launched futures and cash options contracts on three DJ STOXX sector indexes— (banks, energy, and telecommunications)—on March 22, 1999, and intends to apply to both the CFTC and SEC for no-action letters, which allow U.S. investors to trade the listings.

In late January 1999, Morgan Stanley Capital International announced that the two new European indexes it was developing, the

MSCI Euro Index and the MSCI Pan-Euro Index, would be listed for trading in futures and options at LIFFE. The MSCI Euro Index contains 130 stocks in the 10 EMU countries; the MSCI Pan-Euro Index contains 236 securities in 15 European countries. Although the futures contract opened on LIFFE's electronic trading platform on May 25, 1999, the options on the cash indexes were going to be traded by open outcry until they could be moved to the other system. LIFFE has applied to both the CFTC and SEC for no-action letters on these contracts.

The CME announced in March 1999 that it would list two European indexes developed by its long-standing index partner, Standard & Poor's Corporation. The S&P Euro Index includes 158 stocks from 10 EMU countries. The S&P Euro Plus Index adds another 42 stocks from Switzerland, Sweden, Denmark, and Norway to the mix.

Dow Jones STOXX 50; Dow Jones EURO STOXX 50

The Dow Jones STOXX 50 and Dow Jones EURO STOXX 50 Indexes are blue-chip versions of the broader pan-European and pan-Euroland indexes, respectively, in the same family of indexes. Each blue-chip index contains 50 of the largest capitalized stocks in its universe. The STOXX 50 covers the top 50 across all of Europe, and the EURO STOXX 50 represents the market sector leaders in EMU *in* countries.

Index at a Glance.

Index	Dow Jones STOXX 50 Dow Jones EURO STOXX 50
Exchange	MONEP
Weighting	Modified Capitalization
Ticker Symbol	FXS (STOXX 50) FSE (EURO STOXX 50)
Contract Value (Dec. 31, 1998)	3320.3 × €10 = €33,203 (STOXX 50) 3342.3 × €10 = €33,423 (EURO STOXX 50)
Clearinghouse	SBF-Paris Bourse Clearinghouse
Regulator	Conseil des Marchés Financiers (CMF) Commission des Opérations de Bourse (COB) Banque de France
Web Site Information	www.monep.fr www.stoxx.com

Understanding the Index. The component stocks in the blue-chip indexes are established annually, based on market data at the end of July and daily average turnover in euro over the preceding 12 months. Any changes to the index composition become effective on the third Friday in September, after that day's official closing value has been established. Daily charts of the Dow Jones STOXX 50 and Euro STOXX 50 indexes are shown in Figure 7.1 and 7.2, respectively.

To be included in either the STOXX 50 or the EURO STOXX 50, a stock must first be part of its respective broader index, the Dow Jones STOXX (665 companies) or the Dow Jones EURO STOXX (386 companies). The countries in each index, respectively, comprise a region for the purpose of selecting stocks for the blue-chip indexes. All companies in each region are classified by market sector and then sorted by market capitalization within each sector. The largest company in each sector is automatically included in its respective blue-chip index of 50 stocks. Then, stocks in each sector are added until the market capitalization of the index companies comes closest to representing 60% of the sector. For example if the top two companies on the selection list come closer to reaching 60% of the market sector than that of the leading company, then both stocks are included; then their total representation against the 60% benchmark is compared with that of adding a third company, and so on.

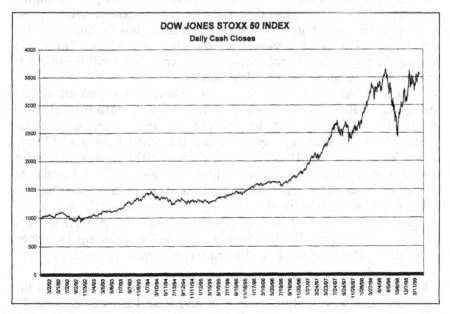

FIGURE 7.1 Dow Jones STOXX 50
Source: Dow Jones

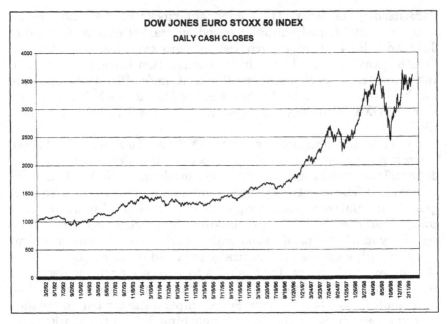

FIGURE 7.2   Dow Jones EURO STOXX 50
Source: Dow Jones

After this selection list is compiled, the stocks are put through a final screening process. The final selection of component stocks must be among the entire group's 60 largest companies on the selection list. Upon component reviews, a noncomponent stock that ranks among the top 40 in capitalization among the group will be added to the index, displacing the smallest stock.

The number of shares used to determine a component stock's market capitalization is reviewed quarterly using data from the end of January, April, July, and October. These weighting changes are introduced on the trading day following the third Friday of March, June, September, and December. No stock in either Index may carry a weight of more than 10% in its calculation (see Tables 7.1 and 7.2).

A selection list for potential replacements in the blue-chip indexes is updated after the last trading day of each month and is published on the first trading day of the following month. These lists indicate which stocks likely would be eligible for replacing a stock either during the year or upon the annual review in August.

STOXX and EURO STOXX Futures and Cash Options. Futures and cash option contracts were listed on both MONEP and Eurex on June 22, 1998, with trading on the two Euro Alliance exchanges intended to meld into a single electronic platform in 1999. Of all the offerings,

TABLE 7.1 Top 10 Stocks in Dow Jones STOXX 50
(December 31, 1998)

Rank	Country	Company	Percent Weight
1	United Kingdom	Glaxo Wellcome	5.02
2	Switzerland	Novartis	4.89
3	Germany	DaimlerChrysler	4.47
4	Netherlands	Royal Dutch Petroleum	4.29
5	United Kingdom	British Telecom	3.90
6	Germany	Allianz	3.65
7	Germany	Deutsche Telekom	3.63
8	United Kingdom	British Petroleum Co.	3.53
9	Switzerland	Nestle	3.45
10	France	France Telecom	3.27

Source: Dow Jones & Company

TABLE 7.2 Top 10 Stocks in Dow Jones EURO STOXX 50
(December 31, 1998)

Rank	Country	Company	Percent Weight
1	Germany	DaimlerChrysler	6.19
2	Netherlands	Royal Dutch Petroleum	5.94
3	Germany	Allianz	5.05
4	Germany	Deutsche Telekom	5.02
5	France	France Telecom	4.53
6	Netherlands	Aegon	3.98
7	Netherlands	ING Group	3.19
8	Finland	Nokia (A)	3.18
9	Netherlands	Unilever	3.04
10	Italy	Ente Nazionale Indrocarburi (ENI)	2.91

Source: Dow Jones & Company

only the option contracts at MONEP received a no-action letter from SEC allowing them to be sold to U.S. customers. Still, trading in the contracts during 1998 was most vibrant at Eurex, which garnered 92% of the trade in the STOXX 50 and 82% in the EURO STOXX 50, including all of the futures trading.

At MONEP, daily price limits are established, both up and down versus the previous day's settlement, at 50 points for the Dow Jones STOXX 50 and 140 points for the Dow Jones EURO STOXX 50. If one of the two nearest futures contracts exceeds the limit, trading is temporarily halted in both futures and options, and additional calls for margin may be made.

MONEP listed futures and options on three market sector indexes from the Dow Jones STOXX family, covering banks, energy, and telecommunication firms beginning March 22, 1999 (see Figure 7.3). The exchange also said it would likely list three or four more sector indexes by year-end 1999. Eurex also plans on listing some of the sector indexes.

Calculating the Index. The same calculation formula applies to both the STOXX 50 and the EURO STOXX 50 Indexes. Each calculation determines the sum of each component stock's market capitalization in euro, using the latest available currency rates and divides by a divisor that relates the index to its base value. Each index had a base value of 1000 on December 31, 1991.

The exchange-listed products are price-return indexes that do not include dividend payments in their calculation. The index values (in euro) are calculated in real-time and distributed every 15 seconds from 8:30 A.M. to 5:45 P.M. (CET); the price-return index figured in U.S. dollars is calculated only at day's end. (Other versions of these two indexes are calculated on a total-return basis, in both euro and U.S. dollars, and are calculated only once a day.) Because the

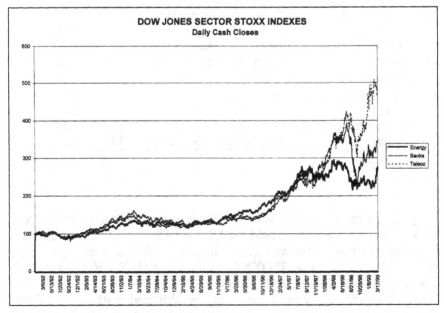

FIGURE 7.3   Dow Jones Sector STOXX Indexes
Source: Dow Jones

component stocks are listed on various exchanges with different holiday schedules, the indexes are calculated only on those days when at least 50% of the underlying market capitalization is available.

FTSE EStars

In an effort to develop a tradable, liquid index of Euroland stock, FTSE International introduced the FTSE EStars index in June 1999. The stocks are the largest, most liquid of those listed on five stock markets in EMU countries, and at its introduction included 29 companies.

Index at a Glance.

Index	FTSE EStars
Exchange	London International Financial Futures and Options Exchange
Weighting	Capitalization
Ticker Symbol	FOE
Contract Value (May 31,1999)	3000.3 × €10 = €30,000
Clearinghouse	London Clearing House
Regulator	Financial Services Authority (FSA) Securities and Futures Authority (SFA)
Web Site Information	www.liffe.com www.ftse.com

Index	FTSE EStars
Exchange	Amsterdam Exchange
Weighting	Capitalization
Contract Value (May 31,1999)	3000.3 × €20 = €60,000
Clearinghouse	AEX-Clearing & Depository
Regulator	Stichting Toezicht Effectenverkeer (Securities Board of the Netherlands)
Web Site Information	www.aex.nl www.ftse.com

Understanding the Index. The stocks in the FTSE EStars index are common to all major cross-border European derivative indexes listed on European exchanges. At its mid-1999 launch, the 29 components equaled almost 40% of the market capitalization of the FT/S&P Eurobloc index value. Of these 29 stocks, eight were listed on the Deutsche Börse, eight on the Paris Bourse, seven on AEX, three on the Italian Exchange and three on the Bolsa de Madrid.

The 10 largest stocks in the index by market capitalization are shown in Table 7.3. These 10 stocks equaled almost 55% of the total index at the end of May 1999.

FTSE EStars Futures and Cash Options. Trading in derivative products on the FTSE EStars index began at LIFFE and AEX on June 29, 1999, each exchange listing both futures and cash option contracts. Both London offerings trade electronically while the AEX products are traded by open outcry. The futures contracts trade the same hours and settle to a similar value at expiration. The London contract has a multiplier of 10 euro for a contract size that is half that traded in Amsterdam. London lists three months from the standard March, June, September, December cycle while Amersterdam trades the three nearest months. The two European-style options contracts are identical.

Calculating the Index. The stocks included in the FTSE EStars index are set annually in December, based on eligible securities on the first trading day that month. The component stocks' full market capitalization on that date results in its base weight, which FTSE International intends to keep constant until the next annual review. However, adjustments will be made for certain corporate events. The changes take effect at the close of business on the third Friday of December.

TABLE 7.3 Top 10 Stocks in FTSE EStars
(May 31, 1999)

Rank	Country	Company	Percent Weight
1	Netherlands	Royal Dutch Petroleum	9.00
2	Germany	Deutsche Telekom	8.68
3	Germany	DaimlerChrysler	6.49
4	France	France Telecom	6.03
5	Germany	Allianz	4.99
6	Italy	Telecom Italia	4.11
7	Germany	Mannesmann	4.05
8	Spain	Telefonica	3.86
9	Netherlands	ING Group	3.83
10	Italy	Ente Nazionale Indrocarburi (ENI)	3.82

Source: LIFFE

The index base value was set at 3000 on May 31, 1999, and has been calculated back to May 31, 1994. A capitalization-weighted index, the assigned number of shares for each component stock (according to its base weight) is multiplied by its current price from its home country exchange, with the sum divided by a divisor. FTSE International calculates and distributes the index value every 15 seconds from 9:30 A.M.to 5:30 P.M. (CET).

FTSE Eurobloc 100

The FTSE Eurobloc 100 Index is designed to represent performance of the 100 largest companies in representative industries from countries that are members of the EMU. These include the 60 largest stocks in the FTSE Eurotop 300 Eurobloc Index as well as 40 others from that pool that are chosen on the basis of sector representation. The final 40 additions are made by figuring the least represented sector in the index on a percent market-capitalization basis and adding the largest stock from the pool in that sector. The process then is repeated until 100 stocks are included in the index.

Index at a Glance.

Index	FTSE Eurobloc 100
Exchange	London International Financial Futures and Options Exchange
Weighting	Capitalization
Ticker Symbol	FOB
Contract Value (Dec. 31, 1998)	998.29 × €20 = € 19,965.80
Clearinghouse	London Clearing House
Regulator	Financial Services Authority (FSA) Securities and Futures Authority (SFA)
Web Site Information	www.liffe.com www.ftse.com

Understanding the Index. Constituent stocks of the FTSE Eurobloc 100 are reviewed annually, in December, with any changes effective on the trading day following the third Friday of the month. In conducting the review, all eligible stocks are first ranked by market capitalization and then cross-checked against the current 60 largest in the index. If the lists are the same, the review is complete. If a nonconstituent stock has become one of the 60 largest, then it is added, and the smallest stock in the most overweight sector of the lowest 40 in the index is removed. This process is repeated until 100 stocks are in the index. A maximum of three stocks may be replaced in the index at each annual review. The 10 largest stocks in the index are shown in Table 7.4.

A company may be deleted due to a delisting, being subject to an unconditional takeover offer or ceasing to have a firm quotation. A vacancy in the index due to merger or takeover between two component stocks brings the largest stock from the most underweighted sector from the FTSE Eurotop 300 Eurobloc Index to take its place. A merger or acquisition between an index stock and a nonconstituent results in removal of the original index stock, with the new stock being the largest one from the most underweighted sector in the larger Eurobloc Index. If a company in the index restructures into two or more companies, each must stand on its own merit against the eligibility criteria to join the index.

FTSE Eurobloc Futures and Cash Options. The FTSE Eurobloc 100 futures and options contracts opened for trading with two other FTSE European indexes on May 25, 1999. Each futures contract carries a 20-euro multiplier, and the options on the cash index have a 10-euro multiplier. The futures contract settles upon expiration to the *Exchange Delivery Settlement value*, the average index value during the last 20 minutes of trading before the contract expires.

The exchange has applied with the CFTC and SEC for no-action letters so that the FTSE Eurobloc 100 can be sold to U.S. customers. It trades from 9 A.M. to 4 P.M. in London on the exchange's electronic LIFFE CONNECT system.

TABLE 7.4 Top 10 Stocks in FTSE Eurobloc 100
(March 23, 1999)

Rank	Country	Company	Percent Weight
1	Netherlands	Royal Dutch Petroleum	4.80
2	Germany	DaimlerChrysler	3.74
3	Germany	Allianz	3.36
4	Finland	Nokia (A)	3.00
5	Netherlands	Aegon	2.39
	Netherlands	ING Group	2.25
7	Italy	Telecom Italia	2.22
8	Italy	Ente Nazionale Indrocarburi (ENI)	2.10
9	Germany	Mannesman	2.07
10	France	AXA-UAP	2.01

Source: FTSE International

Calculating the Index. The FTSE Eurobloc 100 Index figures the current market capitalization for each component stock (adjusted if necessary by a *weighting restraint factor*), adds these figures together, and divides the total by a divisor that represents the total issued share capital in the Index on the base date of May 4, 1998 with a base value of 1000. This divisor can be adjusted to allow for changes in outstanding stock of the component companies without distorting the Index.

Dividends are handled in one of two ways. If they are deemed to be a capital adjustment, the stock's capitalization will be adjusted; if they are deemed to be a redistribution of income, the impact will be absorbed in the adjusted dividend calculation. In order to minimize insignificant weighting changes, the number of shares used to calculate each stock's market capitalization is rounded to the nearest 100,000.

The FTSE Eurobloc 100 Index is calculated in real-time in euro from 10 A.M. to 5:30 P.M. (CET) and distributed every 15 seconds; in addition, it is calculated for 30 minutes before the official index period begins using live prices where available or the preceding day's closing values.

A stock whose trading has been suspended on its home exchange may remain part of the index for up to 10 business days. The price used in the calculation will be the price at which trading was suspended. If removed from the index, the stock may be reinstated if it resumes trading at its home exchange and is larger than the smallest stock in the index; it would be reinstated at the price at which it was removed.

FTSE Eurotop 100

The FTSE Eurotop 100 Index was the first index designed to track major European stocks and was the first pan-European index available to U.S. investors. The Amsterdam Exchanges—formed on January 1, 1997, when the Amsterdam Stock Exchange and European Options Exchange merged—began calculating what was known as the Eurotop 100 in 1990. The index became part of the FTSE International Limited stable of indexes in May 1997.

Understanding the Index. The FTSE Eurotop 100 Index tracks the performance of 100 of Europe's most liquid stocks and represents about 40% of the total market capitalization of European stock markets. The countries included in the index must be members of the Organization for Economic Cooperation and Development (OECD) and are ranked annually by total market capitalization. Starting with the largest market, countries are added to the total as long as a country's market capitalization is at least 2.5% of the combined total capitalization of the selected countries, including the latest addition. For example, Belgium's market capitalization of US$138.9 billion at year-end 1997 brought the total to $5,524 billion and equaled 2.52% of that total, so it was included in the index. The next country on the list, Denmark, would have contributed less than 2.5% of the total if its market capitalization were included, so its stocks were excluded from the index.

Then the country's weighting in the index is figured as equal to the country's capitalization as a percent of the total capitalization of the countries in the index. For example, at year-end 1997, the United Kingdom's market capitalization of US$1,996 billion was 36.14% of the total capitalization of US$5,524 billion from the nine countries included in the index.

For 1998, the countries represented in the index included (along with Index weighting percentage): United Kingdom, 36%; Germany, 15%; France, 12%; Switzerland, 10%; Netherlands, 9%; Italy, 6%; Sweden, 5%; Spain, 4%; and Belgium, 3%. These percentages then are used to determine the number of stocks from each country that are in the FTSE Eurotop 100. For example, 36 U.K. stocks would be in the index, but only three from Belgium. These index points are allocated to the individual stocks on a percentage basis according to their market capitalization and determine each stock's weighting in the index (see Table 7.5).

TABLE 7.5 Top 10 Stocks in FTSE Eurotop 100
(December 31, 1998)

Rank	Country	Company	Percent Weight
1	United Kingdom	Glaxo Wellcome	3.72
2	United Kingdom	British Telecom	2.93
3	Germany	Allianz	2.67
4	United Kingdom	British Petroleum Co.	2.62
5	Switzerland	Novartis	2.62
6	The Netherlands	Royal Dutch Petroleum	2.42
7	United Kingdom	SmithKline Beecham	2.36
8	United Kingdom	Lloyds TSB Group	2.34
9	Belgium	Electrabel	2.32
10	Sweden	Ericsson	2.07

Source: FTSE International

Calculating the Index. The FTSE Eurotop 100 is a market-capitalization-weighted index with a twist. Most indexes of this type multiply a stock's price by the number of outstanding or market-available stocks, sum these values, and divide by a divisor that adjusts to keep the index on an even keel with the index's initial base value. In the FTSE Eurotop 100, the price of each stock in the index is multiplied by an *allotted* number of shares; these totals are summed and divided by 100 to determine the index level. A weekly chart of the index since 1993 is shown in Figure 7.4.

The allotment of shares is determined by first figuring the stock's capitalization as a percent of the country's total market capitalization. This percentage then is multiplied by the euro-denominated market value that country has been assigned in the FTSE Eurotop 100 index according to the index percentage weightings. The resulting figure is divided by the share price in euro. That result is the number of shares that are multiplied by a stock's price to determine its market capitalization value in the FTSE Eurotop 100.

As an example of the share-allotment process, consider the Belgian stock Electrabel, which had 54.4 million outstanding shares at year-end 1997 and accounted for 45.14% of the Belgian stock market's total capitalization. At a 3% weighting in the FTSE Eurotop 100, the Belgian stock market value in Ecus equaled 5,562.37. In the

FIGURE 7.4 FTSE Eurotop 100 Index
Source: CRB-Bridge Information

FTSE Eurotop 100, Electrabel carries the same percentage weight in Belgium's share of the index as it does in the entire Belgian stock market. Thus, Electrabel's number of shares for the FTSE Eurotop 100 formula is determined by giving it 45.14% of the Belgian market's total value of 5,562.37 Ecus in the index and dividing by the stock's Ecu-equivalent price, for the share allotment of 12.78, which is later optimized to 13.30 shares.

The FTSE Eurotop 100 Index is calculated every 15 seconds whenever any of the stock exchanges with index member stocks are open, which spanned from 9 A.M. to 5:30 P.M. (GMT) in early 1999.

Index at a Glance.

Index	FTSE Eurotop 100 futures
Exchange	New York Mercantile Exchange
Weighting	Capitalization
Ticker Symbol	ER
Contract Value (Dec. 31, 1998)	2723.87 × $100 = $272,387
Clearinghouse	NYMEX Clearinghouse
Regulator	Commodity Futures Trading Commission
Web Site Information	www.nymex.com www.ftse.com

Index	FTSE Eurotop 100 futures
Exchange	London International Financial Futures and Options Exchange
Weighting	Capitalization
Ticker Symbol	Q
Contract Value (Dec. 31, 1998)	2723.87 × €20 = €54,477.40
Clearinghouse	London Clearing House
Regulator	Financial Services Authority (FSA) Securities and Futures Authority (SFA)
Web Site Information	www.liffe.com www.ftse.com

Index	FTSE Eurotop 100 options
Exchange	Amsterdam Exchanges
Weighting	Capitalization
Ticker Symbol	E100
Contract Value (Dec. 31, 1999)	2723.87 × €10= € 27,238.70
Clearinghouse	AEX-Clearing & Depository
Regulator	Stichting Toezicht Effectenverkeer (Securities Board of the Netherlands)
Web Site Information	www.aex.nl www.ftse.com

FTSE Eurotop 100 Futures. The first futures contract on the Eurotop 100 Index was listed on June 6, 1991, at the Financial Futures Market of Amsterdam, which later was integrated with the European Options Exchange (EOE). In 1997, the EOE merged with the Amsterdam Stock Exchange to become the Amsterdam Exchanges. FTSE International Limited took over maintenance of the index and added its moniker to it that same year. Trading in the AEX version of the futures contract typically paled in comparison to the volume done in the futures contract at the New York Mercantile Exchange (NYMEX).

Futures contracts on the FTSE Eurotop 100 are available at NYMEX (denominated in dollars) and at LIFFE (denominated in euro). Options on futures were listed at NYMEX but have not traded since 1993. In early 1999, the LIFFE contract was pending approval for U.S. customers at the CFTC. Options on the cash index trade in Amsterdam but are not yet approved for U.S. investors by the SEC. The American Stock Exchange also lists euro-denominated options on the cash index.

The original FTSE Eurotop 100 futures contract (denominated in guilders), which traded at AEX, was approved for U.S. investors by the CFTC in 1996. However, the contract was phased out by year-end 1998 as part of the deal in listing the futures contract exclusively at LIFFE, while AEX lists options on the index.

The Commodity Exchange (COMEX, now a division of the New York Mercantile Exchange) licensed the right to trade the original Eurotop 100 Index from the European Options Exchange and listed a dollar-denominated futures contract on October 26, 1992.

The index trades from 5:30 A.M. to 11:30 A.M. in New York in order to coincide with most of the European trading day. Volume in the futures contract ranged between roughly 25,000 and 50,000 contracts annually from 1992 to 1998.

FTSE Eurotop 300; FTSE Eurotop 300 Ex-U.K.

The FTSE Eurotop 300 Index is designed to measure the performance of the 300 largest capitalized companies in Europe. The FTSE Eurotop 300 Ex-U.K. Index measures the performance of the same list of stocks minus those from the United Kingdom.

Index at a Glance.

Index	FTSE Eurotop 300
	FTSE Eurotop 300 Ex-U.K.
Exchange	London International Financial Futures and Options Exchange
Weighting	Capitalization
Ticker Symbol	FOT (FTSE Eurotop 300)
	FOX (FTSE Eurotop 300 Ex-U.K.)
Contract Value (Dec. 31, 1998)	1182.74 × ℰ 20 = ℰ 23,654.80 (FOT)
	1234.40 × ℰ 20 = ℰ 24,688 (FOX)
Clearinghouse	London Clearing House
Regulator	Financial Services Authority (FSA)
	Securities and Futures Authority (SFA)
Web Site Information	www.liffe.com
	www.ftse.com

Understanding the Indexes. To become eligible for inclusion in either the FTSE Eurotop 300 or Eurotop Ex-U.K. Index, a stock must first be a current constituent of the European Regional Index of the FT/S&P Actuaries World Index. Then each stock must meet investability, price, and liquidity standards to become part of the FTSE Eurotop 300 or FTSE Eurotop 300 Ex-U.K. Indexes. For investability, at least 25% of a company's stock must be publicly available for trading. If so, then a company's entire market capitalization is used in the index calculation; if less than 25% of the shares are publicly available, the market capitalization weight is adjusted accordingly. Prices of component stocks must be considered accurate and reliable. Finally, each stock must have monthly turnover equal to at least 1% of its total shares outstanding for five out the six months preceding a quarterly review.

The FTSE Equity Indices Committee meets the Wednesday after the first Friday of March, June, September, and December to review the index constituents, with any changes implemented on the trading day following the third Friday of that month. A reserve list of the 12 highest ranking nonconstituent stocks is maintained to replace potential index deletions over the upcoming quarter. A company may be deleted due to a delisting, if it becomes subject to an unconditional takeover offer, or if it ceases to have a firm quotation.

A vacancy in the index due to merger or takeover between two component stocks brings the highest ranking stock from the reserve list to the index. A merger or acquisition between an index stock and a non-constituent results in removal of the original index stock, with the new entity eligible to become the replacement if it ranks higher than any other on the reserve list. If a company in the index restructures into two or more companies, each must stand on its own merit against the eligibility criteria to join the index. The 10 most influential stocks in each index are shown in Tables 7.6 and 7.7.

Futures and Cash Options on FTSE Eurotop 300 and FTSE Eurotop Ex-U.K. Indexes. The FTSE Eurotop 300 and FTSE Eurotop Ex-U.K. Index futures and options contracts are similarly constructed. Each futures contract carries a 20-euro multiplier, and the options on the cash indexes have a 10-euro multiplier. Each futures contract settles upon expiration to the Exchange Delivery Settlement value, an average of the index value in the last 20 minutes of trading before the contract expires.

TABLE 7.6 Top 10 Stocks in FTSE Eurotop 300
(March 23, 1999)

Rank	Country	Company	Percent Weight
1	United Kingdom	BP Amoco	2.97
2	Netherlands	Royal Dutch Petroleum	2.09
3	United Kingdom	Glaxo Wellcome	2.06
4	United Kingdom	British Telecommunications	1.94
5	Switzerland	Novartis	1.87
6	Germany	DaimlerChrysler	1.63
7	Switzerland	Roche Holdings	1.58
8	United Kingdom	Lloyds TSB Group	1.50
9	Germany	Allianz	1.46
10	United Kingdom	SmithKline Beecham	1.41

Source: FTSE International

TABLE 7.7 Top 10 Stocks in FTSE Eurotop 300 Ex-U.K.
(March 23, 1999)

Rank	Country	Company	Percent Weight
1	Netherlands	Royal Dutch Petroleum	3.25
2	Switzerland	Novartis	2.90
3	Germany	DaimlerChrysler	2.53
4	Switzerland	Roche Holdings	2.46
5	Germany	Allianz	2.27
6	Switzerland	Nestle	2.07
7	Finland	Nokia (A)	2.03
8	Switzerland	UBS	2.00
9	Netherlands	Aegon	1.61
10	Netherlands	ING Group	1.52

Source: FTSE International

Both indexes opened for trading on May 25, 1999, and the exchange intends to apply with the CFTC and SEC for no-action letters so they can be sold to U.S. customers. They trade from 9 A.M to 4 P.M. in London on the exchange's electronic LIFFE CONNECT system.

A similar set of products is listed at the Amsterdam Exchanges in the Netherlands.

Calculating the Index. The FTSE Eurotop 300 and FTSE Eurotop 300 Ex-U.K. Indexes each figure the current market capitalization for each component stock (adjusted if necessary by a weighting restraint factor), adds these figures together, and divides the total by a divisor that represents the total issued share capital in the index as of the base date. The base date for the FTSE Eurotop 300 is July 25, 1997, and for the FTSE Eurotop 300 Ex-U.K., the date is July 26, 1997; both base values were set at 1000. This divisor can be adjusted to allow for changes in the outstanding stock of the component companies without distorting the index.

Dividends are handled in one of two ways. If they are deemed to be a capital adjustment, the stock's capitalization will be adjusted; if they are deemed to be a redistribution of income, the impact will be absorbed in the adjusted dividend calculation.

In order to minimize insignificant weighting changes, the number of shares used to calculate each stock's market capitalization is rounded to the nearest 1 million for those stocks in the FTSE 100 Index (the large-cap index in the United Kingdom), the nearest 100,000 for all other U.K. stocks, and 1,000 for continental European stocks.

The indexes are calculated in real-time from 10 A.M. to 5:30 P.M. (CET) and distributed every 15 seconds; in addition, they are calculated for 30 minutes before the official index period begins using live prices where available or the preceding day's closing values. Currency cross rates also are used real-time in the calculation.

A stock whose trading has been suspended on its home exchange may remain part of the index for up to 10 business days. The price used in the calculation will be the price at which trading was suspended. If removed from the index, the stock may be reinstated if it is larger than the smallest stock in the index; it would be reinstated at the price at which it was removed.

MSCI Euro; MSCI Pan-Euro

The MSCI Euro and MSCI Pan-Euro Indexes are designed specifically to track the performance of their corresponding benchmarks, the MSCI EMU Index and MSCI Europe Index, respectively. The MSCI EMU Index tracks performance of leading companies in EMU countries, and the MSCI Europe Index covers companies both in and out of EMU. At year-end 1998, the MSCI Euro Index comprised 126 companies (130 securities); the MSCI Pan-Euro comprised 229 companies (236 securities) and captured about 90% of the total capitalization of the MSCI Europe Index.

Index at a Glance.

Index	MSCI Euro
	MSCI Pan-Euro
Exchange	London International Financial Futures and Options Exchange
Weighting	Capitalization
Ticker Symbol	MCU (MSCI Euro)
	MCP (MSCI Pan-Euro)
Contract Value (Dec. 31, 1998)	1000 × € 20 = € 20,000 (MCU)
	1000 × € 20 = € 20,000 (MCP)
Clearinghouse	London Clearing House
Regulator	Financial Services Authority (FSA)
	Securities and Futures Authority (SFA)
Web Site Information	www.liffe.com
	www.msci.com

Understanding the Index. Index constituents are reviewed annually, in November, to coincide with that month's quarterly review of the broader MSCI Europe Index. The broader market's changes go into effect after the end of the last business day in November. Each class of stock listed by a company can be considered for inclusion in the index and must qualify individually.

Stocks are ranked by country via a liquidity screen, which sums the numerical rank each stock achieves in terms of traded-value ratio and traded-value rank. (The traded-value ratio divides a stock's daily traded value, that is, closing price times the day's volume, by the stock's total market capitalization.) Then the number of eligible ranked stocks are included until the total reaches the closest to 95% of the country's total market capitalization. After this list is developed, it is sorted again from largest capitalization stock to smallest until the total capitalization comes closest to 90% of the country's total market capitalization; this is the *constituent list*. A final sorting of the constituent list selects the companies by industry that equal the closest to 90% of the total market capitalization of that industry. This procedure is done for each country in the index.

Each country's final list then is consolidated and ranked strictly by market capitalization, with stocks included until their total capitalization comes closest to 90% of the MSCI Europe Index's total capitalization. Those listings become the constituent stocks of the MSCI Pan-Euro Index. The MSCI Euro Index is a subset of the MSCI Pan-Euro Index and includes only those stocks from EMU *in* countries. The 10 largest stocks in each index at year-end 1998 are shown in Tables 7.8 and 7.9.

TABLE 7.8 Top 10 Stocks in MSCI Euro
(December 31, 1998)

Rank	Country	Company	Percent Weight
1	Netherlands	Royal Dutch Petroleum Co.	3.97
2	Germany	DaimlerChrysler	3.58
3	Germany	Allianz	3.33
4	Germany	Deutsche Telekom	2.68
5	Netherlands	Aegon	2.66
6	France	France Telecom	2.42
7	Finland	Nokia Corp. (A)	2.16
8	Netherlands	ING Group	2.13
9	Netherlands	Unilever NV (Cert)	2.03
10	Italy	Ente Nazionale Indrocarburi (ENI)	1.96

Source: Morgan Stanley Capital International

TABLE 7.9 Top 10 Stocks in MSCI Pan-Euro
(December 31, 1998)

Rank	Country	Company	Percent Weight
1	United Kingdom	Glaxo Wellcome	2.49
2	Switzerland	Novartis	2.47
3	Netherlands	Royal Dutch Petroleum Co.	2.16
4	United Kingdom	British Telecommunications	1.96
5	Germany	DaimlerChrysler	1.95
6	Germany	Allianz	1.82
7	United Kingdom	British Petroleum	1.78
8	Switzerland	Roche Holding	1.74
9	Switzerland	Nestle	1.73
10	United Kingdom	SmithKline Beecham	1.57

Source: Morgan Stanley Capital International

Futures and Cash Options on MSCI Euro and MSCI Pan-Euro Indexes. Futures and cash options on both the MSCI Pan-Euro and MSCI Euro Indexes were listed on May 25, 1999, at the London International Financial Futures and Options Exchange. They trade on the electronic LIFFE CONNECT system from 9 A.M. to 4 P.M. in London. As with the other new European stock index offerings at LIFFE, the MSCI Indexes have a 20-euro multiplier for the futures contract, and the options contract has a multiplier of 10 euros.

The final settlement value is set to the Exchange Delivery Settlement Price, which is the average index level during the last 20 minutes of the contract's last trading day.

Calculating the Indexes. Each index level is calculated by dividing the sum of component stocks' current market capitalization (adjusted for corporate actions such as stock splits, stock dividends, and rights issues) by the previous period's sum of market capitalization for the stocks. This result is multiplied by the preceding period's index level to determine the new index value.

The indexes are calculated in euro in real-time and distributed every 15 seconds. Both indexes have a base date of December 31, 1998, and a base value of 1000. However, each has been calculated back to December 31, 1996. Daily price charts of the indexes since their inception are shown in Figure 7.5.

Stock deletions from the MSCI Euro indexes due to events and situations such as lack of viability or liquidity, bankruptcy, or major corporate restructuring will not be replaced until the annual review unless an eligible stock in the same country and industry is immediately available.

FIGURE 7.5 MSCI Euro & Pan-Euro Indexes
Source: Morgan Stanley Capital International

S&P Euro and S&P Euro Plus

The S&P Euro Index is a capitalization-weighted index of 157 stocks from 10 countries, which are members of the EMU—Austria, Belgium, Finland, France, Germany, Ireland, Italy, Netherlands, Portugal, and Spain. At year-end 1998, the Index represented €1.76 trillion in capitalization.

The S&P Euro Plus Index tracks 200 stocks from the 10 EMU countries as well as Switzerland, Sweden, Denmark, and Norway. At year-end 1998, the index represented €2.26 trillion in capitalization.

Understanding the Indexes. Stocks from 11 industry sectors are included in both indexes. The sectors include basic materials, capital goods, communication services, consumer cyclicals, consumer staples, energy, financials, health care, technology, transportation, and utilities. In developing the Indexes, sector representation was a primary goal.

Stocks are selected based on the following factors: (1) liquidity, measured on a daily, monthly, and annual basis; (2) sector representations; (3) investable shares available for trading, which excludes those held by control groups that own 5% or more of the total; (4) foreign investment limit; and (5) the financial operating condition of the company. The 10 largest stocks in each index at year-end 1998 are shown in Tables 7.10 and 7.11.

Index at a Glance.

Index	S&P Euro
	S&P Euro Plus
Exchange	Chicago Mercantile Exchange
Weighting	Capitalization
Ticker Symbol	(Not available)
Contract Value	1262.708 × €50 = €63,135.40 (S&P Euro)
(Dec. 31, 1998)	1226.876 × €50 = €61,343.80 (S&P Euro Plus)
Clearinghouse	CME Clearinghouse
Regulator	Commodity Futures Trading Commission
Web Site Information	www.cme.com
	www.spglobal.com

TABLE 7.10 Top 10 Stocks in S&P Euro Index
(December 31, 1998)

Rank	Country	Company	Percent Weight
1	Netherlands	Royal Dutch Petroleum	4.77
2	Germany	DaimlerChrysler	3.70
3	Finland	Nokia (A)	2.65
4	Netherlands	ING Group	2.26
5	Germany	Mannesman	2.15
6	Germany	Allianz	2.13
7	Netherlands	Aegon	2.06
8	France	AXA-UAP	1.90
9	Netherlands	Unilever	1.90
10	Spain	Telefonica de Espana	1.88

Source: Standard & Poor's Corporation

S&P Euro and S&P Euro Plus Futures. The two S&P Euro indexes will be the first at the CME to be listed solely on an electronic trading platform, GLOBEX$_2$. They will trade the same hours as the E-mini contracts of the S&P 500 and Nasdaq-100, with the trading day beginning at 3:30 P.M., Sunday through Thursday, and ending the following afternoon at 3:15 P.M. Pending regulatory approval, the two indexes were expected to open for trading in early 2000. As the result of a mid-1999 agreement, members of MEFF in Spain, the Paris Bourse, Italy's IDEM, and Portugal's BDP will have direct electronic access to the contract through EuroGLOBEX.

TABLE 7.11 Top 10 Stocks in S&P Euro Plus
(December 31, 1998)

Rank	Country	Company	Percent Weight
1	Switzerland	Novartis	4.54
2	Netherlands	Royal Dutch Petroleum	3.70
3	Switzerland	Nestle	3.20
4	Germany	DaimlerChrysler	2.87
5	Switzerland	United Bank of Switzerland	2.46
6	Finland	Nokia (A)	2.05
7	Netherlands	ING Group	1.75
8	Germany	Mannesmann	1.66
9	Germany	Allianz	1.66
10	Netherlands	Aegon	1.60

Source: Standard & Poor's Corporation

Calculating the Index. Each country in each index has a minimum market value, determined according to its share of total market capitalization. However, a stock that may dominate its home market could be excluded from the S&P Euro or Euro Plus Indexes if it is not as liquid as another stock in another country from that same industry.

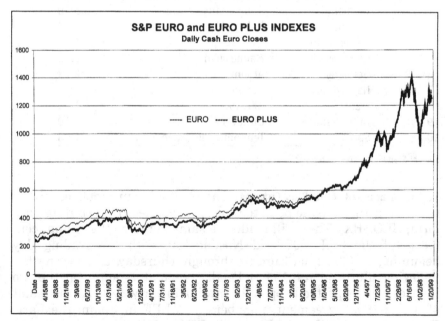

FIGURE 7.6 S & P Euro and S & P Euro Plus Indexes
Source: Standard & Poor's

The number of shares used to determine an individual stock's market capitalization is adjusted to cross-holdings, government restrictions, and closely held situations; this float-adjustment factor is reviewed annually. If these control groups own 5% or more of the company's total outstanding number of shares, those shares are excluded from the market capitalization calculation.

The indexes are managed by the S&P International Index Policy Committee. Stock deletions from the indexes normally occur due to acquisition. However, they also could result from bankruptcy, corporate restructuring, or lack of representation in its industry group. Replacements and additions will be made according to market capitalization and liquidity as well as continuing the index's sector and country representation. Price charts of the two indexes calculated to 1988 are shown in Figure 7.6.

FRANCE

With a market capitalization of $591 billion in 1997, the French stock market ranked fifth in the world and third in Europe, behind the United Kingdom and Germany. France has a long history of providing an index of its capital market.

CAC 40

The CAC 40, developed in 1988, was the first French index to use real-time valuations in its calculation and has become the benchmark for the French stock market. Its 40 blue-chip stocks are among France's largest companies and are weighted in the index by market capitalization (price times shares outstanding). In mid-1998, these 40 stocks represented more than 80% of the Paris market's capital turnover. The move toward stock index futures and options in France was encouraged in the General Report by the Commission on New Financial Instruments and Financial Futures Markets, the DEGUEN Commission report, released in March 1988. CAC comes from a former name of the French stockbrokers association, Compagnie des Agents de Change.

Understanding the Index. The 40 stocks in the CAC 40 index are listed on the Règlement Mensuel (RM), or the monthly settlement market, of the Société des Bourses Françaises (SBF). This market establishes a single buying/selling price on the last trading day of each month for transactions established in a window of about 30 days that closes about a week before the monthly settlement.

Index at a Glance.

Index	CAC 40
Exchange	MONEP
Weighting	Capitalization
Ticker Symbol	FCC (formerly CAC) FCE
Contract Value (Dec. 31, 1998)	FCC: 3942.7 × €1 = €3,942.7 FCE: 3942.7 × €10 = €39,427
Clearinghouse	SBF-Paris Bourse Clearinghouse
Regulator	Conseil des Marchés Financiers (CMF) Commission des Opérations de Bourse (COB) Banque de France
Web Site Information	www.monep.fr www.matif.fr www.bourse-de-paris.fr

The CAC 40 was designed to track the broad French stock market and has a correlation of 97% with the older SBF 240 index, whose index value is set once daily based on opening prices of the component stocks. The smaller number of stocks in the CAC 40 also was deemed advantageous in listing derivative products, such as futures and options, because it would keep costs to arbitrage or hedge stock baskets relatively modest. The 10 largest stocks in the CAC 40 at the end of January 1999 are shown in the Table 7.12.

TABLE 7.12 Top 10 Stocks in CAC 40
(January 29, 1999)

Rank	Company	Market Capitalization (million euro)	Percent Weight
1	France Telecom	84,941	13.21
2	AXA-UAP	44,767	6.96
3	L'Oreal	42,988	6.69
4	Vivendi	41,154	6.40
5	Suez-Lyonnaise des Eaux	26,805	4.17
6	Elf Aquitaine	26,269	4.09
7	Carrefour	22,860	3.56
8	Total	21,908	3.41
9	Alcatel Alstom	20,385	3.17
10	Sanofi	19,368	3.01

Source: SBF

CAC 40 Futures. Futures on the CAC 40 Index began at the Marché à Terme International de France (MATIF) in 1988, first on an over-the-counter basis in August and then to the trading pit on November 9. The original contract multiplier of 200 French francs was cut to 50 francs on July 1, 1998, and then converted to 1 euro on January 4, 1999. At the time of the switch, the ticker symbol for the contract changed to FCC from CAC. In addition, the contract with a multiplier of 10 euro was introduced, under the symbol FCE. The CAC 40 contract was the first stock index futures introduced in continental Europe and is its most heavily traded. The CFTC approved the CAC 40 futures for U.S. investment on December 17, 1991.

Electronic trading of the CAC 40 began as a way to extend trading hours beyond the regular daytime open outcry session. However, on April 8, 1997, the MATIF began trading all its contracts simultaneously in open outcry and on the screen. By month's end, all trading had moved to the screen. Now, CAC 40 futures trade on the NSC electronic platform in three sessions, with the day's settlement at 5 P.M. local time. A new trading day begins with the evening session from 5 P.M. to 10 P.M. A two-hour morning session lasts from 8 to 10 A.M. and the day session runs from 10 A.M. to 5 P.M. If traders do not want their orders available for execution during the evening or morning sessions, they must tell their broker at the time of placement.

Global uncertainty in 1990, particularly surrounding the Persian Gulf war, led to an increased use of the CAC 40 futures that resulted in the annual volume nearly tripling its previous year total. Trading activity has remained hefty since then. Like the parameters for stock index trading in the United States, a daily limit exists on how much the CAC 40 Index may move in a day. The futures contract is limited to a 190-point move, up or down, from the preceding day's settlement. If the limit is exceeded in one of the two nearest futures contracts, trading in both futures and options is halted temporarily.

Beginning on July 10, 1997, the contract has been managed by a company jointly owned by the MATIF, Marché des Options Négocialbes de Paris (MONEP), and SBF and is listed on MONEP, the listed options exchange on which two options on the CAC 40 are traded. This subsidiary company also is charged with expanding the stock index product line, including industry or European offerings. In September 1997, the SBF acquired MATIF by purchasing all shares, investment certificants, and voting rights certificates held by other MATIF shareholders.

In mid-1998, MATIF and the Spanish futures exchange MEFF Renta Fija created an alliance called Euro-GLOBEX, to allow cross access to their interest-rate products by members of the two exchanges; the Italian exchange MIF made it a three-way partnership in December that year. The agreement is expected to be enlarged to include the domestic stock index products of the MONEP, MEFF Renta Variable, and Italy's IDEM in 1999, adding to the cross access already available with the Dow Jones STOXX Index products. Also in 1998, the SBF, MATIF and MONEP signed a memorandum of understanding with Eurex to form EURO Alliance, which would allow the exchanges to work toward full convergence of their electronic trading platforms to allow equal and standardized access by all their members by January 2002.

CAC 40 Cash Options. Two options on the cash CAC 40 Index trade at MONEP. The short-term option, ticker symbol PX1, with a European exercise style, was listed the same day as the futures contract at MATIF, on November 9, 1988. The long-term option, ticker symbol PXL, with European-style exercise and listing as far out as two years, joined on October 17, 1991. Both contracts were recognized by the SEC in June 1996 as suitable for U.S. investment.

Other than the contract months available and strike price increments, contract specifications for both options are identical. Like the futures contract, the option multipliers are 1 euro, making arbitrage easy among the three offerings. Also like the futures contract, trading in the options halts when the futures contract reaches a daily price limit of 190 index points.

Short-term options are available for the nearest three months plus the next month from the quarterly March, June, September, and December cycle. Long-term options trade only for March and September expiration. Strike price intervals are 25 index points for the short-term and 150 index points for the long-term option.

Each options contract has traded more than 1 million in volume every year since 1993. However, over that same period, activity in the CAC 40 futures contract has outpaced trading in both options combined. For three years, 1989 to 1991, volume in short-term CAC 40 options surpassed trading in the futures contract.

Calculating the Index. To figure the CAC 40 Index level, sum the current market capitalization of each component stock and divide by the adjusted base capitalization figure. The base value for the CAC 40 was set on December 31, 1987, at 1000. Then multiply that result by 1,000. The index value is calculated in real-time and quoted every 30 seconds by the SBF-Paris Bourse. The underlying index is quoted to two decimal points, but the futures contract (and its final settlement price) are quoted to just a single decimal point (see Figure 7.7).

The SBF releases a trend indicator called an éclaireur ("scout" in French) whenever stocks representing more than 35% of the index capitalization cannot be quoted, for example, due to a trading halt or

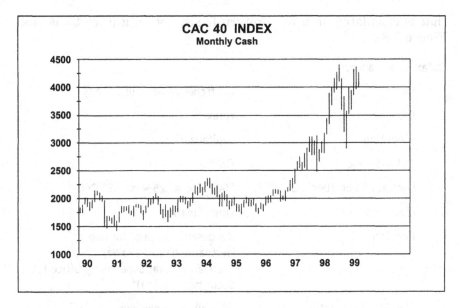

FIGURE 7.7   CAC 40 Index
Source: CRB-Bridge Information

a technical snafu. In that case, the published index value represents only those stocks that have current quotes.

A panel of experts in finance and statistics periodically review the index components and recommend changes. The panel includes representatives from the following organizations: Bank of France; INSEE, the economic forecasting agency; the COB, the exchange trading commission; and the French Association of Financial Analysts (SFAF). Only the top 100 RM stocks in terms of market capitalization are considered for inclusion in the CAC 40, with volume and volatility also part of the decision-making process.

GERMANY

Germany's stock market in 1997 was the fourth largest in the world and second only to the United Kingdom in Europe with $671 billion in capitalization. With the advent of EMU, Germany is Euroland's most significant stock market.

DAX

The Deutscher Aktienindex (DAX) is Germany's blue-chip index of 30 leading stocks. It is one of the few indexes with listed derivatives that is claculated on a total-return basis, not on a price basis (see Figure 7.8).

Index at a Glance.

Index	Deutscher Aktienindex (DAX)
Exchange	Eurex
Weighting	Capitalization
Ticker Symbol	FDAX
Contract Value (Dec. 30, 1998)	5002.4 × ≈€ 25 = ≈€ 125,060
Clearinghouse	Eurex Clearing AG
Regulator	Bundesaufsichtsamt für den Wertpapierhandel (BaWe) (German Federal Supervisory Office for Securities Trading)
Web Site Information	www.eurexchange.com www.exchange.de

Understanding the Index. DAX stocks represent: (1) more than 75% of market capitalization of all listed stocks at the Frankfurter

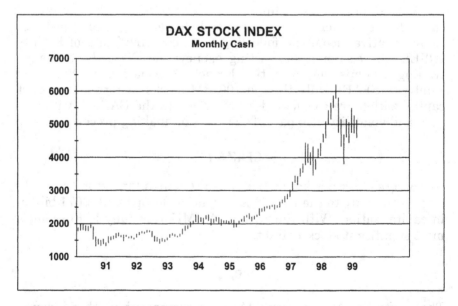

FIGURE 7.8 DAX Stock Index
Source: CRB-Bridge Information

Wertpapierbörse (FWB, or Frankfurt Stock Exchange); and (2) more than 70% of the market capitalization of all listed German stocks at the eight German stock exchanges. Unlike most market-cap indexes, the DAX tracks total return rather than strictly price return. Thus, income from dividends and rights issues are reinvested in the index portfolio and are reflected in the index value.

The DAX is based at 1000 points on December 30, 1987, and was designed as an extension of the Börsen-Zeitung Index, which dates to 1959. The 10 largest stocks as measured by market capitalization in euro on the first trading day of 1999 are shown in Table 7.13.

DAX Futures and Cash Options. Futures on the DAX Index were first listed on November 23, 1990, at the Deutsche Terminbörse (DTB and forerunner to Eurex Deutschland) in the exchange's first year of operation. Options on the futures contract were listed on January 24, 1992, but were delisted in 1997. Options on the cash index are the most popular vehicle as measured by trading volume but are not available to U.S. investors.

The DAX Index is the leading European stock index in terms of futures and options volume combined. The futures contract was approved for trading by the CFTC effective January 1, 1995, following the enactment of reforms to Germany's financial market regulations. Although DTB has sought approval from the SEC to allow similar access to the cash option on DAX, it has yet to receive the necessary no-action letter. Trading got another boost in 1996 when the CFTC allowed DTB to install trading terminals in the United

TABLE 7.13 Top 10 Stocks in DAX
(January 4, 1999)

Rank	Company	Market Capitalization (million euro)	Percent Weight
1	DaimlerChrysler	86,736	12.04
2	Allianz	83,076	11.53
3	Mannesmann	42,887	5.95
4	SAP	41,048	5.70
5	Muench.Rueckvers	38,336	5.32
6	Siemens	32,795	4.55
7	Deutsche Telekom	31,800	4.41
8	Volkswagen	31,435	4.36
9	Deutsche Bank	28,278	3.93
10	RWE	27,543	3.82

Source: Deutsche Börse

States. By November 1997, DTB terminals had reached the trading floor of the CME so that firms that are members of both exchanges could trade DAX from their floor booth. (DAX trading hours extend to 10 A.M. in Chicago.)

The Eurex electronic platform is available before trading begins, the pretrading period, from 7:30 to 8:25 A.M. so traders can make inquiries or enter, change, or delete orders and quotes. Trades are executed from 8:30 A.M. to 5 P.M. (CET) in the main trading period. In the post-trading period (5:00 to 7:30 P.M.), market, limit, or stop orders can be placed for the next day's trading session; all inquiry functions also are available.

Final settlement of a futures contract is in cash, based on prices of the underlying stocks during an intra-day auction on Xetra, the electronic cash-market trading system for German securities.

As of January 1999, the DAX multiplier changed to €25 from 100 Deutsche marks, effectively halving the contract size of the DAX future.

Calculating the Index. Domestic stocks eligible for inclusion in DAX must be listed on the continuously traded first or second segment of the FWB, with less than 85% of their shares in company hands and no more than 75% of its stock held by another company in the DAX. In addition, market capitalization, the stock's volume over the last 12 months, and a stock's sector are determining factors for inclusion. Finally, stocks eligible for DAX must be among the top 35 in both 12-month volume and capitalization and accept the takeover code for rules regarding voluntary public tender offers. On a quarterly basis, the index goes through a *chaining*, or reweighting, process to reflect updates in market capitalization. Changes in the DAX composition are reviewed semiannually and made by the Board of Directors of Deutsche Börse, which, together with the Swiss derivatives exchange SOFFEX, are the parent company of Eurex. These changes are based on proposals submitted by a working committee.

In figuring a stock's market capitalization, DAX uses all classes of stocks that are deliverable on the FWB official market and multiplies that total by the price of the most liquid class of stock. As a performance, or total return index, all income from dividend payments and rights issues are reinvested. During an annual chaining procedure in September, the yield from dividends and capital changes is spread over all index companies according to their new weights.

The index is computed every 15 seconds during the FWB trading day, which runs from 8:30 A.M. to 5 P.M. for both floor trading and electronic trading on Xetra.

ITALY

The Italian Exchange was founded in 1808, and 190 years later listed the stocks of 243 domestic companies, with a market value of ∈ 485 billion. Market reforms in the early 1990s, including a move to electronic trading, as well as increased privatization, have resulted in increased trading volume. The stock market is open for trading from 9 A.M. to 5 P.M., with a pre-opening session that begins at 8 A.M. Derivatives products on the Italian stock market were first developed in the mid-1990s. The Italian stock market was Europe's sixth largest in 1997 with capitalization of $258 billion; it ranks fourth among EMU countries.

MIB 30

The MIB 30 is a capitalization-weighted index of 30 blue-chip stocks listed on the Italian Exchange. (MIB originally was an acronym for Milano-Indice Borsa, but now stands for Mercato Italiano di Borsa, that is, Italian Exchange.) The stocks typically account for more than 70% of the market's total capitalization and correlate highly with the broader MIBTEL Index. Several over-the-counter products have been developed based on the MIB 30.

Index at a Glance.

Index	MIB 30
Exchange	The Italian Derivatives Market (IDEM)
Weighting	Capitalization
Ticker Symbol	MIB30
Contract Value (Dec. 31, 1998)	35,152 × ∈ 5 = ∈ 175,760
Clearinghouse	The Italian Clearing House (Cassa di Compensazione e Garanzia)
Regulator	National Commission for Companies and the Stock Exchange (Commissione Nazionale per le Societa e la Borsa)
Web Site Information	www.borsaitalia.it

Understanding the Index. Stocks included in the MIB 30 Index must be both highly capitalized and highly liquid. Stocks are ranked semiannually (usually March and September) by an Indicator of Liquidity and Capitalization (ILC), with the top 30 comprising the MIB 30. The ILC is determined by first finding each stock's *share alpha*, which divides average capitalization over the previous six months by average volume over the same period. (Stocks with a share alpha greater than 10,000 are automatically excluded from the index in order to avoid stocks with high capitalization, but low liquidity.) A similar ratio, *market alpha*, is calculated for the market as a whole. Each stock's ILC is found by multiplying the market alpha by the stock's average six-month volume and adding that to the stock's average six-month capitalization. The 10 most heavily weighted stocks at year-end 1998 are shown in Table 7.14.

MIB 30 Futures and Cash Options. Both a futures contract and an option on the cash index are listed by the Italian Derivatives Market (IDEM), organized as a division of the Italian Exchange in 1994, and both are approved by the appropriate U.S. authorities for trading by U.S. investors. Based in Milan, IDEM is the only derivatives market in Italy. Trading is done on an electronic platform identical to the Swedish OM system, with the futures contract being the dominant product.

Futures trading occurs from 9:30 A.M. to 5:30 P.M., with the index option opening five minutes later and closing five minutes earlier. A pretrading session for the index option overlaps the first five minutes of trading in futures; a posttrading session runs from the options close until 6 P.M. In those two sessions, participants can manage but cannot execute their orders. The pre-trading session in

TABLE 7.14 Top 10 Stocks in MIB 30
(December 31, 1998)

Rank	Company	Market Capitalization (million euro)	Percent Weight
1	Ente Nazionale Indrocarburi (ENI)	40,367	13.9
2	T.I.M. (TIM)	32,573	11.2
3	Telecom Italia (TI)	32,026	11.0
4	Generali Assicurazioni (G)	30,888	10.6
5	Unicredito Italiano (UC)	21,416	7.3
6	Sanpaolo-IMI (SPI)	17,416	6.0
7	Banca Commerciale Italiana (COM)	9,354	3.2
8	Fiat (F)	8,823	3.0
9	Ina (INA)	8,181	2.8
10	Banca Intesa (BIN)	7,967	2.7

Source: Italian Exchange

futures is from 9:00 A.M. to 9:30 A.M.; the post-trading session runs for 30 minutes following the close.

In December 1998, Italy's fixed-income futures exchange, MIF, joined with comparable organizations, MATIF of France and MEFF Renta Fija of Spain, in an alliance called Euro-GLOBEX, to allow cross access to their interest-rate products. The agreement is expected to be enlarged to include the domestic stock index products of IDEM, the French MONEP, and Spanish MEFF Renta Variable in 1999.

Calculating the Index. The MIB 30 Index base was set at 10,000 on December 31, 1992. A weekly price chart since 1995 is shown in Figure 7.9. The index value is determined by summing the component stocks' current capitalization then dividing by the base date total capitalization, and multiplying the result by the last value with the old composition. The index is quoted in full points. The index is adjusted to reflect changes in the number of outstanding shares in the event of stock splits and rights issues so as not to affect the stock's capitalization. The index does not take into account an ordinary dividend but is adjusted in case of an extraordinary dividend.

The index is calculated and disseminated once a minute by the Diffusione Dati di Borsa (DDB) of Ced borsa, a private company

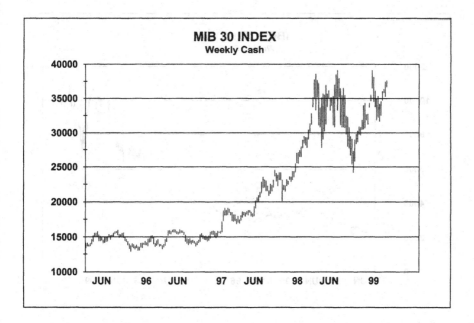

FIGURE 7.9   MIB 30 Index
Source: CRB-Bridge Information

under contract with the Italian Exchange to manage the electronic trading system and trading data. In addition to the index level, the following information also is available with each update: percent change, number of stocks trading, percentage of stocks in the basket that are trading, time of calculation, trend of latest quote versus the previous, and the session high and low.

SPAIN

The Spanish stock market ranked eighth in Europe with $243 billion in capitalization in 1997. Among EMU countries, it is the fifth largest marketplace.

IBEX-35

The IBEX-35 stock index tracks Spain's 35 most liquid stocks. It is capitalization-weighted and equals about 80% of the market's total value. A chart of weekly prices since 1995 is shown in Figure 7.10.

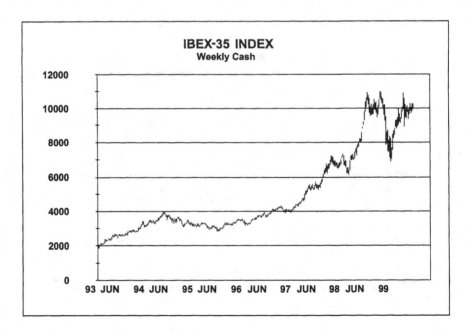

FIGURE 7.10   IBEX-35 Index
Source: CRB-Bridge Information

Index at a Glance

Index	IBEX-35
Exchange	MEFF-RV
Weighting	Capitalization
Ticker Symbol	X
Contract Value (Dec. 31, 1998)	9836.60 × ₠ 10 = ₠ 98,366
Clearinghouse	MEFF-RV Clearing House
Regulator	Comisión Nacional del Mercado de Valores (CNMV) (Spanish Securities Exchange Commission)
Web Site Information	www.meffrv.es www.bolsamadrid.es

The index covers more than 80% of the total market capitalization and total turnover on the Spanish Stock Market. The 10 largest stocks in the index at year-end 1998 are shown in Table 7.15.

IBEX-35 Futures. Futures and options on futures contracts for the IBEX-35 Index began trading on January 14, 1992. Five years later, on January 10, 1997, the index multiplier was increased to 1,000 pesetas from 100 pesetas and was briefly known as the IBEX-35 Plus before going back to the original moniker. The increase in contract

TABLE 7.15 Top 10 Stocks in IBEX-35
(December 31, 1998)

Rank	Company	Market Capitalization (million euro)	Percent Weight
1	Telefonica	39,645	17.33
2	Banco Bilbao Vizcaya	27,292	11.93
3	Endesa	21,577	9.43
4	Banco Santander	19,837	8.67
5	Iberdrola	14,386	6.29
6	Gas Natural	13,860	6.06
7	Repsol	13,649	5.97
8	Banco Central Hispano	11,198	4.90
9	Argentaria	10,823	4.73
10	Banco Popular	7,124	3.11

Source: MEFF-RV

size attracted the attention of institutional investors, and volume (on a comparable basis) more than doubled in 1997 versus 1996. The multiplier changed to 10 euros with the start of European Monetary Union in 1999, increasing the value of a contract by 68% compared with the value when the multiplier was 1,000 pesetas. Both the futures and options on futures contracts are available for trade by U.S. customers.

Trading in IBEX-35 futures is conducted on a computerized system, MEFF S/MART, which displays the six best bid/ask prices. Orders at equal prices are matched on a first-in/first-out basis. In all option months, orders of at least 50 contracts are eligible for execution at a single price by requesting a FAST order. The system was established in 1995 to encourage liquidity in the options market. Trading in futures and options at MEFF-RV is expected to become accessible by exchange members at the French equity derivatives exchange, MONEP, and the Italian exchange IDEM, due to a 1998 agreement among the derivative exchanges in all three countries to create an alliance called Euro-GLOBEX.

Unlike the majority of exchanges with position limits based on the number of contracts that can be held, MEFF-RV limits position concentration based on the amount of margin money a firm or customer has in the market. No single entity can have total margin that equals more than 25% of the total margin required by MEFF-RV for all positions in that market. In addition, each member of the exchange has a daily trading limit that encompasses both proprietary and customer orders.

Customer business in IBEX-35 Index futures, often in the range of 50% to 60% of the total monthly volume, runs about 10 to 15 percentage points above proprietary trading. In options, the situation is reversed, with proprietary business greater than customer volume by about the same degree as in futures.

In futures, customer business is about equally divided between those in Spain and those outside the country; in options, nonresident customers are about 66% of the market's volume. For both contracts, the customer category *other financial investors* is the largest component and equals about 33% of customer trading. Other large participants include banks and mutual funds. Individuals account for nearly 20% of customer volume in futures but less than 10% in options.

Calculating the Index. The IBEX-35 Index focuses on Spain's most liquid stocks and is reviewed each January and July. An independent index manager, Sociedad de Bolsas, S.A., is responsible for index maintenance, review, real-time calculation, and distribution. Recommendations for changing any of the index components must be approved by a five-person Committee of Experts.

The IBEX-35 Index base was set to equal 3,000 on December 29, 1989. The current index level is obtained by dividing the current sum of market capitalization for all 35 stocks by the previous market-cap sum and then multiplying the result by the previous Index value.

Adjustments are made for rights issues, stock splits or consolidation, and issues of convertible bonds or any other type of debenture loan. No adjustments are made for dividend payments.

SWEDEN

The Swedish stock market, with market capitalization of $247 billion in 1997, is similar in size to the Spanish market. Sweden's market ranks seventh in Europe and 13th in the world. Although eligible to join EMU, the country had not yet become a member as of mid-1999.

Swedish Equity Index

The Swedish Equity Index (OMX) is a capital-weighted index of the 30 stocks with the most trading volume at the Stockholm Stock Exchange (SSE). These 30 stocks, out of a total of about 250, typically account for about 66% of total market capitalization of companies listed on the stock exchange (see Table 7.16).

TABLE 7.16 Top 10 Stocks in Swedish Equity Index (OMX)
(January 28, 1999)

Rank	Company	Market Capitalization (million krona)	Percent Weight
1	Ericsson (B)	742.0	22.62
2	Astra (A)	224.7	13.54
3	Hennes & M. (B)	118.5	7.14
4	FörenSparbank (A)	73.9	4.45
5	Nordbank (H)	70.1	4.23
6	SHB (A)	67.3	4.05
7	Nokia (A)	66.0	3.98
8	Volvo (B)	63.9	3.85
9	Skandia	63.5	3.82
10	Astra (B)	50.8	3.06

Source: OM Group

Index at a Glance.

Index	Swedish Equity Index
Exchange	OM Stockholm (OMS)
	OM London (OML)
Weighting	Capitalization
Ticker Symbol	OMX
Contract Value (Dec. 31, 1998)	701.31 × 100 krona = 70,131 krona
Clearinghouse	OM Stockholm Clearing House
	OML Clearing House
Regulator	OMS—Swedish Financial Supervisory Authority (FSA)
	OML—Financial Services Authority (FSA)
Web Site Information	www.omgroup.com

Understanding the Index. The OMX component stocks are changed on the first of January and July each year, based on trading volume from June–November and December–May, respectively. SIX AB, a Nordic financial information and systems company, manages the index updates. The firm also calculates the index and disseminates it every minute during market hours.

The SSE was established in 1863 and is the leading Nordic stock exchange in terms of market capitalization and volume. In 1992, the exchange was privatized as a public limited liability company. In 1998, OM Stockholm, which lists the OMX, merged with the SSE to become the OM Stockholm Exchange; however, the spot and derivatives markets are not linked electronically on the same trading system.

OMX Futures and Cash Options. The OM Stockholm Exchange introduced futures and cash options on the OMX in 1986, and a daily price chart since then is shown in Figure 7.11. In 1989, no volume existed in OMX futures, and OM Stockholm formed OM London (OML) that year in order to access a more international market. The link between OM London and OM Stockholm was the world's first electronic link-up of exchanges to create a single real-time marketplace. Still, the contracts clear at each exchange's individual clearinghouse. Trades on OML are cleared on a member-firm basis at the OML Clearing House while trades on OMS are cleared on an individual account basis at the OM Stockholm Clearing House.

Futures contracts trade electronically on the OM CLICK Exchange System. The system accepts the following types of orders: fill-or-kill, immediate or cancel, rest-of-day, or until expiration. For

FIGURE 7.11 OMX Index
Source: Copyright OM Gruppen AB (publ) 1999, all rights reserved. OMX is a trademark of OM Gruppen AB (publ)

more complex orders, exchange employees handle execution via the Market Place Service (MPS). The market is open from 10 A.M. to 5 P.M. (CET), and although there had been discussion about expanding the trading hours, no decision had been made as of early 1999.

Futures contracts at OM are similar to forward contracts in the United States, because they are three-month contracts with a settlement on the fourth Friday of each month. Although open positions are marked-to-market daily in terms of margin transfers between firms, futures and options contracts on OMX do not settle until contract expiration, at which time trading profits and losses are distributed to customers. Another nonconventional practice involves expiration month codes for the contracts. Both futures and call options use the letters A–L to designate the contract trading month from January–December, respectively; for put options, the letters run from M–X.

Calculating the Index. The OMX base was set at 500 on September 30, 1986, and was split by four on April 27, 1998. Index values are calculated continuously during each Swedish banking day, based on the last paid prices for the underlying stocks. The current index level is determined by dividing the total current market capitalization of the stocks in the index by the previous period's total market capitalization plus any necessary adjustments due to changes in share capital (e.g., as a result of merger or share redemptions). Then that result is multiplied by the previous period's index value.

Although Sweden is not one of the first 11 participants in the EMU and did not switch to the euro as its currency from the krona in January 1999, the stock and derivatives exchanges have made preparations for dealing with individual companies that decide to switch to the euro. When switching to the euro, a company must notify the OM Stockholm Exchange at least three months in advance; in October 1998, no company had announced such plans, so the OMX calculation was not affected by euro conversion in January 1999. In early 1999, two companies in OMX were expected to begin a parallel listing of their stock in euro sometime that year.

The OMX at both OMS and OML will continue to be calculated in Swedish krona until 67% of the market capitalization for one month is traded in euro at the stock exchange. Then the index will be calculated in both krona and euro. Index calculation will switch entirely to euro only when all the component stocks are traded in the new currency; then, either the index multiplier will be adjusted to the current exchange rate, or the index will be split.

UNITED KINGDOM

The London stock market is the largest in Europe and third largest in the world, with market capitalization of $1.7 trillion in 1997. Performance of certain sections of stocks is tracked by two indexes, the FTSE 100 and the FTSE 250, which trade at LIFFE. The FTSE 100 (originally named for the joint developers, the *Financial Times* and the Stock Exchange in London) tracks the 100 largest capitalized stocks on the London Stock Exchange; the FTSE 250 follows the next 250 largest, or mid-cap stocks. The indexes are maintained and distributed by FTSE International Limited.

Trading in the FTSE 100 and FTSE 250 moved entirely to LIFFE's electronic platform, LIFFE CONNECT, on May 10, 1999. Previously, the bulk of trading occurred during a daytime open outcry session on the LIFFE trading floor; a short electronic trading session took place after the stock market closed. On the system, orders are matched according to price and time priority, with posted prices representing firm bids and offers. All products at LIFFE on the FTSE 100 and FTSE 250 are approved for U.S. investment.

FTSE 100

Developed just two years after the first U.S. stock index contract traded, the FTSE 100, also known as *Footsie*, was the first index to trade in Europe. It was listed in May 1984 at LIFFE when the exchange was less than two years old. The index was developed jointly by the London Stock Exchange (LSE), the *Financial Times*, and the Institute and Faculty of Actuaries and was the first of a family of indexes that now represent different segments of the U.K. market.

Understanding the Index. The FTSE 100 represents the value of the 100 largest companies listed on the LSE. These blue-chip stocks typically equal about 66% of the market's total capitalization. In 1998, the 100 stocks in the index each had a market capitalization that exceeded about £2.2 billion, representing nearly 74% of the market's total. The 10 largest stocks in the index are shown in Table 7.17.

Index at a Glance.

Index	FTSE 100
Exchange	London International Financial Futures and Options Exchange
Weighting	Capitalization
Ticker Symbol	Z
Contract Value (Dec. 31, 1998)	5882.60 x £10 = £58,826
Clearinghouse	London Clearing House
Regulator	Financial Services Authority (FSA) Securities and Futures Authority (SFA)
Web Site Information	www.liffe.com www.ftse.com

TABLE 7.17 Top 10 Stocks in FTSE 100
(December 31, 1998)

Rank	Company	Market Capitalization (million pounds)	Percent Weight
1	Glaxo Wellcome (GLXO)	74,944	6.98
2	British Telecommunications (BT.A)	58,513	5.45
3	British Petroleum Co. (BPA)	52,827	4.92
4	SmithKline Beecham (SB.A)	46,864	4.37
5	Lloyds TSB Group (LLOY)	46,469	4.33
6	Shell Transport & Trading Co. (SHEL)	36,718	3.42
7	Vodafone Group (VOD)	30,197	2.81
8	HSBC Holdings (HK$10) (HSB)	27,603	2.57
9	ZENECA Group (ZEN)	24,862	2.32
10	Diageo (DGE)	24,494	2.28

Source: London International Financial Futures and Options Exchange

FTSE 100 Futures and Cash Options. The FTSE 100 futures contract was an immediate hit when it opened at LIFFE in 1984, trading an average 18,500 contract per day after only two months. The futures contract received a no-action letter from CFTC in 1990, which opened up trading to Americans.

Three types of cash options are available on the FTSE 100, and all have been granted a no-action letter from the SEC, permitting investment by U.S. citizens. The option with the American-style exercise has been on the board the longest, since 1984. Trading in the American-style option moved to LIFFE after the exchange's merger with the London Traded Options Market (LTOM) in March 1992. It was joined by a European-style option in 1990 and FLEX options in 1995, which are flexible or customizable. Like the futures contract, the contract multiplier for all the options is £10.

Calculating the Index. Today, the FTSE 100 is maintained by FTSE International Limited, a company formed in 1995 and jointly owned by the LSE and the *Financial Times*. Committees comprising representatives of the fund management, derivative, actuarial, and end-user communities work independently of FTSE International and review all changes to the index as well as make recommendations concerning index calculation and company classifications. Constituent stocks are reviewed quarterly, in March, June, September, and December.

The formula for calculating the current index value is simply the sum of each constituent stock's market capitalization (outstanding shares multiplied by current price) divided by the latest index divisor. The FTSE 100 divisor was initially set at 100.034 in 1984 and is adjusted to reflect capitalization changes in the underlying stocks, for example, dividends, enhanced scrip dividends, issue of new shares, share repurchases, or rights issues. Company additions or deletions also require an adjustment in the divisor. A monthly chart since 1987 is shown in Figure 7.12.

FTSE 250

The FTSE 250 Index picks up where the FTSE 100 Index leaves off, tracking the second tier of public, U.K. stocks listed on the LSE. The index, considered the benchmark for medium-size U.K. companies, was launched in October 1992, with futures arriving in February 1994 (see Figure 7.13). Together, the FTSE 100 and FTSE 250 comprise the FTSE Actuaries 350 Index.

Understanding the Index. With data calculated back to 1985, the FTSE 250 in early 1998 included companies with market capitalization ranging from about £280 million to £2.2 billion, which equaled about 17% of the market's total capitalization. The 10 largest stocks in the index at year-end 1998 are shown in Table 7.18.

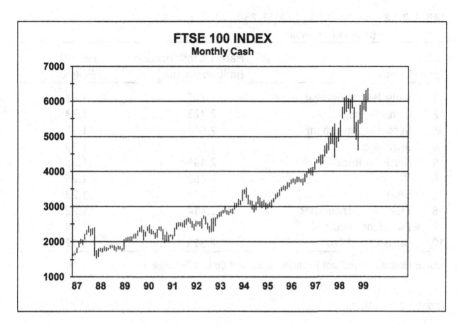

FIGURE 7.12 FTSE 100 Index
Source: CRB-Bridge Information

FIGURE 7.13 FTSE 250 Index
Source: CRB-Bridge Information

TABLE 7.18 Top 10 Stocks in FTSE 250
(December 31, 1998)

Rank	Company	Market Capitalization (million pounds)	Percent Weight
1	Daily Mail & General Trust	2,775	1.41
2	Dema Group	2,723	1.38
3	Nycomed Amersham	2,612	1.32
4	Britannic	2,540	1.29
5	Northern Rock	2,495	1.26
6	Misys	2,463	1.25
7	EMAP	2,417	1.22
8	Blue Circle Industries	2,414	1.22
9	Provident Financial	2,325	1.18
10	British Land Co.	2,315	1.17

Source: London International Financial Futures and Options Exchange

Index at a Glance.

Index	FTSE 250
Exchange	London International Financial Futures & Options Exchange (LIFFE)
Weighting	Capitalization
Ticker Symbol	Y
Contract Value (Dec. 31, 1998)	4854.73 × £10 = £48,547.30
Clearinghouse	London Clearing House
Regulator	Financial Services Authority (FSA) Securities and Futures Authority (SFA)
Web Site Information	www.liffe.com www.ftse.com

FTSE 250 Futures. Futures on the FTSE 250 were listed on February 25, 1994, at LIFFE and got the CFTC's approval just five months later. No option contracts on the index are listed at LIFFE. Like the FTSE 100, the FTSE 250 Index is cash settled to the exchange delivery settlement price (EDSP), which is determined on the contract's last trading day, usually the third Friday of the month, based on the average of the index levels traded between 11:40 A.M. and noon.

Traders with positions in both the FTSE 100 and FTSE 250 are eligible for margin offsets when appropriate.

Calculating the Index. The FTSE 250 is maintained by FTSE International Limited, a company formed in 1995 and jointly owned by the LSE and the *Financial Times*. Committees comprising representatives of the fund management, derivative, actuarial, and end-user communities work independently of FTSE International and review all changes to the index as well as make recommendations concerning Index calculation and company classifications. Constituent stocks are reviewed quarterly, in March, June, September, and December.

The formula for calculating the current index value is simply the sum of each constituent stock's market capitalization (outstanding shares multiplied by current price) divided by the latest index divisor. The FTSE 250 base value was initially set at 1412.60 on December 31, 1985 and is adjusted to reflect capitalization changes in the underlying stocks, for example, dividends, enhanced scrip dividends, issue of new shares, share repurchases, or rights issues. Company additions or deletions also require an adjustment in the divisor.

8

TRADING FROM THE BEACH

Technology is a beautiful thing for traders who don't want to be tied to a desk, an office, or even a trading pit. Armed with a laptop computer, cellular phone, and plenty of batteries, a trader can get quotes, enter orders, and in some cases, access stock index markets directly over the Internet—all from the comfort of the nearest beach chair. Add in a special card that slips into one of the slots on the laptop, and for a monthly fee, real-time quotes make it almost exactly like being there.

ONLINE TRADING

Online trading is a child of the 1990s. Until the Internet began leveling the investment playing field—both for gaining information and executing transactions—individual investors were tied to their brokers and their telephones. No more.

Both the securities and futures industries have felt the impact of individual investors feeling their oats in this new trading medium. In the United States, where the electronic infrastructure of futures exchanges lags that of the securities industry, it is the latter that is on the front lines of learning how to deal with online investors.

Securities Industry

Online trading has taken the U.S. securities industry by storm since the mid-1990s and was estimated to account for about 14% of all securities trades on the NYSE and Nasdaq in the fourth quarter of 1998, or one in seven trades.[1] Charles Schwab, the market share leader in online securities accounts, counted 2.2 million online account holders and $175 billion in online customer assets as of March 1999. In January 1999, Schwab customers placed an average of 153,000 trades a day. Although slow to embrace online trading for fear of alienating their brokers, full-service brokerage firms are jumping on the bandwagon, too, for "what many believe is a once-in-a-generation technology breakthrough that will transform the investment world."[2] A Securities Industry Association study in November 1998 revealed that 43% of investors had used the Internet to get information; 10% had traded online; and 30% non-online traders said they would do so in 1999.

The spotlight has shone on a particular breed of online securities trader, the day-trader who has made a new career of trading stocks full time sitting in front of a computer. Some traders stay at home while others congregate with like-minded entrepreneurs at an office that caters to the new online crowd and supplies necessary equipment and data. In either case, these day-traders rely on gut instincts, gossip from Internet chat rooms, and an occasional peep at the stock index futures markets for trading signals. However, they remain at a disadvantage to more mainstream professional traders, because commission costs take a significant bite out of short-term trading profits.

These day-traders are having an impact on U.S. securities trading. Their influence is particularly evident in stocks of Internet-oriented companies, where online trading volume can be more than 50% of the total.[3] Larger stocks are not immune either. Online traders have been credited with more than 10% of the volume in Microsoft Corp. and nearly 25% in Dell Computer.[4] Although the online traders favor the Small Order Execution System (SOES) at Nasdaq, it appears they're not afraid of trading Big Board stocks. Indeed, the share of total volume attributed to block trading (10,000 shares or more) at the NYSE fell under 50% in 1998, down seven percentage points in three years,[5] and had not been above 50% through the first three months of 1999.

One of the downsides to this online trading fever is that some newcomers have gotten in over their heads, prompting the topic of online trading to be addressed by gambling hotlines, addiction treatment centers, and compulsive gambling seminars. Even SEC Chairman Arthur Leavitt warned in a January 1999 speech that day-trading can be highly risky and should be employed only with funds an investor can afford to lose. On another front, even the best of the online brokerages have had their systems crash due to order overload.

Technology also is supporting the growth of *electronic communication networks* (ECNs), which have offered after-hours stock trade crossing for years and now appear to be positioned to become exchanges themselves. The two largest ECNs at year-end 1998 were Instinet, run by Reuters Group PLC, and The Island, ECN, Inc. owned and operated by Datek Online Holdings Corp. Ultimately, the ECNs may be responsible for laying the foundation for a global, 24-hour trading network in equities.[6]

Futures Industry

The online trading boom in the U.S. securities industry is more like a pop in the futures industry, mainly because so few contracts trade on an electronic platform, but also because of fledgling online order-entry capabilities from brokerage firms and electronic order-routing systems at the exchanges. The securities industry has been forced by trading volume demands over the last 20 years to develop common electronic systems that accept and route orders efficiently. In addition, the Nasdaq market has always emphasized a nonfloor trading environment. The U.S. futures industry has not been under similar pressure, even though trading volumes set a new record on an almost annual basis. Still, the industry is working toward developing a common message switch similar to that found in the securities industry, which would set a standard for electronic communication at the brokerage firms and exchanges.

Electronic networks for futures trading flourished in the late 1980s as non-U.S. exchanges began to form (often to trade a stock index contract) without benefit of either the physical or human capital available to traditional open-outcry futures exchanges in the United States. As a result, these electronic exchanges had a cost structure that enabled them to reduce their fees and to attract trading from anyone who had access to their systems. By the late 1990s, electronic trading platforms were not only considered the way to go for any entity that wanted to develop a new exchange, but also were replacing venerable, successful open-outcry platforms, most notably in London and Sydney. In mid-1999, Deutsche Bank AG announced it would launch Exchange Link, an Internet-based service that enables access to all major electronically traded products in the United States and Europe from one screen.

Competitive pressures from the upstart electronic exchanges also prompted U.S. markets to develop electronic trading capabilities, initially to expand their trading hours around the clock and to prevent an exchange in a different time zone from launching a look-alike contract that would pilfer potential volume and liquidity. Then came the E-mini S&P 500 Index at the CME. It was the first contract in U.S. futures trading history to trade on an electronic platform during regular market hours; in total, traders can reach the market nearly 24 hours a day, from late Sunday through Friday afternoon. Launched in September 1997, the E-mini S&P 500 caught the dual waves of a bullish stock market and online investing popularity. By the end of 1998, it was the third most traded stock index product in the United States, behind the S&P 500 futures and options on futures contracts, which primarily trade in open outcry.

From most accounts, the popularity of the E-mini S&P 500 lies in an individual trader's ability to enter an order online at a brokerage firm, have it routed directly to the GLOBEX$_2$ trading platform, and receive a fill back in less than 10 seconds. It's easy and it's fast. In mid-1999, with the exception of the newly introduced E-mini Nasdaq-100 at CME, other U.S. stock index futures or options contracts were not hooked up to an electronic trading platform during regular market hours. For those markets, a trader could use online order entry at a brokerage firm, but the best that could happen is that the order would be electronically routed to a broker in the trading pit, who would then fill it by open outcry and send it back through the system. At worst, the electronically entered order would go to a clerk who would call the trading floor, have it written down, and run into the trading pit for execution. However, the CBOT intended to introduce side-by-side trading in the DJIA by year-end 1999.

After the U.S. stock market closes, investors can electronically trade all U.S. stock index contracts at the CME and CBOT, including the S&P 500 and the DJIA, throughout the night and into the following morning. The only other contracts that trade more than 12 hours a day with the use of an electronic system include the All Ordinaries at the Sydney Futures Exchange and three contracts at MONEP in Paris, including the CAC 40, Dow Jones STOXX 50, and Dow Jones EURO STOXX 50. The NYSE Composite Index and the Russell 1000 from the New York Board of Trade are open for open outcry trading nearly 12 hours in New York and more than six hours a day on a satellite trading floor in Dublin, Ireland. Surprisingly, stock index contracts traded on all-electronic systems often are not open much longer than the underlying stock market.

MAJOR ELECTRONIC TRADING PLATFORMS

Although some movement has occurred among international futures exchanges to coordinate the development of electronic trading platforms, the effort as of early 1999 has not been very fruitful. Indeed, the four largest exchanges in the world each sport their own system, and for a variety of reasons (mainly political and competitive) appeared mostly unable to veer from that course as they headed into the new millennium.

Eurex

Eurex debuted in 1998 as the electronic trading and clearing systems of the Deutsche Terminbörse (DTB) and Swiss Options and Futures Exchange (SOFFEX) merged. The DTB opened in January 1990 as an electronic exchange, partly as a solution to the problem of having multiple financial centers and traders spread throughout Germany. In addition to the DAX stock index product discussed in this book, Eurex lists options on dozens of German and Swiss stocks, Swiss and German interest rates, and other stock index products. Eurex is the largest futures and options exchange in Europe and the world's largest computerized exchange. In March 1999, monthly futures volume on Eurex first exceeded that of the CBOT, which typically holds that spot.

Only three types of participants are granted direct access to a Eurex trading terminal: a general clearing member, a direct clearing member (which must be a German or Swiss company), and a nonclearing member. Individuals are not permitted to become members but may trade as a market maker through one of the three types of members. The exchange's host computer is located in Frankfurt, Germany, with other access points in Amsterdam, Chicago, Helsinki, London, Madrid, New York, Paris, and Zurich.

Orders with equal prices are matched on a first-come, first-served basis. Orders are sorted by type, price, and entry time, with market orders having the highest matching priority. The system constantly updates the 10 best bids and offers and makes that information available to traders. Limit orders are sorted by highest bid and lowest offer and can be identified as immediate-or-cancel, fill-or-kill, good-till-canceled, or good-till-date. Stop orders are not identified as such to the marketplace.

After taking a close look at the costs involved in upgrading Project A versus working together with a partner, the CBOT agreed to an alliance with Eurex to develop a common electronic trading platform in mid-1999. A previous agreement reached in 1998 had been voted down by CBOT members in January 1999. The alliance is scheduled to launch in mid-2000.

GLOBEX$_2$

The move toward after-hours electronic trading of open outcry futures products began in 1987 when the CME announced it would work with Reuters Holdings PLC to develop GLOBEX. When GLOBEX finally opened, nearly five years later on June 25, 1992, the CBOT and the French MATIF exchange also had signed on. Two years later, the CBOT left the group to concentrate on its own system, Project A.

In 1997, the CME signed a deal that would swap its state-of-the-art clearing software for the electronic trading platform software Nouveau Systeme de Cotation (NSC) developed by the Paris Bourse (SBF). The NSC platform became the basis for GLOBEX$_2$, introduced in September 1998, and covered trading at the CME as well as SBF and its subsidiaries, MONEP and MATIF. In February 1999, SIMEX agreed to join in what now is called the GLOBEX Alliance, in which all members use the NSC platform.

The GLOBEX$_2$ system features customizable trading screens, the ability to use charts and spreadsheets, and a wide variety of accepted orders. These orders include market, stop limit (triggered by a trade, not a new bid or offer), one-cancels-other, market-if-touched, fill-or-kill, good-till-canceled, and good-till-date. Orders also can be designated for either the current electronic trading session or for a single trading day. The order book shown to traders is five deep on either side of the market.

GLOBEX$_2$ trading terminals are available only to members of futures exchanges. However, a growing number of brokerage firms have developed customer access to GLOBEX$_2$ via the Internet.

LIFFE CONNECT

This open architecture platform, launched to trade equity options in November 1998 at the London International Financial Futures and Options Exchange, is the successor system to the exchange's first electronic trading platform, Automated Pit Trading (APT), begun in 1989 and mainly used for after-hours trading. The German bund contract was the world's battleground between open outcry floor trading (at LIFFE) and electronic screen trading (at DTB, now Eurex) in 1997 and 1998. The electronic system's victory sent seat prices plummeting at open-outcry exchanges worldwide.

Losing the bund contract also prompted LIFFE members to take the drastic step in mid-1998 of voting to move the exchange's trading to an electronic platform from open outcry, a change that was scheduled to be mostly complete by mid-1999. Indeed, all LIFFE's stock index contracts went electronic in May 1999.

Several software vendors have developed front-end systems for LIFFE CONNECT so that the market is accessible from an individual's personal computer. Network hubs are in Chicago, Frankfurt,

New York, and Paris. Orders on the system are matched according to price and time priority, and the system displays the aggregate size of all bids and offers on a real-time basis. Calendar spreads are treated as a single trade. Expected functionality includes the ability to perform several different types of option spread trades.

OM CLICK Exchange System

The OM Stockholm Exchange developed its own electronic trading platform, the OM CLICK Exchange System, in 1985 and has pursued selling the technology package to other exchanges that needed a platform but didn't want to develop their own. Besides OMS and OM London, other exchanges that used the OM CLICK system as of April 1999 included Wiener Börse of Austria, Italian Exchange, American Stock Exchange, Hong Kong Futures Exchange, Australian Stock Exchange, Korea Futures Exchange, Toronto Stock Exchange, Nord-Pool (PowerCLICK), and EL-EX (PowerCLICK).

The system allows for integration of users' trading and analytical and back-office systems. The system also boasts that a new product can be designed and listed in a single day. To a user, the system reveals the market's orders five deep and can accept the following order types: fill-or-kill, immediate or cancel, rest-of-day, until expiration, and combinations.

Project A

The Chicago Board of Trade launched its electronic after-hours trading network, Project A, in October 1994, six months after leaving the GLOBEX partnership. Since then, average daily volume has more than doubled every year and was more than 50,000 contracts through the first quarter of 1999. Although U.S. Treasury products trade side-by-side on Project A with the open outcry trading pits, virtually all of Project A volume is handled after the open outcry markets in Treasuries, the DJIA, and agricultural markets are closed. Project A workstations are concentrated in Chicago but also have been set up in New York and other U.S. states, London, Paris, and Tokyo. In addition, CBOT members can access the system via personal computers. Project A originally was designed in the late 1980s as an alternative trading platform for low-volume contracts that could not yet support an open-outcry trading forum.

Unlike most electronic trading arenas, Project A uses a matching algorithm to determine which orders get matched rather than a price/time priority method. Essentially, matching occurs when a buy order is placed at a price equal to or higher than the price of an existing sell order. Orders get priority when they better the market, that is when a bid order is entered above the current bid or a sell order is entered below the current offer. Priority orders get filled first, with remaining orders at the same price matched by quantity allocation, based on a percentage of the total quantity of orders at that price.

Four types of orders are accepted on Project A: limit bid, limit offer, hit the bid, and take the offer. The system accepts two-leg, non-ratio calendar and intercommodity spread orders. Orders can be designated as day orders, good only for that Project A session, or good-till-canceled, which will roll over to the next Project A session. Orders on Project A do not automatically roll to the open outcry forum, or vice versa.

SYCOM

The Sydney Computerized Market (SYCOM) opened in November 1989 for after-hours trading at the Sydney Futures Exchange, and its fourth version allowed all trading on the exchange to move to an electronic platform in 1999. The system also is used for trading on the New Zealand Futures and Options Exchange, an SFE subsidiary.

Exchange members have access to SYCOM workstations, and orders can be entered manually into the workstation or electronically via an automated order entry interface. The latter would allow order-entry from member offices around the globe via the firm's own order entry system. Orders for both individual contracts and spreads are matched on a first-in/first-out priority. Custom orders of up to four legs in futures and/or options can be traded at a user-defined ratio at the prices specified by the trader.

APPENDIX 1

READING THE FINE PRINT

FINDING THE RIGHT BROKER

Finding a U.S. broker to handle stock index futures and options trades may be as easy as asking whether your current stock broker handles futures trading accounts. Since 1997, Series 7 registered securities brokers can register as an associated person (AP) to offer stock index futures and options on futures by passing the Series 33 exam. Brokers, who want to sell all types of futures contracts, must pass the Series 3 exam, which is twice as long as the Series 33 test for financial instruments.

Unless you are a member of a futures exchange, trading stock index futures or options requires placing an order through a brokerage firm. Most major brokerage firms have the ability to execute both securities and futures orders. Other brokerage firms specialize in handling only futures and options on futures trades, and many of these firms feature discounted commission rates. The futures exchange that lists the product you want to trade probably has a list of firms that are members of the exchange on the exchange's web site, often with a link to that firm's individual web site.

When choosing a brokerage firm, you might want to consider more than the commission rate you will be charged. Compare the services the firms offer, such as research, educational materials, and information that may be available online. Certainly, the quality of order executions and fill reports is a priority but is hard to judge without prior trading experience. Still, understand how the firm you're considering routes stock index orders to the respective markets and the path they take to get executed and reported back to you. Does the firm send orders to its own brokers (employees), or do they use independent brokers? What relationships has the firm established to execute orders on markets where it is not a member? If the firm is not a clearing member of an exchange, find out what brokerage company clears your firm's trades.

If online order entry is important to you, check out each firm's web site. You'll probably find at least a demonstration of how online trading would work if not a full-blown, downloadable version to test.

Information about a U.S.-registered firm's financial wherewithal and its regulatory status (and that of its brokers) is available from the CFTC and the National Futures Association (NFA), the industry's self-regulatory organization. The CFTC publishes a semiannual report on the financial condition of registered brokerage firms which is available on its web site (www.cftc.gov). Among other information, the report shows how much money the firm holds for customers (segregated funds) and how much capital it holds in excess of government-required minimums.

An absolute must before opening an account in the United States should be to check on the registration status of the firm and broker you are considering. This is easily done by visiting the NFA's web site (www.nfa.futures.org) and accessing the Background Affiliation Status Information Center (BASIC). The database includes information about every entity required to be registered to do business in the futures industry and can be accessed by a company or individual's name. You should not do business with any U.S. brokerage firm or individual that is not properly registered with the CFTC and NFA. Check out whether your broker is registered and whether your broker or firm has ever been disciplined by the NFA, CFTC, or any of the 14 futures exchanges in the United States. The database does not include criminal background information, such as felony convictions, but that information can be requested from the CFTC. It also does not include any civil lawsuits with which the firm or broker might have been involved. Although some information before 1990 may not be available, a record of enforcement cases filed by the CFTC extends to 1975. You also can use BASIC to file a complaint regarding potentially improper activity by your broker or brokerage firm.

OPENING AN ACCOUNT

Opening a futures trading account requires a lot of reading and a lot of signatures, mainly because of the nature of the futures markets.

Futures trades are highly leveraged, and changes in the value of your account are marked-to-the-market daily. That combination means that a market move against your position can make a major dent in your account that must be repaired right away if you want to hold the position into the next day. In addition, there is no limit as to how much the market might move against your position before you can execute an offsetting order. Thus, unlimited risk exists in holding an open futures position. Even if markets have daily price limits, or circuit breakers, it doesn't guarantee that your order to close out a losing position will be able to be executed at that limit, or even that day.

Somewhere in the papers you are asked to sign with your brokerage firm likely will be a statement to the effect that you are entirely liable for all losses in your trading account, up to and beyond your deposited margin monies. The firm probably also will want to know that you understand that money you devote to a futures trading account should be purely risk capital and that its loss should not impair your lifestyle or other financial obligations. Investors who have never traded futures before, have relatively low income or net worth, or who want to assign power of attorney over their account may be required to sign additional documents.

On the low end of account sizes, some firms may accept an initial deposit of $3,000 to $5,000. A firm likely will require the deposit be made by check or wire transfer, not in cash. Considering that professional futures money managers typically believe it is prudent to devote no more than 20% to 30% of their total deposited funds to margin for open positions, a small account size may limit which markets you can trade and the number of contracts you can hold.

COSTS OF TRADING

Although experienced traders may say that there are emotional costs to trading futures, most people are mainly concerned with the financial costs. The big one is margin, but fees and commissions are what eat into a trade's profitability. In addition, the idle money in your margin account may be earning interest for your brokerage firm, not you. If you trade contracts denominated in a foreign currency, your broker likely will be able to handle the conversion of funds, but your money will be subject to currency risk.

Margin

Margin requirements are one of the main considerations for an individual contemplating a stock index futures trade. In the futures markets, margin may be more accurately described as a performance bond or good-faith deposit. In the securities markets, margin represents a loan from broker to customer to buy stocks. Buying a futures option requires paying the entire premium in full, up front.

Futures margin levels typically are set by individual exchanges and reviewed on a daily basis in order to accurately reflect market volatility; initial stock index margin rates tend to be about 10% of the underlying contract value. Your brokerage firm probably will require margin from you that exceeds these exchange-set minimums. Part of the reason that futures markets can be so leveraged is that losses do not accumulate because every position is marked-to-the-market daily, with debits and credits available to customers also on a daily basis. Any shortfall in margin requirements must be met immediately for a position to remain open. (The Federal Reserve Board, which sets securities margin requirements in the United States, has held the rate steady at 50% since 1974.)

Control over setting margins for U.S. stock index futures contracts was one of the obstacles to listing the products in 1982, with the Federal Reserve Board finally agreeing that futures exchanges could continue their practice of setting contract margin levels. Value Line futures, the first stock index futures contract to open, started with an initial margin requirement of $6,500 (up from the originally proposed $4,000). In early 1999, the initial margin requirement for the Value Line was $8,750, but the contract multiplier was half its size compared with 1982.

The bull market since stock index futures began brought contract values sky high, and many exchanges opted to cut the contract multipliers in order to increase affordability. Even so, with the S&P 500 Index contract multiplier halved in late 1997, the initial margin required by the exchange was more than $20,000 per contract in early 1999. The affordability factor was partly behind the move toward the E-mini S&P 500, which carried an initial margin requirement of $4,125 at the exchange level in early 1999.

Initial margin is the amount of money you need in your account to open a position. Maintenance margin is the amount that determines when you get a call to deposit more funds. For example, you might need $5,000 to buy (or sell) one lot of a stock index futures contract (initial margin) and $4,000 in the account to keep holding the position (maintenance margin). That means you'll get a margin call if the balance in your account drops below $4,000, and you'll have to deposit funds to bring the account back up to the initial requirement of $5,000 to keep the position open.

The clearinghouses used to clear trades at futures exchanges are the ultimate protection against trading defaults. The clearinghouse, which can be an exchange department, subsidiary company, or a stand-alone corporation, is the counterparty to every trade made on an exchange. This ensures that customers can exit their positions without having to settle up with the original counterparty. Clearing members of an exchange have accounts with the clearinghouse and must meet strict financial standards. The clearinghouse monitors the financial conditions of its members constantly during market hours and may make intraday calls for increased funds if necessary.

Fees and Commissions

Commission fees to your broker typically are charged on a round-turn basis for futures contracts (payable when you exit the position) and on a per-side basis for options on futures. Commission fees vary by brokerage firm and are negotiable. Other charges that will be passed along to you include nominal fees imposed by the exchanges and the NFA.

If you have a managed futures fund, its profitability will be affected by the level of management fees and incentive fees charged, both typically on a percentage basis of assets or profits, respectively. Management fees cover the fund's administration and overhead, and incentive fees are paid to the fund's traders when they make money for the fund.

Understanding Your P&S Statement

In the United States, your brokerage firm is required to send you a written purchase-and-sale (P&S) statement each month that tracks your account's activity. The statement will show the date of each transaction, the quantity bought or sold in the number of contracts, the contract month and market, the execution price, the exchange, the currency, and the net debit or credit to your account. Commission fees debited also will be noted, as will option premium debits or credits. If the trade is still open at the date of the statement, the open trade equity (debit or credit) will be determined versus the most recent closing price of the market you're trading.

Like a bank statement, you should see a summary of activity in your account, with beginning balance, net activity, ending balance, and the account's value at current market prices. If necessary, the account value will be converted into your domestic currency.

IF THINGS GO WRONG

In the United States, if you have a serious dispute with your broker over the handling of your account, you may choose to bring a lawsuit, go to arbitration, or file a reparations claim with the CFTC. Arbitration disputes usually center on disagreements about trades in an account, but a reparations claim is more serious in that customer losses are alleged to have occurred due to commodity law violations.

Arbitration

Arbitration is often the preferred method of handling disputes because the length of time needed to come to a decision typically is less than that needed to file a lawsuit or go through an extended reparations claim. In addition, arbitration decisions are final, so no time is needed for appeals. Although your brokerage firm may ask you to sign a form agreeing that disputes will go to arbitration, you are not required to do so in the United States in order to open an account.

Futures exchanges and the NFA both handle futures trading arbitration cases. The exchanges tend to arbitrate trading disputes between exchange members, and the NFA focuses on customer/broker disputes; it worked on about 450 cases in both 1997 and 1998, with less than 50 going to a hearing in each year.

In NFA arbitrations, the number of arbitrators, one to three, on a panel is determined by the size of the claim. Arbitrators may be industry experts or those with no connection to an NFA member or associate, depending on the size of the claim and the request of the person filing for arbitration. An arbitration hearing's final decision will be made within 30 days after the panel has all the information it needs. The panel does not reveal how it arrived at its decision, and the decision may not be appealed. The NFA has an extensive amount of information available about its arbitration process that you should request and review if you are considering arbitration.

CFTC Reparations

Reparation proceedings to recover actual damages may be brought against only those registered to handle futures business, which only emphasizes the reason to make sure that your broker and firm are properly registered before opening an account. Three types of reparations proceedings exist, all of which must be filed within two years of the customer's knowledge of the wrongdoing. In each type of proceeding, the customer may choose to have legal representation.

Voluntary. These claims are judged solely on written evidence, and the decision is final, with no appeal. They can move quickly because no hearings or appeals are possible, and these claims are the cheapest to file. No dollar limitation exists in this reparation proceeding.

Summary. This proceeding is for claims of no more than $30,000, and oral hearings may be conducted by conference telephone call. The decision may be appealed first to the full CFTC and then to a federal court of appeals.

Formal. A formal proceeding involves claims of more than $30,000 with an in-person hearing. Like the summary reparations proceeding, the losing party may appeal to the full CFTC or a federal court of appeals.

APPENDIX 2

STOCK INDEX CONTRACT
SPECIFICATIONS
AND
HISTORICAL STOCK INDEX
ANNUAL VOLUME

BROAD-BASED U.S. STOCK INDEX FUTURES AND OPTIONS CONTRACT SPECIFICATIONS

	S&P 500	E-mini S&P 500	Value Line
Exchange	CME	CME	KCBT
FUTURES			
Index weighting	Capitalization	Capitalization	Equal
Date Opened	April 21, 1982	September 9, 1997	February 24, 1982
Ticker Symbol	SP	ES (All-or-none: EG)	KV
Multiplier	$250	$50	$250
Months*	HMUZ	HMUZ	HMUZ
Hours (local)	8:30 A.M.–3:15 P.M. (OO); 3:45 P.M.– 8:15 A.M. (EL) Friday–5:30 P.M. Sun.	24–hours except: 3:15–3:30 P.M., Mon.–Thurs.; 3:15 P.M.	8:30 A.M.–3:15 P.M.
Tick size	0.10	0.25	0.05
Tick value	$25	$12.50	$12.50
Price limit	**	**	2% and 5% versus previous settlement
Last trading day	Thursday prior to third Friday of contract month	Thursday prior to third Friday of contract month	Third Friday of contract month
Settlement	Cash; To special opening quotation on third Friday's stock opening	Cash; To special opening quotation on third Friday's stock opening	Cash; To closing value of underlying index on last trading day
Position limit	20,000 net long or short in all contracts combined	In conjuction with S&P 500 limits	5,000 contracts net long or short in all contracts combined
OPTIONS			
Date Opened	January 28, 1983	September 9, 1997	No KV option
Ticker Symbol	CS, PS	ES, ES	
Contract Size	1 S&P 500 futures contract	1 E-mini S&P 500 futures contract	
Months	All 12 calendar months	All 12 calendar months	
Hours (local)	8:30 A.M.–3:15 P.M. (OO); 3:45 P.M.–8:15 A.M. (EL)	24–hours except: 3:15–3:30 P.M., Mon.–Thurs.; 3:15 P.M. Friday–5:30 P.M. Sun.	
Tick size	0.10	0.25	
Tick value	$25	$12.50	
Strike price intervals	5 points for two nearest; 10 points for deferreds	5 points for two nearest; 10 points for deferreds	
Last trading day	HMUZ are same as underlying futures; Third Friday of month for others	HMUZ are same as underlying futures; Third Friday of month for others	
Settlement	Cash	Cash	
Exercise style	American	American	
Position limit	Combined with SP futures on a delta-equivalent basis	Combined with SP futures on a delta-equivalent basis	

*Standard abbreviations for contract months: January, F; February, G; March, H; April, J; May, K; June, M; July, N; August, Q; September, U; October, V; November, X; December, Z.
**Price limits coordinated with New York Stock Exchange; see text for circuit-breaker information
Source: Individual exchanges; Futures Industry Institute

Mini Value Line	NYSE Composite	NYSE Large Composite	NYSE Small Composite
KCBT	NYBOT	NYBOT	NYBOT
Equal	Capitalization	Capitalization	Capitalization
July 29, 1983	May 6, 1982	September 26, 1997	June 26, 1998
MV	YX	YL	YS
$100	$500	$1,000	$250
HMUZ	HMUZ	HMUZ	HMUZ
8:30 A.M.–3:15 P.M.	4:45–10 P.M.; 3–9:15 A.M.; 9:30A.M.–4:15 P.M.	4:45–10 P.M.; 3–9:15 A.M.; 9:30A.M.–4:15 P.M.	4:45–10 P.M.; 3–9:15 A.M.; 9:30 .A.M.–4:15 P.M.
0.05	0.05	0.05	0.05
$5	$25	$50	$12.50
2% and 5% versus previous settlement	**	**	**
Third Friday of contract month	Thursday prior to third Friday of contract month	Thursday prior to third Friday of contract month	Thursday prior to third Friday of contract month
Cash; To closing value of underlying index on last trading day	Cash; To special opening on third Friday's stock opening	Cash; To special opening on third Friday's stock opening	Cash; To special opening on third Friday's stock opening
5,000 contracts net long or short in all contracts combined	10,000 contracts net long or short in delivery month; 10,000 contracts net long or short in all months combined	Figured as part of Regular contract limit; one Large contract equals two Regular	Figured as part of Regular contract limit; two Small contracts equal one Regular
July 1, 1992	January 28, 1983	No YL option	No YS option
MVC, MVP	YX, YX		
1 Mini Value Line futures contract	1 NYSE Composite futures contract		
2 near serial months and 3 nearest HMUZ	3 near serial months and 3 nearest HMUZ		
8:30 A.M.–3:15 P.M.	4:45–10 P.M.; 3–9:15 A.M.;9:30A.M.–4:15 P.M.		
0.05	0.05		
$5	$25		
5 points	2 points, even only; deferreds, 10 points, even only		
Third Friday of month	HMUZ are same as underlying futures; Third Friday of month for others		
Cash	Cash		
American	American		
Combined with MV futures on a delta-equivalent basis	Combined with YX futures on a delta-equivalent basis		

LARGE-, MID- AND SMALL-CAP U.S. STOCK INDEX FUTURES AND OPTIONS CONTRACT SPECIFICATIONS

	Dow Jones Industrial Average (Large-cap stocks)	Standard & Poor's MidCap 400 Index (Mid-cap stocks)
Exchange	CBOT	CME
FUTURES		
Index Weighting	Price	Capitalization
Date Opened	October 6, 1997	February 13, 1992
Ticker Symbol	DJ ZD on Project A	MD
Multiplier	$10	$500
Months*	HMUZ	HMUZ
Hours (local)	8 A.M.–3:15 P.M. (OO) 3:30–4:30 P.M., M-Th; 6:05 P.M.–5 A.M., Sun-Th; 5:35-7:50 A.M., M-F(EL)	8:30 A.M.–3:15 P.M. (OO) 3:45 P.M.–8:15 A.M. (EL)
Tick size	1.0 point	0.05 point
Tick value	$10	$25
Price limit**	**	**
Last trading day	Trading day preceding the third Friday of the contract month	Thursday prior to third Friday of contract month
Settlement	Cash; To special opening quotation on third Friday of contract month	Cash; To special opening quotation on third Friday of contract month
Position Limit	50,000 net long or short in all contract months combined	5,000 net long or short in all contract months combined
OPTIONS		
Date Opened	October 6, 1997	February 13, 1992
Ticker Symbol	DJC, DJP	MD, MD
Contract Size	1 DJIA futures contract	1 S&P MidCap 400 futures contract
Months*	3 serial months + next 3 from HMUZ quarterly cycle	All 12 calendar months
Hours (local)	8 A.M.–3:15 P.M. (OO) 3:30-4:30 P.M., M-Th; 6:05 P.M.–5 A.M., Sun-Th (EL)	8:30 A.M.–3:15 P.M. (OO) 3:45 P.M.–8:15 A.M. (EL)
Tick Size	0.05 point	0.05 point
Tick Value	$5	$25
Strike Price Intervals	100 points	2.5 points for two nearest months; 5 points for deferreds
Last Trading Day	For HMUZ, trading day preceding final settlement day; for serial options, third Friday of contract month	For HMUZ, same date as underlying futures; other 8 months, third Friday of contract month
Settlement	Cash	Cash
Exercise Style	American	American
Position limit	Combined with DJ futures on a delta-equivalent basis	Combined with MD futures on a delta-equivalent basis

*Standard abbreviations for contract months: January, F; February, G; March, H; April, J; May, K; June, M; July, N; August, Q; September, U; October, V; November, X; December, Z
**Price limits coordinated with New York Stock Exchange; see text for circuit-breaker information
Source: Individual exchanges; Futures Industry Institute

Russell 2000 (Small-cap stocks)	Russell 1000 (Large-cap stocks)
CME	NYBOT
Capitalization	Capitalization
February 4, 1993	March 5, 1999
RL	R for Regular RQ for Large
$500	$500 for R $1,000 for RQ
HMUZ	HMUZ
8:30 A.M.–3:15 P.M. (OO) 3:45 P.M.–8:15 A.M. (EL)	9:30 A.M.–4:15 P.M.; 4:45 P.M.–10 P.M. and 3 A.M.–9:15 P.M.
0.05 point	0.05 point
$25	$25 for R $50 for RQ
***	***
Thursday prior to third Friday of contract month	Thursday prior to third Friday of contract month
Cash; To special opening quotation on third Friday of contract month	Cash; To close on third Friday of contract month
5,000 net long or short in all contract months combined	5,000 net long or short in all contract months combined
February 4, 1993	March 8, 1999
RL, RL	R
1 Russell 2000 futures contract	1 Russell "Regular" 1000 futures contract
All 12 calendar months	3 serial months + next 3 from HMUZ quarterly cycle
8:30 A.M.–3:15 P.M. (OO); 3:45 P.M.–8:15 A.M. (EL)	4:45–10 P.M.; 3–9:15 A.M.; 9:30 A.M.–4:15 P.M.
0.05 point	0.05 point
$25	$25
2.5 points for two nearest contracts; 5 points for deferreds	Integers divisible by two for nearest contracts; divisible by 10 for deferreds
For HMUZ, same date as underlying futures; other 8 months, third Friday of contract month	For HMUZ, same date as underlying futures; for other months, third Friday of contract month
Cash	Cash
American	American
Combined with RL futures on a delta-equivalent basis	Combined with R futures on a delta-equivalent basis

U.S. STYLE AND SECTOR STOCK INDEX FUTURES AND OPTIONS CONTRACT SPECIFICATIONS

	S&P 500/Barra Growth	S&P 500/Barra Value
Exchange	CME	CME
FUTURES		
Index weighting	Capitalization	Capitalization
Date Opened	November 6, 1995	November 6, 1995
Ticker Symbol	SG	SU
Multiplier	$250	$250
Months*	HMUZ	HMUZ
Hours (local)	8:30 A.M.–3:15 P.M. (00); 3:45 P.M.–8:15 A.M. (EL)	8:30 A.M.–3:15 P.M. (00); 3:45 P.M.–8:15 A.M. (EL)
Tick size	0.10 point	0.10 point
Tick value	$25	$25
Price limit	**	**
Last trading day	Thursday prior to third Friday of the contract month	Thursday prior to third Friday of the contract month
Settlement	Cash; To special opening quotation on third Friday of expiry month	Cash; To special opening quotation on third Friday of expiry month
Position limit	Combined with S&P 500 futures	Combined with S&P 500 futures
OPTIONS		
Date Opened	November 6, 1995	November 6, 1995
Ticker Symbol	SG, SG	SU, SU
Contract Size	1 SG futures contract	1 SU futures contract
Months	All 12 calendar months	All 12 calendar months
Hours (local)	8:30 A.M.–3:15 P.M. (00); 3:45 P.M.–8:15 A.M. (ET)	8:30 A.M.–3:15 P.M. (00); 3:45 P.M.–8:15 A.M. (ET)
Tick size	0.10	0.10
Tick value	$25	$25
Strike price intervals	2.5 points for two nearest contracts; 5 points for deferreds	2.5 points for two nearest months; 5 points for deferred months
Last trading day	Same date as underlying futures in HMUZ; third Friday of contract month otherwise	Same date as underlying futures in HMUZ: third Friday of contract month otherwise
Settlement	Cash	Cash
Exercise style	American	American
Position limit	Combined with S&P 500 futures on a delta-equivalent basis	Combined with S&P 500 futures on a delta-equivalent basis

*Standard abbreviations for contract months: January, F; February, G; March, H; April, J; May, K; June, M; July, N; August, Q; September, U; October, V; November, X; December, Z
**Price limits coordinated with New York Stock Exchange; see text for circuit-breaker information
Source: Individual exchanges; Futures Industry Institute

Nasdaq-100	E-mini Nasdaq-100	PSE Tech 100	Internet Stock Index
CME	CME	NYBOT	KCBT
Modified Capitalization	Modified Capitalization	Price	Modified Capitalization
April 10, 1996	June 21, 1999	April 23, 1996	June 1, 1999
ND	NQ (NV for All-or-none)	TK	IS
$100	$20	$100	$100
HMUZ	HMUZ	HMUZ	HMUZ
8:30 A.M.–3:15 P.M. (OO); 3:45 P.M.–8:15 A.M. (EL)	On Globex₂: 3:30 P.M. to 3:15 P.M. the following day, Sun–Thur	9:30 A.M.–4:15 P.M.	8:30 A.M.–3:15 P.M.
0.05 point	0.50 point	0.10 point	0.05 point
$5	$10	$10	$5
**	**	**	No upside limits; Downside limits at 5%, 10%, 15% and 20% below previous settlement
Thursday prior to third Friday of the contract month	8:30 A.M. on third Friday of contract month	Thursday prior to third Friday of the contract month	Third Friday of contract month
Cash; To special opening quotation on third Friday of expiry month based on five-minute, volume-weighted average of each stock price	Cash; To special opening quotation on third Friday of expiry month based on five-minute, volume-weighted average of each stock price	Cash	Cash
5,000 net long or short in all contract months	Combined with ND futures on a delta-equivalent basis	5,000 net long or short in all contract months combined	5,000 net long or short in all contract months combined
April 10, 1996	June 21, 1999	April 23, 1996	June 1, 1999
ND, ND XHC, XHP (American FLEX) YHC, YHP (European FLEX)	NQ, NQ	TK, TK	ISC, ISP
1 ND futures contract	1 NQ futures contract	1 TK futures contract	1 IS futures contract
All 12 calendar months	HMUZ	3 serial plus next three in HMUZ quarterly cycle	2 serial + 3 nearest HMUZ quarterly months
8:30 A.M.–3:15 P.M. (OO); 3:45 P.M.–8:15 A.M. (ET)	On Globex₂: 3:30 P.M. to 3:15 P.M. the following day, Sun–Th	9:30 A.M.–4:15 P.M.	8:30 A.M.–3:15 P.M.
0.05	0.05	0.10	0.05
$5	$10	$10	$5
10 points	25 points	Integers evenly divided by two; integers evenly divisible by 10 for most deferred contract	Integral multiples of five index points
Same date as underlying futures in HMUZ; third Friday of contract month otherwise	Same date as underlying futures in HMUZ; third Friday of contract month otherwise	Same date as underlying futures in HMUZ; third Friday of contract month otherwise	Third Friday of contract month
Cash	Cash	Cash	Cash
American	American	American	American
Combined with ND futures on a delta-equivalent basis	Combined with ND futures on a delta-equivalent basis	Combined with TK futures on a delta-equivalent basis	Combined with IS futures on a delta-equivalent basis

U.S. STYLE AND SECTOR STOCK INDEX FUTURES AND OPTIONS CONTRACT SPECIFICATIONS

	Australia	Canada	Canada
Index S&P Euro Plus	All Ordinaries Share Price	Toronto 35	TSE 100
Exchange	SFE	TFE	TFE

FUTURES

	Australia	Canada	Canada
Index weighting	Capitalization	Modified Capitalization	Capitalization
Date Opened	Feburary 16, 1983	May 27, 1987	May 20, 1994
CFTC Approved	September 5, 1991	October 6, 1988	April 14, 1994
Ticker Symbol SA on SYCOM	AO TXF	TOF	SXF
Multiplier	A$25	C$500	C$500
Months*	HMUZ	2 serial + next 2 from HMUZ cycle	2 serial + next 2 from HMUZ cycle
Hours (local)	9:50 A.M.–12:30 P.M.; 2 P.M.–4:15 P.M. (OO); 4:40 P.M.–7 A.M. (EL)	9:15 A.M.–4:15 P.M.	9:15 A.M.–4:15 P.M.
Tick size	1.0 point	0.05 points	0.05 points
Tick value	A$25	C$25	C$25
Price limit	None	None	None
Last trading day	Last business day of contract month	Thursday before third Friday of expiry month	Thursday before third Friday of expiry month
Settlement	Cash, to closing index value on Australian Stock Exchange	Cash, to official opening level of the Toronto 35 Index on third Friday of contract month	Cash, to official opening level of the TSE 100 Index on third Friday of contract month
Position limit	None	Hedge: 30,000 for all contract months combined; Speculative: 15,000 for all contract months combined	Hedge: 30,000 for all contract months combined; Speculative: 15,000 for all contract months combined

OPTIONS

	Australia	Canada	Canada
Date Opened	June 18, 1985	May 27, 1987	May 20, 1994 (no longer active)
SEC Approved	NA	NA	NA
Ticker Symbol SA on SYCOM (Year code)SX for LEAPS	AO TXO E100	EQ	SXO (European) Not available
Contract Size	1 futures contract	$100 x Toronto 35 Index	
Months	HMUZ + serial months	Two serial + next 2 from HMUZ quarterly cycle	
Hours (local)	9:50 A.M.–12:30 P.M.; 2 P.M.–4:15 P.M. (OO); 4:40 P.M.–6 A.M. (EL)	9:30 A.M.–4:15 P.M.	
Tick size	0.1	C$0.01 on premiums to C$0.10; C$0.05 on premiums at C$0.10 and higher	
Tick value	A$25	C$1; C$5	
Strike price intervals Index level	25 points	5 points	
Last trading day	Last business day of contract month	Thursday before the third Friday of an expiry month	
Settlement	Cash	Cash, to official opening level of the Toronto 35 Index on third Friday of contract month	
Exercise style	American	European	
Position limit	None	25,000 contracts, with no more than 15,000 in the nearest expiry month	

*Standard abbreviations for contract months: January, F; February, G; March, H; April, J; May, K; June, M; July, N; August, Q; September, U; October, V; November, X; December, Z
**Pending regulatory approval
Source: Individual exchanges; Futures Industry Institute

Canada	Europe	Europe	Europe
S&P/Canada 60	FTSE Eurotop 100	FTSE Eurotop 100	S&P Euro
ME	LIFFE	NYMEX	CME
Capitalization September 7, 1999 pending	Capitalization May 12, 1998 pending	Capitalization October 26, 1992 (U.S. exchange)	Capitalization 2000** (U.S. exchange)
Q	ER	Not available	
C$250	20 euro	$100	50 euro
HMUZ	3 nearest of HMUZ	HMUZ	3 nearest of HMUZ
9:15 A.M.–4:15 P.M.	9 A.M.–4 P.M.	5 A.M.–11 A.M.	3:30 P.M. Sun-Thus to 3:15 P.M. Mon-Fri (EL)
0.05 points	0.5 point	0.1 point	0.25 point
C$12.50	10 euro	$10	12.5 euro
None	None	None	Not available
Thursday before third Friday of expiry month	Third Fridy of contract month	Third Friday of contract month until 7 A.M.	Not available
Cash, to official opening value of Index on third Friday of contract month (to two decimal points)	Cash to Exchange Delivery Settlement Price, taken between 11:40 A.M. and noon on expiration day	Cash, to settlement price determined by FT-SE International based on closing prices on third Friday of the delivery month	Cash
Hedge: 30,000 for all contract months combined; Speculative: 15,000 for all contract months combined	None months combined	10,000 contracts, all short, in all contract months	5,000 contracts, net long or short combined
September 7, 1999	AEX May 12, 1998	January 8, 1993	2000**
pending	pending	(U.S. exchange)	(U.S. exchange)
C$100 x S&P/TSE 60 Index	10 euro x FTSE Eurotop 100 Index	1 FTSE Eurotop 100 futures contract	1 S&P Euro futures contract; 1 S&P Euro Plus futures contract
SXO: 2 serial + next 2 from HMUZ quarterly cycle; LAPS: Z	3 serial + next 2 from HMUZ	HMUZ + next two nearest non-regular trading months	2 nearest serial months + HMUZ
9:30 A.M.–4:15 P.M.	10 A.M.–5 P.M.	5 A.M.–11 A.M.	3:30 P.M. Sun-Thurs to 3:15 P.M. Mon–Fri (EL)
C$0.01 on premiums to C$0.10; C$0.05 on premiums at C$0.10 and higher	0.01 points	0.05 points	0.25 points
C$1; C$5	1 euro	$5	12.5 euro
5 points	50 euro	10 points	200, 500 or 600 points depending on
Thursday before third Friday of expiry month	Third Friday of contract month	Third Friday of contract month until 7 A.M. in HMUZ; in non-regular trading months, the Thursday preceding the third Friday	Not available
Cash, to official opening level of S&P/TSE 60 on expiration date, to two decimal points	Cash, to Exchange Delivery Settlement Price. Based on average index values during close on last trading day	Cash	Cash
European	European	American	American
50,000 contracts, net long or short, European and LEAPS combined	None	10,000 futures-equivalent in all months combined (including futures positions); No limit in spot month	Combined with futures on a delta-equivalent basis

INTERNATIONAL STOCK INDEX FUTURES AND OPTIONS CONTRACT SPECIFICATIONS

	Europe	Europe	Europe
Index	Dow Jones STOXX 50	Dow Jones EURO STOXX 50	FTSE Eurotop 300
Exchange	MONEP	MONEP	LIFFE
FUTURES			
Index weighting	Modified Capitalization	Modified Capitalization	Capitalization
Date Opened	June 22, 1998	June 22, 1998	May 25, 1999
CFTC Approved	pending	pending	pending
Ticker Symbol	FXS	FXE	FOT
Multiplier	10 euro	10 euro	20 euro
Months*	3 nearest of HMUZ	3 nearest of HMUZ	3 nearest of HMUZ
Hours (local)	8 A.M.–10 P.M.	8 A.M.–10 P.M.	9 A.M.–4 P.M.
Tick size	1 point	1 point	0.5 points
Tick value	10 euro	10 euro	10 euro
Price limit	50 points	140 points	None
Last trading day	Third Friday of expiry month	Third Friday of expiry month	Noon on third Friday of expiry month
Settlement	Cash, to mean Index value from 11:50 A.M. to 12 noon on last trading day	Cash, to mean Index value from 11:50 A.M. to 12 noon on last trading day	Cash, to the Exchange Delivery Settlement Price
Position limit	None	None	None
OPTIONS			
Date Opened	June 22, 1998	June 22, 1998	May 25, 1999
SEC Approved	1998	1998	pending
Ticker Symbol	OSX	OEX	FOT
Contract Size	10 euro	10 euro	10 euro
Months	Maturities of 1, 2, 3, 6, 9, 12, 18 and 24 months	Maturities of 1, 2, 3, 6, 9, 12, 18 and 24 months	3 serial plus HMUZ
Hours (local)	10 A.M.–5 P.M.	10 A.M.–5 P.M.	9 A.M.–4 P.M.
Tick size	0.1 point	0.1 point	0.5 points
Tick value	1 euro	1 euro	5 euro
Strike price intervals	50 points for serial months; 100 points for quarterlies; 200 points for half-yearlies	50 points for serial months; 100 points for quarterlies; 200 points for half-yearlies	50 or 100 points
Price limit	with futures	with futures	None
Last trading day	Third Friday of expiry month	Third Friday of expiry month	Noon on third Friday of expiry month
Settlement	Cash	Cash	Cash
Exercise style	European	European	European
Position limit	None	None	None

*Standard abbreviations for contract months: January, F; February, G; March, H; April, J; May, K; June, M; July, N; August, Q; September, U; October, V; November, X; December, Z
Source: Individual exchanges; Future Industry Institute

Europe	Europe	Europe	Europe
FTSE Eurotop 300 Ex-U.K.	FTSE Eurobloc 100	MSCI Euro	MSCI Pan Euro
LIFFE	LIFFE	LIFFE	LIFFE
Capitalization	Capitalization	Capitalization	Capitalization
May 25, 1999	May 25, 1999	May 25, 1999	May 25, 1999
pending	pending	pending	pending
FOX	FOB	MCU	MCP
20 euro	20 euro	20 euro	20 euro
3 nearest of HMUZ	3 nearest of HMUZ	3 nearest of HMUZ	3 nearest of HMUZ
9 A.M.–4 P.M.	9 A.M.–4 P.M.	9 A.M.–4 P.M.	9 A.M.–4 P.M.
0.5 points	0.5 points	0.5 points	0.5 points
10 euro	10 euro	10 euro	10 euro
None	None	None	None
Noon on third Friday of expiry month	Noon on third Friday of expiry month	Noon on third Friday of expiry month	Noon on third Friday of expiry month
Cash, to the Exchange Delivery Settlement Price	Cash, to the Exchange Delivery Settlement Price	Cash, to the Exchange Delivery Settlement Price	Cash, to the Exchange Delivery Settlement Price
None	None	None	None
May 25, 1999	May 25, 1999	May 25, 1999	May 25, 1999
pending	pending	pending	pending
FOX	FOB	MCU	MCP
10 euro	10 euro	10 euro	10 euro
3 serial plus HMUZ	3 serial plus HMUZ	3 serial plus HMUZ	3 serial plus HMUZ
9 A.M.–4 P.M.	9 A.M.–4 P.M.	9 A.M.–4P.M.	9 A.M.–4 P.M.
0.5 points	0.5 points	0.5 points	0.5 points
5 euro	5 euro	5 euro	5 euro
50 or 100 points	50 or 100 points	50 or 100 points	50 or 100 points
None	None	None	None
Noon on third Friday of expiry month	Noon on third Friday of expiry month	Noon on third Friday of expiry month	Noon on third Friday of expiry month
Cash	Cash	Cash	Cash
European	European	European	European
None	None	None	None

INTERNATIONAL STOCK INDEX FUTURES AND OPTIONS CONTRACT SPECIFICATIONS

	Europe	Europe	France	France
Index	EStars	EStars	CAC 40	CAC 40
Exchange	LIFFE	AEX	MONEP	MONEP
FUTURES				
Index weighting	Capitalization	Capitalization	Capitalization	
Date Opened	June 29, 1999	June 29, 1999	November 9, 1988	
CFTC Approved	pending	pending	December 17, 1991	
Ticker Symbol	FOE	FTES	FCC (1 euro); FCE (10 euro)	
Multiplier	10 euro	1/10 x 200 euro	1 euro; 10 euro	
Months*	3 nearest of HMUZ	3 serial	3 spot months, 3 from HMUZ quarterly cycle and 2 half-yearly maturities (H,U)	
Hours (local)	9 A.M.–4 P.M.	10 A.M.–5 P.M.	Three sessions: Evening: 5 P.M.–10 P.M. Morning: 8 A.M.–10 A.M. Daytime: 10 A.M.–5 P.M.	
Tick size	0.5 points	0.5 points	0.5 points	
Tick value	5 euro	10 euro	0.5 euro (FCC); 5 euro (FCE)	
Price limit	None	None	190 points	
Last trading day	Noon on third Friday of expiry month	1 P.M. on third Friday of expiry month	Last trading day of contract month	
Settlement	Cash, to the Exchange Delivery Settlement Price	Cash, to the Exchange Delivery Settlement Price	Cash to arithmetic mean of closing values on last trading day, to one decimal point	
Position limit	None	10 for local traders	20% of open interest in nearby contract; 30% in next expiration; none in any other contract months	
OPTIONS			Short-term	Long-term
Date Opened	June 29, 1999	June 29, 1999	November 9, 1988	October 17, 1991
SEC Approved	pending	pending	June 17, 1996	June 17, 1996
Ticker Symbol	FOE	STAR	PX1	PXL
Contract Size	10 euro	1/10 x 100 euro	1 euro x CAC 40 Index	1 euro x CAC 40 Index H and U
Months	3 serial plus HMUZ	3 serial + 3 from HMUZ	3 nearby months + next from HMUZ quarterly cycle	out two years
Hours (local)	9 A.M.–4 P.M.	10 A.M.–5 P.M.	10 A.M.–5 P.M.	10 A.M.–5 P.M.
Tick size	0.5 points	0.5 points	0.10 euro	0.10 euro
Tick value	5 euro	5 euro	0.10 euro	0.10 euro
Strike price intervals	50 or 100 points	5 points	25 points	150 points
Price limit	None	None	190 points	190 points
Last trading day	Noon on third Friday of expiry month	1 P.M. on third Friday of expiry month	Last business day of contract month	Last business day of contract month
Settlement	Cash	Cash	Cash	Cash
Exercise style	European	European	European	European
Position limit	None	None	30% of daily open interest	30% of daily open interest

*Standard abbreviations for contract months: January, F; February, G; March, H; April, J; May, K; June, M; July, N; August, Q; September, U; October, V; November, X; December, Z
Source: Individual exchanges; Futures Industry Institute

Germany	Hong Kong	Hong Kong
DAX	Hang Seng	MSCI Hong Kong+
Eurex	HKFE	SIMEX
Capitalization	Capitalization	Capitalization
November 23, 1990	May 6, 1986	November 23, 1998
January 5, 1995	June 1, 1994	June 1, 1994 (with MSCI Hong Kong Index)
FDAX	HSI	HK
25 euro	HK$50	US$5
3 nearest from HMUZ quarterly cycle	Spot month, next month and next two from HMUZ quarterly cycle	2 serial months + HMUZ quarterly cycle
8:30 A.M.–5 P.M.	9:45 A.M.–12:30 P.M.; 2:30 P.M.–4:15 P.M.	9:45 A.M.–12:30 P.M.; 2:30 P.M.–4:15 P.M.
0.5 points	1 point	1 point
12.50 euro	HK$50	US$5
None	None	10-minute halt on 15% move, then no limits
Third Friday of contract month	Business day immediately preceding last business day of contract month	Second last business day of contract month
Cash to the intra-day trading rotation on the electronic system (Xetra) of the Frankfurt Stock Exchange	Cash, to average of quotations of Index taken at five-minute intervals on last trading day	Cash, to average of quotations of Index taken at one-minute intervals during last hour of trading on last trading day (excluding high and low values), rounded to nearest single decimal point
None	500 contracts in any single month (Effective Aug. 29, 1998, number temporarily reduced to 250 contracts.)	5,000 contracts
DAX	Hang Seng	No option listed
August 16, 1991	March 5, 1993	
Not approved	December 14, 1995	
ODAX	HK$50	
5 euro x DAX Index	Short-dated: Spot month, next two months, next 3 from HMUZ cycle. Long-dated: two years out	
3 serial + next 3 from HMUZ + next 2 from MZ		
8:30 A.M.–5 P.M.	10 A.M.–12:30 P.M.; 2:30 P.M.–4 P.M.	
0.1 euro	1 point	
0.5 euro	HK$50	
50, 100 and 200 depending on time to expiration	Short-dated: 50 (index under 2,000), 100 (index 2,000-8,000) and 200 points (index above 8,000). Long-dated: 5% on either side of index at time of introduction, rounded down to nearest multiples used for short-dated	
None	None	
Third Friday of contract month	Business day immediately preceding last business day of contract month	
Cash	Cash	
European	European	
None	None	

INTERNATIONAL STOCK INDEX FUTURES AND OPTIONS CONTRACT SPECIFICATIONS

	Italy	Japan	Japan
Index	MIB 30	Nikkei 225	Nikkei 225
Exchange	IDEM	CME	OSE
FUTURES			
Index weighting	Capitalization	Price	Price
Date Opened	November 28, 1994	September 25, 1990	September 3, 1988
CFTC Approved	September 6, 1995	U.S. exchange	January 16, 1992
Ticker Symbol	MIB30	NK	None
Multiplier	5 euro	$5	¥1,000
Months*	3 nearest in HMUZ cycle	HMUZ	5 nearest in HMUZ cycle
Hours (local)	9:30 A.M.–5:30 P.M.	8 A.M.–3:15 P.M.	9–11 A.M. 12:30-3:10 P.M.
Tick size	5 index points	5 index points	¥10
Tick value	25 euros	$25	¥10,000
Price limit	None	1,000–2,000 points based on closing index level of front-month futures at Osaka Stock Exchange on last business day of preceding month	About 5% from previous close
Last trading day	10 A.M., third Friday of contract month	Day preceding day when final settlement price set, usually the second Friday of the contract month	Day preceding second Friday of contract month
Settlement	Cash, to opening prices of shares on last trading day	Cash, to special opening quotation of index, usually on second Friday of contract month	Cash, to special opening quotation of index based on opening prices of each component stock on second Friday of contract month
Position limit	None	5,000 net long or short in all contract months combined	None
OPTIONS	MIB 30	Nikkei 225 (CME)	Nikkei 225 (OSE)
Date Opened	November 15, 1995	September 25, 1990	June 12, 1989
SEC Approved	September 1, 1998	U.S. exchange	Information unavailable
Ticker Symbol	MIB	KN (calls)	
JN (puts)	None	CNK, PNK	None
Contract Size	5 euros x MIB 30	1 Nikkei 225 futures contract	¥1,000 x Nikkei 225 index
Months	2 serial + next three from HMUZ quarterly cycle	2 serial + 4 from HMUZ	4 serial
Hours (local)	9:35 A.M.–5:25 P.M.	8 A.M.–3:15 P.M.	9–11 A.M. 12:30-3:10 P.M.
Tick size	1 index point when option price less than 100 index points; 2 index points from 102–500; 5 index points above 505 points	5 index points	¥5 when index at 1,000 or less; –10 above 1,000
Tick value	5 euros, 10 euros, 15 euros, depending on option price level	$25	¥5,000 when index at 1,000 or less; ¥10,000 above 1,000
Strike price intervals	500 index points	500 index points	¥500
Price limit	None	No trading when futures contract is locked limit up or down	About 5% from previous day's close; no trading when futures contract in trading halt
Last trading day	10 A.M. on third Friday of contract month	Same as futures for HMUZ; third Friday of contract month for others	Day preceding second Friday of contract month
Settlement	Cash, to MIB 30 Index based on value of opening prices of shares on last trading day	Cash. Exercise into futures position	Cash, to special opening quotation of index on second Friday of month
Exercise style	European	American	European
Position limit	None	Combined with NK futures on a delta-equivalent basis	None

*Standard abbreviations for contract months: January, F; February, G; March, H; April, J; May, K; June, M; July, N; August, Q; September, U; October, V; November, X; December, Z
Source: Individual exchanges; Futures Industry Institute

Japan	Japan	Japan	Japan
Nikkei 225	Nikkei 300	Nikkei 300	TOPIX
SIMEX	OSE	SIMEX	TSE
Price	Capitalization	Capitalization	Capitalization
September 3, 1986	February 14, 1994	February 3, 1995	September 3, 1988
December 5, 1986	May 17, 1994	December 13, 1995	January 16, 1992
NK	None	N3	HTPX
¥500	¥10,000	¥10,000	¥10,000
5 nearest in HMUZ cycle	5 nearest in HMUZ cycle	5 nearest in HMUZ cycle	4 serial months
7:55 A.M.–10:15 A.M.	9–11 A.M.	8–10:15 A.M.	9–11 A.M.
11:15 A.M.–2:25 P.M.	12:30-3:15 P.M.	11:15 A.M.–2:15 P.M.	12:30-3:10 P.M.
3-7 P.M. (Electronic)		3-7 P.M. (Electronic)	
5 index points	0.1 index point	0.1 index point	0.5 index points
¥2,500	¥1,000	¥1,000	¥5,000
7.5% from previous close induces 15-min. halt; then 12.5% limit for rest of day	About 5% from previous close	7.5% from previous close induces 15-min. halt; then 12.5% limit for rest of day	50–250 points depending on level of index
Day preceding second Friday of contract month	Day preceding second Friday of contract month	Day preceding second Friday of contract month	Day preceding second Friday of contract month
Cash, to special opening quotation of index based on opening prices of each component stock on second Friday of contract month	Cash, to special opening quotation of index based on opening prices of each component stock on second Friday of contract month	Cash, to opening prices of shares on second Friday of contract month	Cash, to opening prices of shares on second Friday of contract month
10,000 net long or short in all contract months combined	None	5,000 net long or short in all contract months combined	None
Nikkei 225 (SIMEX)	Nikkei 300 (OSE)	Nikkei 300 (SIMEX)	TOPIX
March 19, 1992	February 14, 1994	February 3, 1995	October 20, 1989
CFTC: January 23, 1992	Information unavailable	CFTC: Jan 23, 1996	Not approved
CN3, PN3	HTPX		
1 Nikkei 225 futures contract	¥10,000 x Nikkei 300 index	1 Nikkei 300 futures contract	¥10,000 x TOPIX index
5 serial months + 5 from HMUZ quarterly cycle	2 serial + 4 from HMUZ cycle + MZ out two years	5 serial months + 5 from HMUZ quarterly cycle	4 serial months
7:55 –10:15 A.M.	9–10:15 A.M.	8 A.M.–10:15 A.M.	9–11 A.M.
11:15 A.M.–2:25 P.M.	12:30-3:15 P.M.	11:15 A.M.–2:15 P.M.	12:30-3:10 P.M.
5 index points	0.1 index point	0.1 index point	0.5 index points
¥2,500	¥1,000	¥1,000	¥5,000
500 index points	5 index points for two nearest serial months; 25 points for others	5 index points	25 index points
No trading when futures contract in trading halt	About 5% from previous day's close; no trading when futures contract in trading halt	No trading when futures contract in trading halt	50–250 points depending on index level
Day preceding second Friday of contract month	Day preceding second Friday of contract month	Day preceding second Friday of contract month	Day preceding second Friday of contract month
Cash. Exercise into futures position	Cash, to special opening quotation of index on second Friday of month	Cash. Exercise into futures position	Cash, to opening prices of shares on secondFriday of contract month
American	European	American	European
Combined with NK futures on a delta-equivalent basis	None	Combined with N3 futures on a delta-equivalent basis	None

INTERNATIONAL STOCK INDEX FUTURES AND OPTIONS CONTRACT SPECIFICATIONS

	Spain	Sweden
Index	IBEX-35	OMX
Exchange	MEFF-RV	OM Stockholm
FUTURES		
Index weighting	Capitalization	Capitalization
Date Opened	January 14, 1992	April 3, 1987
CFTC Approved	August 16, 1994	June 3, 1998
Ticker Symbol	X	OMX
Multiplier	10 euro	100 krona
Months*	3 serial + 3 from HMUZ quarterly cycle	All calendar months. Two-year contract listed every January
Hours (local)	10 A.M.-5:15 P.M.	10 A.M.-5 P.M.
Tick size	1 index point	0.25 krona
Tick value	10 euro	25 krona
Price limit	None. Underlying stock market has a 15% limit	None
Last trading day	Third Friday of contract month	Fourth Friday of contract month
Settlement	Cash, to average index value on last trading day taken once per minute from 4:15 P.M.-4:45 P.M.	Cash, to index fix value, which is the average value for the Index during the last trading day
Position limit	Margin monies in market cannot exceed 25% of total market margins	None

*Standard abbreviations for contract months: January, F; February, G; March, H; April, J; May, K; June, M; July, N; August, Q; September, U; October, V; November, X; December, Z
Source: Individual exchanges; Futures Industry Institute

Sweden	Taiwan	United Kingdom	United Kingdom
OMX	MSCI Taiwan	FTSE 100	FTSE 250
OM London	SIMEX	LIFFE	LIFFE
Capitalization	Capitalization	Capitalization	Capitalization
December 1989	January 9, 1997	May 3, 1984	February 25, 1994
July 23, 1996	August 29, 1997	January 16, 1990	July 27, 1994
OMX	TW	Z	Y
100 krona	US$100	£10	£10
All calendar months. Six-month contract listed every June; two-year contract listed every January	2 serial + 4 nearest from HMUZ quarterly cycle	Nearest 3 from HMUZ quarterly cycle	Nearest 2 from HMUZ quarterly cycle
9 A.M.-4 P.M.	8:45 A.M.-12:15 P.M. (Mon.-Sat.) Elec: 2:45 P.M.-7 P.M. (Mon.-Fri.)		
0.25 krona	0.1 point	0.5 point	0.5 point
25 krona	US$10	£5	£5
None	7% from previous pit session close for 10 min., then 10% from previous close for 10 min., then 15% from previous close. During ATS session, 7% from previous pit session's settlement	None	None
Fourth Friday of contract month	Second last business day of contract month, unless it is a Saturday. If so, then the preceding business day	10:30 A.M. on third Friday of contract month	10:30 A.M. on third Friday of contract month
Cash, to index fix value, which is the average value for the Index during the last trading day	Cash, to official closing price on last trading day	Cash, to Exchange Delivery Settlement Price (EDSP), based on index level between 10:10 A.M. and 10:30 A.M. on last trading day	Cash to Exchange Delivery Settlement Price (EDSP), based on index level between 10:10 A.M. and 10:30 A.M. on last trading day
None	5,000 contracts net long or short in all months combined	None	None

INTERNATIONAL STOCK INDEX FUTURES AND OPTIONS CONTRACT SPECIFICATIONS

	Spain	Sweden
OPTIONS		
Index	IBEX-35	OMX
Exchange	MEFF-RV	OM Stockholm
Date Opened	January 14, 1992	December 18, 1986
SEC Approved	CFTC: yes	yes
Ticker Symbol	X	OMX
Contract Size	1 IBEX-35 futures contract	100 krona x OMX
Months	3 serial + 3 from HMUZ quarterly cycle	All calendar months
Hours (local)	10 A.M.-5:15 P.M.	10 A.M.-5 P.M.
Tick size	1 index point	0.1-0.25 krona, depending on premium level
Tick value	10 euros	1-25 krona, depending on premium level
Strike price intervals	50 points, ending in 50 or 00	10 or 20 points, depending on level of Index
Price limit	None. Underlying stock market has 15% limit	None
Last trading day	Third Friday of contract month	Fourth Friday of contract month
Settlement	Cash. Exercise into futures position	Cash, to index fix value
Exercise style	European	European
Position limit	None	None

*Standard abbreviations for contract months: January, F; February, G; March, H; April, J; May, K; June, M; July, N; August, Q; September, U; October, V; November, X; December, Z
Source: Individual exchanges; Futures Industry Institute

Sweden	Taiwan	United Kingdom	United Kingdom
OMX OM London December 1989	MSCI Taiwan SIMEX January 9, 1997	FTSE 100 LIFFE SEI: May 3, 1984 ESX: February 1, 1990 FLX: June 30, 1995	FTSE 250 LIFFE No option traded
yes	CFTC: August 29, 1997	SEI & ESX: May 1, 1992 FLX: March 6, 1996	
OMX OMX (Long)	CTW (Calls) PTW (Puts)	SEI (American) ESX (European) FLX (Flex)	
100 krona x OMX	1 MSCI Taiwan futures contract	£10 per index point	
All calendar months; two-year contract (long) listed every January; flex equals any Swedishbanking day up to three years out	2 serial + 4 from HMUZ quarterly cycle	SEI: 4 serial + June and December ESX: 3 serial + HMUZ FLX: Any business day up to two years out	
9 A.M.-4 P.M.	8:45 A.M.-12:15 P.M., Mon.-Sat.	SEI and ESX: 8:35 A.M.-4:30 P.M. FLX: 9:15 A.M.-4:15 P.M.	
0.01-0.25 kroner, depending on premium level	0.1 index point	0.5 points	
1-25 krona, depending on premium level	US$10	£5	
10 or 20 points, depending on level of Index	5 points	SEI and ESX: 50 or 100 points, depending on time to maturity FLX: 1 point	
None	No options trading when underlying futures is at daily or expanded price limit	None	
Fourth Fridy of contract month	Second last business day of month unless a Saturday, then preceding business day	SEI and ESX: 10:30 A.M. on third Friday of contract month FLX: 10:30 A.M. on any business day	
Cash, to index fix value	Cash, to official index closing price on last trading day	Cash	
European Flex: American or European	American; no option exercise on Saturday	American (SEI) European (ESX) European Flexible (FLX)	
None	Combined with TW futures on a delta-equivalent basis	None	

STOCK INDEX FUTURES ANNUAL VOLUME

	Listed	1982	1983	1984	1985	1986	1987	1988
All Ordinaries Share Price Index Futures (SFE)	Feb. 16, 1983		180,014	237,031	284,421	486,139	624,699	292,065
All Ordinaries Share Price Index Options	June 18, 1985				3,720	27,091	137,078	82,234
Total All Ordinaries Share Price Index					288,141	513,230	761,777	374,299
CAC 40 Futures (MONEP; MATIF)	Nov. 9, 1988							64,688
CAC 40 Short-term Cash Options	Nov. 9, 1988							49,716
CAC 40 Long-term Cash Options	Oct. 17, 1991							
Total CAC 40								114,404
CBOE 250 Futures (CBOT)	Nov. 1998							55,840
DAX Futures Index (EUREX)	Nov. 23, 1990							
DAX Options on Futures Index	Jan. 1992							
DAX Options on Cash Index	Aug. 16, 1991							
Total DAX								
Dow Jones Industrial Average Futures (CBOT)	Oct. 6, 1997							
Dow Jones Industrial Average Options	Oct. 6, 1997							
Total Dow Jones Industrial Average								
Dow Jones Taiwan Futures (CME)	Jan. 8, 1997							
Dow Jones Taiwan Options	Jan. 8, 1997							
Total Dow Jones Taiwan								
Eurotop 100 Futures (AE)	June 06, 1991							
Eurotop 100 Options	June 06, 1991							
Total Eurotop 100								

1989	1990	1991	1992	1993	1994	1995	1996	1997	1998
325,846	313,761	388,174	342,013	980,866	2,552,546	2,476,331	2,675,754	3,204,266	3,678,151
139,834	185,996	247,982	154,149	466,896	833,667	652,607	896,880	896,340	847,375
465,680	499,757	636,156	496,162	1,447,762	3,386,213	3,128,938	3,572,634	4,100,606	4,525,526
581,473	1,641,398	2,311,196	3,601,476	5,908,739	7,464,449	6,549,953	5,853,172	6,461,308	16,443,276
816,025	2,470,394	3,717,515	3,170,782	2,451,512	2,755,289	2,425,363	2,465,497	2,683,025	5,108,041
		86,881	547,485	1,760,763	2,996,181	3,013,926	2,126,001	2,267,084	2,752,536
1,397,498	4,111,792	6,115,592	7,319,743	10,121,014	13,215,919	11,989,242	10,444,670	11,411,417	24,303,853
13,945									
	51,363	1,251,453	3,271,055	3,976,882	5,140,803	4,788,661	5,452,505	6,623,287	6,937,139
		136,439	62,976	49,642	21,073	24,574	3,415	0
		2,045,707	13,944,986	21,419,890	23,499,552	24,299,078	26,042,463	31,521,286	29,948,503
	51,363	3,297,160	17,352,480	25,459,748	28,689,997	29,108,812	31,519,542	38,147,988	36,885,642
								755,476	3,567,512
								156,132	245,398
								911,608	3,812,910
								8,558	0
								146	0
								8,704	0
		1,265	2,003	1,102	435	233	31	249	2,026
		9,632	10,424	2,647	853	5,204	5,090	12,127	33,586
		10,897	12,427	3,749	1,288	5,437	5,121	12,376	35,612

STOCK INDEX FUTURES ANNUAL VOLUME

	Listed	1982	1983	1984	1985	1986	1987	1988
FTSE 100 Futures (LIFFE) LIFFE	May 03, 1984			73,178	88,646	122,343	458,045	465,103
FTSE 100 Options (SEI) LIFFE	May 03, 1984			159,037	232,156	417,071	883,637	1,175,192
FTSE 100 Options (ESX)	Feb. 1, 1990							
FTSE 100 Flex Options	June 30, 1995							
Total FTSE 100				232,215	320,802	539,414	1,341,682	1,640,295
FTSE 100 Futures (CME)	Oct. 1992							
FTSE 100 Options	Oct. 1992							
Total FTSE 100								
FTSE Eurotop 100 Futures (COMEX)	Oct. 26, 1992							
FTSE Eurotop 100 Options (COMEX)	Jan. 8, 1993							
Total FTSE Eurotop 100								
FTSE Eurotop 100 Futures (LIFFE)	6/91 & 5/12/98							
FTSE MidCap 250 Futures (LIFFE)	Feb. 25, 1994							
Hang Seng Futures (HKFE)	May 06, 1986					791,305	3,611,329	140,155
Hang Seng Cash Options	Mar. 5, 1993							
Total Hang Seng						791,305	3,611,329	140,155
IBEX-35 Futures (MEFF-RV)	Jan. 14, 1992							
IBEX-35 Options	Jan. 14, 1992							
Total IBEX-35								
(92-96 levels converted)								
International Index Futures (CBOT)	Oct. 1987						175	
Major Market Index Futures (CBOT)	July 23, 1984			1,514,737	2,062,083	36,292		
MMI Maxi Futures (CBOT)	Aug. 8, 1985				422,091	1,738,916	2,630,887	1,175,531
MMI Maxi Options	Oct. 1991							
Total MMI Maxi								

1989	1990	1991	1992	1993	1994	1995	1996	1997	1998
1,028,014	1,443,829	1,727,382	2,618,629	3,119,971	4,227,490	3,373,259	3,627,044	3,698,368	6,955,096
2,356,764	2,412,083	1,849,346	2,607,815	2,647,304	3,640,668	2,915,214	3,764,079	2,988,158	1,001,428
	294,206	383,253	454,772	792,156	1,145,988	1,518,872	2,974,876	4,200,191	3,512,173
						60,699	65,701	32,985	27,855
3,384,778	4,150,118	3,959,981	5,681,216	6,559,431	9,014,146	7,868,044	10,431,700	10,919,702	11,496,552
			1,057	94					
			73	2					
			1,130	96					
			26,453	56,497	62,231	49,328	38,925	47,427	50,619
				533					
			26,453	57,030	62,231	49,328	38,925	47,427	50,619
		2,721	87						42,058
					40,674	35,068	34,068	68,280	65,219
235,976	236,002	499,262	1,089,027	2,415,739	4,192,571	4,546,613	4,656,084	6,446,696	6,969,708
				295,217	606,679	645,538	1,093,871	1,147,374	798,712
235,976	236,002	499,262	1,089,027	2,710,956	4,799,250	5,192,151	5,749,955	7,594,070	7,768,420
			286,353	1,085,601	2,764,728	2,809,670	2,924,367	6,053,283	8,627,374
			244,666	356,349	756,637	817,960	863,961	1,411,101	1,681,205
			531,019	1,441,950	3,521,365	3,627,630	3,788,328	7,464,384	10,308,579
1,086,550	951,325	702,927	360,879	155,338					
		3,059	2,215	1,368					
		705,986	363,094	156,706					

STOCK INDEX FUTURES ANNUAL VOLUME

	Listed	1982	1983	1984	1985	1986	1987	1988
Major Market Index Futures (CME)	Sept. 7, 1993							
Major Market Index Options	Sept. 7, 1993							
Total Major Market Index								
Mexican IPC Futures (CME)	May 30, 1996							
Mexican IPC Options	May 30, 1996							
Total Mexican IPC								
MIB 30 Futures (IDEM)	Nov. 28, 1994							
MIB 30 Cash Options	Nov. 15, 1995							
Total MIB 30								
Moody's Index Futures (COMEX)	Oct. 1987						11,482	
MSCI Hong Kong Futures (SIMEX)	3/93 & 11/23/98							
MSCI Taiwan (SIMEX)	Jan. 9, 1997							
MSCI Taiwan Options	Jan. 9, 1997							
Total MSCI Taiwan								
Nasdaq-100 Futures (CBOT)	Oct. 25, 1985				139,888	3,743		
Nasdaq-100 Futures (CME)	April 10, 1996							
Nasdaq-100 Options	April 10, 1996							
Total Nasdaq-100								
Nikkei 225 Futures (CME)	Sept. 25, 1990							
Nikkei 225 Options	Sept. 25, 1990							
Total Nikkei 225								
Nikkei 225 Futures (OSE)	Sept. 3, 1988							1,892,394
Nikkei 225 Cash Options	June 12, 1989							
Total Nikkei 225								1,892,394
Nikkei 225 Futures (SIMEX)	Sept. 3, 1986					33,593	363,439	586,921
Nikkei 225 Options	Mar. 19, 1992							
Total Nikkei 225						33,593	363,439	586,921

1989	1990	1991	1992	1993	1994	1995	1996	1997	1998
				49,286	150,308	58,048	4,592	732	4
				251	804	289	729	20	
				49,537	151,112	58,337	5,321	752	4
							4,481	88	
							75		
							4,556	88	
					36,155	1,144,754	2,675,236	4,463,042	5,896,238
						12,540	476,237	1,159,040	1,616,635
					36,155	1,157,294	3,151,473	5,622,082	7,512,873
				80,245	317				6,124
								677,295	1,842,977
								7,550	20,521
								684,845	1,863,498
							380,963	807,604	1,063,328
							23,992	108,922	127,532
							404,955	916,526	1,190,860
	52,046	246,948	383,755	356,523	548,233	609,720	502,072	417,541	479,248
	8,793	12,378	13,971	9,684	7,982	8,986	5,722	7,834	7,725
	60,839	259,326	397,726	366,207	556,215	618,706	507,794	425,375	486,973
5,442,647	13,588,779	21,643,085	11,927,329	8,461,458	6,208,754	7,220,900	7,043,977	7,484,182	8,191,130
6,610,435	9,187,741	11,835,611	9,256,981	6,090,375	4,273,641	5,174,571	3,924,543	4,910,359	5,230,046
12,053,082	22,776,520	33,478,696	21,184,310	14,551,833	10,482,395	12,395,471	10,968,520	12,394,541	13,421,176
858,965	880,513	721,751	3,349,243	5,162,199	5,801,098	6,456,984	4,887,912	4,844,495	5,537,558
			269,039	897,545	1,496,922	1,943,096	586,660	628,222	838,891
858,965	880,513	721,751	3,618,282	6,059,744	7,298,020	8,400,080	5,474,572	5,472,717	6,376,449

STOCK INDEX FUTURES ANNUAL VOLUME

	Listed	1982	1983	1984	1985	1986	1987	1988
Nikkei 300 Futures (OSE)	Feb. 14, 1994							
Nikkei 300 Cash Options	Feb. 14, 1994							
Total Nikkei 300								
Nikkei 300 Futures (SIMEX)	Feb. 3, 1995							
Nikkei 300 Options	Feb. 3, 1995							
Total Nikei 300								
NYSE Composite Futures (NYFE)	May 6, 1982	1,432,913	3,506,439	3,456,798	2,833,614	3,123,668	2,915,915	1,668,732
NYSE Composite Options	Jan. 28, 1983		306,602	246,359	195,634	296,303	206,631	23,304
Total NYSE Composite		1,432,913	3,813,041	3,703,157	3,029,248	3,419,971	3,122,546	1,692,036
NYSE Financial Futures (NYFE)	Nov. 12,1982	13,933	3,828					
NYSE Utility Futures (NYFE)	Nov. 15, 1993							
OSF 50 (OSE)	June 09, 1987						200,480	540,857
PSE Tech 100 Futures (NYBT)	April 23, 1996							
PSE Tech 100 Options	April 23, 1996							
Total PSE Tech 100								
Russell 2000 Futures (CME)	Feb. 4, 1993							
Russell 2000 Options	Feb. 4, 1993							
Total Russell 200								
Russell 2000 Futures (NYFE)	Sept. 1987						5,644	32
Russell 3000 Futures (NYFE)	Sept. 1987						10,734	
S&P 100 Futures (CME)	July 14, 1983		390,902	166,202	1,662	3,514		
S&P 400 Futures (CME)	Feb. 13, 1992							
S&P 400 Options	Feb. 13, 1992							
Total S&P 400								
S&P 500 Futures (CME)	April 21, 1982	2,935,532	8,101,697	12,363,592	15,055,955	19,505,273	19,044,673	11,353,898
S&P 500 Options	Jan. 28, 1983	0	281,090	672,884	1,090,068	1,886,445	1,877,295	734,827
Total S&P 500		2,935,532	8,382,787	13,036,476	16,146,023	21,391,718	20,921,968	12,088,725

1989	1990	1991	1992	1993	1994	1995	1996	1997	1998
					4,184,480	2,318,652	1,872,983	1,526,538	1,531,004
					269,067	122,084	44,254	7,798	2,577
					4,453,547	2,440,736	1,917,237	1,534,336	1,533,581
						174,234	156,482	129,695	95,255
						3,160			
					177,394	156,482	129,695	95,255	
1,579,704	1,574,641	1,486,166	1,315,438	848,522	729,231	685,922	791,325	916,716	590,327
39,482	25,501	34,570	43,386	29,571	26,636	26,457	48,714	81,038	93,343
1,619,186	1,600,142	1,520,736	1,358,824	878,093	755,867	712,379	840,039	997,754	683,670
				10	11				
355	270	253	49						
							8,663	9,848	20,764
						-	2,211	8,801	75,166
							10,874	18,649	95,930
				19,479	36,239	43,857	78,353	182,717	276,662
				1,428	2,793	1,532	2,089	2,849	2,656
				20,907	39,032	45,389	80,442	185,566	279,318
			102,708	218,531	285,962	253,741	289,989	262,017	310,008
			2,933	5,129	3,622	5,435	2,201	3,272	1,899
			105,641	223,660	289,584	259,176	292,190	265,289	311,907
10,560,455	12,139,209	12,340,380	12,414,157	13,204,413	18,708,599	18,852,149	19,899,999	21,294,584	31,430,523
1,161,629	1,638,131	1,813,118	2,209,529	2,916,047	3,820,893	4,568,232	4,636,236	4,734,950	4,986,687
11,722,084	13,777,340	14,153,498	14,623,686	16,120,460	22,529,492	23,420,381	24,536,235	26,029,534	36,417,210

STOCK INDEX FUTURES ANNUAL VOLUME

	Listed	1982	1983	1984	1985	1986	1987	1988
E-mini S&P 500 Futures (CME)	Sept. 9, 1997							
E-mini S&P 500 Options	Sept. 9, 1997							
Total E-mini S&P 500								
S&P 500 Barra Growth Futures (CME)	Nov. 6, 1995							
S&P 500 Barra Growth Options	Nov. 6, 1995							
Total S&P 500 Barra Growth								
S&P 500 Barra Value Futures (CME)	Nov. 6, 1995							
S&P 500 Barra Value Options	Nov. 6, 1995							
Total S&P 500 Barra Value								
S&P OTC 250 Futures (CME)	Oct. 25, 1985				94,919	5,270		
Swedish Equity Index, OMX (OMLX)	Apr. 3, 1987						159,447	312,096
Swedish Equity Index Options	Dec. 18, 1986					15,401	6,738,654	4,466,763
Total Swedish Equity Index						15,401	6,898,101	4,778,859
TSE 300 Futures (TFE)	1984			19,014	25,050	51,491	6,373	
TSE 300 Spot Futures	1985				23,680	75,081	25,187	654
Total TSE 300				19,014	48,730	126,572	31,560	654
Toronto 35 Futures (TFE)	May 27, 1987						35,524	27,284
Toronto 35 Options	May 27, 1987						227,404	428,713
Total Toronto 35							262,928	455,997
TSE 100 Futures (TFE)	May 20, 1994							
TSE 100 Options	May 20, 1994							
Total TSE 100								
TOPIX Futures (CBOT)	Sept. 1990							
TOPIX Futures (TSE)	Sept. 3, 1988							1,887,140
TOPIX Options	Oct. 20, 1989							
Total TOPIX								1,887,140

1989	1990	1991	1992	1993	1994	1995	1996	1997	1998
								885,825	4,466,032
								8,661	20,629
								894,486	4,486,661
						1,240	3,400	6,196	9,816
							2,960	962	82
						1,240	6,360	7,158	9,898
						1,478	7,531	11,203	21,245
						50	4,765	1,791	40
						1,528	12,296	12,994	21,285
0	3,675	114,176	450,031	627,706	1,706,984	1,593,408	1,625,391	2,163,560	9,265,510
5,016,222	5,168,766	4,826,172	5,605,059	4,073,452	5,812,435	6,067,268	5,399,227	3,545,967	4,947,486
5,016,222	5,172,441	4,940,348	6,055,090	4,701,158	7,519,419	7,660,676	7,024,618	5,709,527	14,212,996
1,191	22		2						
1,191	22		2						
34,814	52,687	60,950	59,049	69,058	104,209	110,011	155,652	317,408	440,851
487,488	692,878	465,124	302,444	221,232	247,482	337,764	254,199	431,623	388,273
522,302	745,565	526,074	361,493	290,290	351,691	447,775	409,851	749,031	829,124
					10,819	2,963	8,135	19,317	16,900
					13,200	7,824	845	51	
					24,019	10,787	8,980	19,368	16,900
	230								
3,727,512	3,091,014	1,676,798	1,358,723	2,156,960	2,623,067	2,745,614	2,857,272	3,035,724	2,727,070
2,883,264	193,893	49,027	48,576	37,831	20,078	16,742	13,444	9,356	583
6,610,776	3,284,907	1,725,825	1,407,299	2,194,791	2,643,145	2,762,356	2,870,716	3,045,080	2,727,653

STOCK INDEX FUTURES ANNUAL VOLUME

	Listed	1982	1983	1984	1985	1986	1987	1988
Value Line Futures (KCBT)	Feb. 24, 1982		724,979	910,956	1,204,659	953,985	505,551	79,872
Value Line Options (CBOT floor)	Mar. 4, 1983		168					
Total Value Line			725,147	910,956	1,204,659	953,985	505,551	79,872
Mini Value Line Futures (KCBT)	July 29, 1983		25,092	30,179	19,032	18,678	28,457	14,171
Mini Value Line Options	July 01, 1992							
Total Mini Value Line			25,092	30,179	19,032	18,678	28,457	14,171
Wilshire Small-Cap Futures (CBOT)	Jan. 1993							
Wilshire Small-Cap Options	Jan. 1993							
Total Wilshire Small-Cap								

Source: FIA and Individual Exchanges

1989	1990	1991	1992	1993	1994	1995	1996	1997	1998
41,268	35,558	57,705	46,195	45,806	50,259	35,185	28,663	14,047	4,485
41,268	35,558	57,705	46,195	45,806	50,259	35,185	28,663	14,047	4,485
8,390	14,081	26,941	34,454	40,662	51,901	74,346	135,848	154,784	76,345
			918	1,797	3,404	3,014	1,439	4,547	1,662
8,390	14,081	26,941	35,372	42,459	55,305	77,360	137,287	159,331	78,007
				1,626					
				52					
				1,678					

APPENDIX 3

RESOURCES

EXCHANGES

Exchanges worldwide should be able to supply you with current information about their stock index products.

Amsterdam Exchanges (AEX)

Marketing Research & Development
P.O. Box 19163
1000 GD Amsterdam
Netherlands
Tel: 31-20-550-4199
Fax: 31-20-550-4912
www.aex.nl

Chicago Board of Trade (CBOT)

141 W. Jackson Blvd.
Chicago, IL 60604
Tel: 312-435-3500
Fax: 312-341-3306
www.cbot.com

Chicago Mercantile Exchange (CME)

30 S. Wacker Dr.
Chicago, IL 60606
Tel: 312-930-1000
Fax: 312-930-3439
www.cme.com

Eurex

Eurex Frankfurt AG
Borsenplatz 7–11
D–60313 Frankfurt/Main
Germany
Tel: 49-069-2101-1510
Fax: 49-069-2101-1511
www.eurexchange.com

Kansas City Board of Trade (KCBT)

4800 Main Street
Suite 303
Kansas City, Missouri 64112
Tel: 816-753-7500
Fax: 816-753-3944
www.kcbt.com

Hong Kong Futures Exchange (HKFE)

Asia Pacific Finance Tower,
  6th Floor
Citibank Plaza, 3 Garden Road
Hong Kong
Tel: 852-2842-9333
Fax: 852-2509-0555
E-mail: prm@hkfe.com
www.hkfe.com

London International Financial Futures and Options Exchange (LIFFE)

Cannon Bridge
London EC4R 3XX
England
Tel: 44-171-623-0444
Fax: 44-171-379-2818 (index
  department)
E-mail:
equity.products@liffe.com
www.liffe.com

Italian Derivatives Market (IDEM)

Piazza degli Affari, 6
20123 - Milan
Italy
Tel: 392-7242-6207
Fax: 392-7242-6279
www.borsaitalia.it

Marche des Options Negociables de Paris (MONEP SA)

39, Rue Cambon
75039 Paris Cedex 01
France
Tel: 33-1-4927-1800
Fax: 33-1-4927-1823
www.monep.fr

MEFF Renta Variable (MEFF-RV)

Spanish Equity Derivatives
  Exchange
Plaza Pablo Ruiz Picasso, s/n
Torre Picasso, Planta 26
28020 Madrid
Spain
Tel: 34-91-585-08-00
Fax: 34-91-571-95-42
www.meffrv.es

Montreal Exchange (ME)

800 Victoria Square
P.O. Box 61
Montreal, Quebec H4Z 1A9
Canada
Tel: 514-871-2424
Fax: 514-871-3553
www.me.org

New York Board of Trade (NYBOT)

NYFE Division
Four World Trade Center
Suite 5572
New York, NY 10048
Tel: 212-748-1248
Fax: 212-742-5026
www.nybot.com

New York Mercantile Exchange (NYMEX)

One North End Avenue
World Financial Center
New York, NY 10282-1101
Tel: 212-299-2000
Fax: 212-301-4700
E-mail:
exchangeinfo@nymex.com
www.nymex.com

OM London (OML)

107 Cannon Street
London EC4N 5AD
England
Tel: 44-171-283-0678
Fax: 44-171-815-8508
www.omgroup.com

OM Stockholm (OMS)

Box 16305
S–103
26 Stockholm
Sweden
Tel: 46-8-700-06-00
Fax: 46-8-723-10-92
www.omgroup.com

Osaka Securities Exchange (OSE)

8–16, Kitahama 1-chome,
Chuo-ku
Osaka 541-0041
Japan
Tel: 81-6-229-8643
Fax: 81-6-231-2639
www.ose.or.jp

Singapore International Monetary Exchange Limited (SIMEX)

1 Raffles Place #07-00
OUB Centre
Singapore 048616
Tel: 65 535-7382
Fax: 65-535-7282
E-mail: simex@pacific.net.sg
www.simex.com.sg

SIMEX America Ltd
10 E. 40th St.
Suite 4205
New York, NY 10016
Tel: 212-481-8080
Fax: 212-481-7373

Sydney Futures Exchange (SFE)

Level 3
30–32 Grosvenor Street
Sydney NSW 2000
Australia
Tel: 61-2-9256-0555
Fax: 61-2-9256-0666
www.sfe.com.au

Tokyo Stock Exchange (TSE)

Equity Derivatives Department
2–1, Nihombashi-Kabuto-cho,
Chuo-ku, Tokyo, 103-8220
Japan
Tel: 81-3-3665-1261
Fax: 81-3-3665-1405
www.tse.or.jp

U.S. Office
45 Broadway
New York, NY 10006
Tel: 212-363-2350
Fax: 212-363-2354

Toronto Stock Exchange (TSE)

Derivative Markets
The Exchange Tower
2 First Canadian Place
Toronto, ON
M5X 1J2
Canada
Tel: 416-947-4487
Fax: 416-947-4272
www.tse.com

STOCK INDEX DEVELOPERS

Stock index development is largely in the hands of companies that specialize in designing and maintaining the indexes.

Dow Jones & Co.

Dow Jones Indexes
P.O. Box 300
Princeton, NJ 08543-0300
Tel: 609-520-7799
Fax: 609-520-7030
www.dj.com

FTSE International

St Alphage House,
   Podium Floor
2 Fore Street
London EC2Y 5DA
England
Tel: 44-171-448-1810
Fax: 44-171-448-1804
E-mail: info@ftse.com
www.ftse.com

HSI Services Ltd.

Division of Hang Seng Bank
Head Office
83 Des Voeux Road Central
Hong Kong
Tel: 852-2877-0704
Fax: 852-2845-8919
www.hsiservices.com

internet.com LLC

20 Ketchum Street
Westport, CT 06880
Tel: 203-226-6967
Fax: 203-454-5840
E-mail: info@internet.com
www.internet.com

Morgan Stanley Capital International

1221 Avenue of the Americas
New York, NY 10020
Tel: 212-762-5790
Fax: 212-762-9160
www.msci.com

Nihon Keizai Shimbun, Inc. (Nikkei)

1-9-5 Otemachi, Chiyoda-ku
Tokyo 100-66, Japan
Tel: 03-3270-0251
Fax: 03-5255-2661
www.nikkei.co.jp

1325 Avenue of the Americas
Suite 2500
New York, NY 10019
Tel: 212-261-6200
Fax: 212-261-6209

Frank Russell and Company

909 A Street
Tacoma, WA 98402
Tel: 253-572-9500
E-mail: webmaster@russell.com
www.russell.com

Standard & Poor's Corporation

55 Water St.
42nd Floor
New York, NY 10041
Tel: 212-438-2000
Fax: 212-438-3539
www.spglobal.com

STOXX Ltd.

Selnaustrasse 30
P.O. Box
CH-8021, Zurich
Switzerland
Tel: 41-1-229-2300
Fax: 41-1-229-2301
E-mail: stoxx@stoxx.com
www.stoxx.com

Value Line

220 East 42nd Street
New York, NY 10017
Tel: 212-907-1500

Customer Service
Tel: 800-634-3583
Fax: 201-939-9079
www.valueline.com

REGULATORS

The exchanges that list stock
index products are all subject to
federal regulation in their respective countries.

Australian Securities and Investments Commission

GPO Box 4866
Sydney NSW 2001
Australia
Tel: 61-2-9911-2000
Fax: 61-2-9911-2634
E-mail: infoline@asic.gov.au
www.asic.gov.au

France Commission des Operations de Bourse (COB)

17 Place de la Bourse
75082 Paris Cedex 02
France
Tel: 33-1-53-45-6000
Fax: 33-1-53-45-6100
www.cob.fr

Germany The Federal Securities Supervisory Office [Bundesaufsichtsamt für den Wertpapierhandel (BAWe)]

P.O. Box 50 01 54
D-60391 Frankfurt am Main
Germany
Tel: 49-69-959-520
Fax: 49-69-959-52123
E-mail: mail @bawe.de
www.bawe.de

Hong Kong Securities and Futures Commission

11th–13th Floor
Edinburgh Tower, The Landmark
15 Queen's Road
Central Hong Kong
China
Tel: 852-2840-9222
Fax: 852-2521-7836

Italy National Commission for Companies and the Stock Exchange [Commissione Nazionale per le Societa e la Borsa, or (Consob)]

Via Isonzo
19/d
Rome 00198
Italy
Tel: 39-6-847-7611
Fax: 39-6-841-6703
www.consob.it

Japanese Ministry of Finance

3–1–1 Kasumigaseki
Chiyoda-ku, Tokyo 100-8940
Japan
Tel: 81-3-3591-2874
Fax: 81-3-3501-3720
www.mof.go.jp

Monetary Authority of Singapore

10 Shenton Way
MAS Building
Singapore 079117
Tel: 65-229-9220
Fax: 65-229-9697
www.mas.gov.sg

Ontario Securities Commission

20 Queen Street West
Suite 800
Toronto, Ontario M5H 3S8
Canada
Tel: 416-597-0681
Fax: 416-593-8122
www.osc.gov.on.ca

Quebec Securities Commission (Commission des valears mobilieres du Quebec)

800 Victoria Square
P.O. Box 246
Tour de la Bourse
Montreal, Quebec H4Z 1G3
Canada
Tel: 514-940-2150
Fax: 514-873-3090
www.cvmq.com

Securities Board of the Netherlands [Stichting Toezicht Effectenverkeer]

Singel 542
10017 AZ Amsterdam
The Netherlands
Tel: 31-20-553-5200
Fax: 31-20-620-6649
www.ste.nl

Spanish Securities Exchange Commission [Comisión Nacionel del Mercado de Valores (CNMV)]

Paseo de la Castellana, 19
28046 Madrid
Spain
Tel: 34-1-585-1500
Fax: 34-1-319-3373
www.cnmv.es

Swedish Financial Supervisory Authority [Finansinspektionen]

P.O. Box 7831
103 98 Stockholm
Sweden
Tel: 46-8-787-8000
Fax: 46-8-24-1335
www.fi.se

United Kingdom
The Financial Services Authority

25 The North Colonnade
Canary Wharf
London, U.K. E14 5HS
Tel: 44-171-676-1000
Fax: 44-171-676-1099
www.fsa.gov.uk

United Kingdom
The Securities and Futures Authority

25 The North Colonnade
Canary Wharf
London, U.K. E14 5HS
Tel: 44-171-676-1000
Fax: 44-171-676-1099
www.sfa.org.uk

United States Commodity Futures Trading Commission

Three Lafayette Centre
1155 21st Street, N.W.
Washington, DC 20581
Tel: 202-418-5498
Fax: 202-254-6265
www.cftc.gov

United States National Futures Association

200 W. Madison St.
Suite 1600
Chicago, IL 60606-3447
Tel: 800-621-3570 or
        800-676-4NFA
        312-781-1300
Fax: 312-781-1467
www.nfa.futures.org

ASSOCIATIONS

The following associations may be able to provide further information about trading in stock index futures and options as well as the participants who use the markets.

Electronic Traders Association

1800 Bering
Suite 750
Houston, TX 77057
Tel: 713-706-3300
Fax: 713-977-7975
www.electronic-traders.org

End-Users of Derivatives Association

P.O. Box 14467
Washington, DC 20044-4467
Tel: 202-383-0639
Fax: 202-637-0229
www.numa.com/euda

Futures and Options Association

One American Square
17 Crosswall
London EC3N 2PP
England
Tel: 44-171-426-7250
Fax: 44-171-426-7251
E-mail: info@foa.co.uk
www.foa.co.uk

Futures Industry Association

2001 Pennsylvania, N.W.
Suite 600
Washington, D.C. 20006
Tel: 202-466-5460
Fax: 202-296-3184
www.fiafii.org

Managed Funds Association

1200 19th Street, N.W.
Suite 300
Washington, D.C. 20036-2422
Tel: 202-828-6040
Fax: 202-828-6041
www.mfainfo.org

PUBLICATIONS

The following publications are the major ones that specialize in covering the futures trading arena. Hundreds of newsletters about trading exist, but are not listed here.

Futures

250 S. Wacker Drive
Suite 1150
Chicago, IL 60606
Tel: 312-977-0999
Fax: 312-977-1042
futuresmag.com

Futures Industry

2001 Pennsylvania, N.W.
Suite 600
Washington, D.C. 20006-1807
Tel: 202-466-5460
Fax: 202-296-3184
www.fiafii.org

Futures and OTC World

16 Lower Marsh
London, SE1 7SJ
England
Tel: 44-171-827-9977
Fax: 44-171-928-6539
www.fow.com

Hedge Fund Research, Inc.

208 South LaSalle Street
Suite 766
Chicago, IL 60604
Tel: 312-658-0955
Fax: 312-658-1019
E-mail: inc@hfr.com
www.hfr.com

Managed Account Reports

220 Fifth Ave.
19th Floor
New York, NY 10001-7781
Tel: 212-213-6202
Fax: 212-213-1870
www.marhedge.com

Technical Analysis of Stocks and Commodities

Technical Analysis, Inc.
4757 California Ave. S.W.
Seattle, WA 98116-4499
Tel: 206-938-0570
Fax: 206-938-1307
E-mail: editor@traders.com
www.traders.com

GLOSSARY

American-style option. An option that can be exercised at any time up to and including expiration.

Arbitrage. Simultaneous buying and selling of similar instruments in different markets to profit from a price discrepancy.

Arbitration. The process of settling a trade dispute between two parties in which the parties agree to be bound by the decision of the arbitration panel that judges the evidence.

Ask. Price at which a market participant is willing to sell.

Asset allocation. A trading strategy that uses futures to synthetically implement a switch among asset classes.

Associated person (AP). An individual registered with the Commodity Futures Trading Commission who solicits orders, customers, or customer funds on behalf of a futures commission merchant, introducing broker, commodity trading advisor, or commodity pool operator.

At-the-market. An order requesting immediate execution at the best possible price upon receipt.

At-the-money. An option whose strike price is closest to the price of the underlying futures contract.

Automatic exercise. The process by which all in-the-money option positions are exercised at expiration.

B

Bear market. A market in which prices are declining.

Bear spread. A position intended to profit from a price decline.

Bid. Price at which a market participant is willing to buy.

Bid-ask spread. The difference between the highest current buying price (bid) and the lowest current selling price (ask).

Broad-based indexes. Market indexes based on a large number of underlying equities in a variety of industry sectors to represent overall market trend.

Broker. A person paid a fee or commission for executing buy and sell orders for a customer.

Bull market. A market in which prices are rising.

Bull spread. A position intended to profit from a price rise.

C

Call. An option contract that grants the right, but not the obligation, to buy a specified futures contract at the strike price on or before the expiration date.

Capitalization-weighted index. A stock index whose value is based on multiplying the number of shares outstanding in each underlying stock by each stock's price.

Cash settlement. A method of settling a futures contract whereby the seller pays the buyer the cash value of the contract and in which no physical delivery of the underlying market occurs.

CFTC. See *Commodity Futures Trading Commission.*

Circuit breakers. Price limits and trading halts designed to slow rapid stock index price movement.

Clearing. The procedure through which a clearinghouse matches corresponding buy and sell records and becomes the buyer to each seller and the seller to each buyer.

Clearinghouse. The entity through which all futures and options on futures transactions are settled. It is responsible for ensuring the transfer of funds and guaranteeing the financial performance of each open contract.

Clearing member. A firm that has met the financial requirements to clear trades at a futures exchange.

Closing transaction. A trade that liquidates an existing long or short position with an equal and opposite transaction.

Commission. Fee a brokerage firm charges a customer for executing an order.

Commodity Futures Trading Commission (CFTC). The federal agency formed in 1974 to administer the Commodity Exchange Act and to regulate the U.S. futures industry. Its five commissioners are appointed to five-year terms by the President, subject to Senate confirmation.

Contract. One unit of futures or option trading.

Contract month. The month and year in which performance on a futures contract is required.

Contract specifications. Key trading details for each contract market established by the exchange upon which it is listed.

Convergence. The movement of futures and cash prices toward a common price as the futures contract's expiration nears.

Cover. See *offset*.

D

Day trade. A round-turn trade completed in one trading session.

Day trader. A speculator who initiates and offsets a position in one trading session.

Deferred month. A contract trading month other than the one closest to expiration.

Delta. A statistical measure of the rate of change in an option's theoretical value versus a change in the underlying futures price.

Divisor. The base number used to determine the value of a stock index. This number is adjusted as stocks in the index change.

E

European-style option. An option that can be exercised only on its expiration date.

Exercise. The process by which a long option holder invokes the right granted by the option contract and assumes an underlying futures position on the day following the exercise.

Exercise price. See *strike price.*

F

Fair value. The theoretical price for a stock index futures contract based on a formula that includes time to expiration, interest rates, and dividend yield.

Floor broker. Any member on the trading floor of an exchange who is licensed to execute customer orders in the trading pit for one or more clearing firms.

Fundamental analysis. The study of a market's economic supply and demand factors.

Futures commission merchant (FCM). Entities that solicit or accept customer orders to trade futures and options on futures and that accept payment from or to customers.

Futures contract. In stock indexes, a standardized agreement between buyer and seller to transfer the cash value of the contract at a future date.

Futures exchange. An organization designated by a governmental regulatory body to provide trading in futures and options on futures markets.

Futures option. An option contract that converts to a futures position upon exercise.

Futures price. The price quote determined at a futures exchange by trading among participants.

H

Hedge. A futures or option position taken opposite of a cash market position in order to reduce the risk of financial loss.

Holder. An option buyer.

I

In-the-money. An option with intrinsic value, that is a call option with a strike price below the current futures price or a put option with strike price above the current futures price.

Index arbitrage. The simultaneous purchase (sale) of stock index futures against the sale (purchase) of stocks that make up the index.

Index portfolio. A cash portfolio structured to exactly replicate a stock index.

Initial margin. See *margin.*

Introducing broker (IB). A firm or individual registered with the CFTC that solicits and accepts futures and option trading orders from customers but does not accept any money, securities, or property from customers.

L

Last trading day. The final day of trading in a futures or option contract.

Leverage. The ability to control large dollar amounts of a market with a relatively small amount of capital.

Limit move. A price that has advanced or declined the daily trading limit permissible by rules of a futures exchange.

Liquid. A characteristic of a market with enough open interest or volume to allow large transactions without a substantial change in price.

Liquidate. To close out a futures position.

Long. The buying side of a transaction.

Long hedge. A risk-management technique that involves buying a futures contract, buying a call option, or selling a put option to protect against future price increases in the underlying market.

M

Maintenance margin. See *margin*.

Managed futures fund. A fund that raises money from investors, distributes monies to one or several commodity trading advisors who invest in futures and options markets, and charges an annual management fee as well as a trading incentive fee.

Margin. The amount of money or collateral deposited by a customer with a broker, by a broker with a clearing member, or by a clearing member with the clearinghouse to act as a performance bond, not a downpayment, in insuring the receiving party against loss on open futures or option positions.

- *Initial margin.* Customer funds required to initiate a futures or short option position to ensure the performance of the customer's obligations.

- *Maintenance margin.* The amount of money that must be on deposit at all times in order to maintain the account's open positions.

- *Variation margin.* The daily payment made by a clearing member to a clearinghouse based on adverse price movement in positions carried by the clearing member.

Margin call. The request by a brokerage firm for a customer to deposit funds that will bring margin deposits back to initial levels.

Mark-to-market. The daily adjustment of a margin account's open positions to reflect the day's settlement prices.

N

Naked option. The sale of a put or a call without holding an offsetting position in the underlying futures or cash market.

Nearby month. The contract month closest to expiration. Also referred to as the spot month.

O

Offer. The price at which a market participant is willing to sell.

Offset. To close an open futures or option position with an equal and opposite position.

Open interest. The total number of contracts in a market that have not been offset.

Open outcry. Method of public auction required to make bids or offers in the trading pits of futures exchanges.

Option. A contract that gives the buyer the right, but not the obligation, to buy or sell the underlying futures contract at a specific price within a specified period of time.

Option buyer. One who pays the option premium to own call or put options.

Option premium. The price a buyer pays and a seller receives for the rights granted by the option.

Option seller. See *writer*.

Order. Instructions regarding execution of a futures or option transaction.

Order types.

- *Cancel Orders.* An order removing a previously placed order that has not yet been executed.

  Cancel-replace. An order canceling a previously placed order and replacing it with an order that has a slightly changed quantity or price before the original order has been executed.

  Cancel former order (CFO). Similar to a straight cancel order.

  Fill-or-kill (FIK). An order that is canceled if it cannot be immediately filled.

  One-cancels-other (OCO). A combination of two orders in which the execution of either one automatically cancels the other.

■ *Contingency orders.* Orders that specify limits in executing price and/or time of execution.

Day order. An order that automatically expires if it is not executed on the day it is entered.

Good-till-canceled (GTC). An order that remains in force until canceled or until the contract expires.

Resting order. Any order held by a floor broker that is outside the current market price, that is, buy orders below current values and sell orders above current values. These can be either day or GTC orders.

■ *Discretionary orders.* An order authorizing a broker to use best judgment as to its execution, including price, time, and quantity.

Disregard tape (DRT) order. This is the specific wording for a not-held order, for which the broker is not held liable.

■ *Limit orders.* An order that can be executed only at a specified price or better.

Or better order. Part of a limit order that carries instructions for an order to be executed at the specified price or one that is more advantageous to the customer.

■ *Market orders (MKT).* An order to be executed immediately at the current market price.

Market-if-touched (MIT). An order that becomes a market order for immediate execution if a specified price is reached. A sell MIT is placed above the current market; a buy MIT is placed below the current market.

Market-on-close (MOC). An order that is to be executed as a market order at the end of the trading session at a price within the closing range.

Market-on-open. An order that is to be executed at the beginning of the trading session at a price within the opening range.

■ *Spread orders.* An order to simultaneously buy and sell at least two different contracts at a quoted differential.

■ *Stop orders.* An order that becomes a market order only when the market trades at a specified price, but can be filled only at the specified price or better. A sell stop order is placed below the market; a buy stop order is placed above the market. Also known as a *stop-loss order*.

Stop-close-only (SCO). A stop order that is in effect only during the closing range. If the market has reached or reaches the stop price at the closing range, it becomes a market order.

Out-of-the-money. A term used to describe an option with no intrinsic value; call option with a strike price higher than the current futures price or a put option with a strike price lower than the current futures price.

P

Portfolio insurance. A generic term used to describe the use of futures, options, other derivatives, or asset allocation strategies to protect a stock index portfolio from an adverse price move.

Position limit. The maximum net long or net short contracts one person or entity may hold according to exchange rules.

Position trader. One who holds long or short contracts for an extended period of time in anticipation of a major trend.

Premium 1. The price of an option contract. 2. The amount by which a cash price or a futures contract is trading above another cash price or futures contract.

Price limit. The largest amount a futures price is allowed to move up or down from the previous day's settlement within a single trading session.

Price-weighted index. A stock index value that gives equal weight to the price of each stock.

Program trading. The computer-assisted buying or selling of 15 or more stocks, with a total market value of at least $1 million.

Put option. The right, but not the obligation, to sell a futures contract at the option's strike price on or before the expiration date.

R

Range. The difference between a market's high and low prices in a certain time period.

Resistance. A technical term for an area that prices have difficulty rising above. Also see *support*.

Round turn. A completed transaction that includes the initial long or short position and the corresponding offsetting position.

Round-turn commission. The single charge for entering and exiting a futures position.

S

Scalp. To buy or sell rapidly for small, short-term profits, typically by professional speculative traders.

Settlement price. The official daily closing price at which all trades in a futures or option contract are cleared on a daily basis.

Short. The selling side of a transaction.

Short covering. Buying contracts to offset initial short positions.

Short hedge. A risk-management strategy in which futures are sold to protect against a possible decrease in the price of the underlying market.

Short side of the market. Positions that gain as prices fall: short futures, short call options, and long put options.

Speculate. To attempt to profit from buying or selling a futures or option contract by anticipating future price moves.

Spread. A position containing multiple, related instruments with some degree of offsetting risk.

Spread margin. A reduced margin rate assessed accounts that hold simultaneous long and short positions in markets with similar price movement, in recognition of the position's reduced risk versus outright positions.

Stock index futures. Futures contracts based on cash stock indexes, which are settled in cash.

Strike price. The price at which the buyer of a call (put) option may choose to exercise the right to purchase (sell) the underlying futures contract.

Support. An area that prices have difficulty falling below. Also see *resistance*.

T

Tactical asset allocation. A technique that estimates the return on various asset classes, such as stocks, bonds, or cash, and that shifts a particular asset mix in favor of a relatively attractive asset class.

Technical analysis. An approach to forecasting prices that examines price patterns, volume, open interest, momentum, and other statistical indicators.

Tick. A contract's minimum price fluctuation.

U

Underlying futures contract. The futures contract that must be bought or sold upon exercise of an option.

V

Variation margin. See *margin*.

Volume. The total number of contracts traded in a session, a figure used as a measure of liquidity.

W

Write. To sell an option.

Writer. One who sells an option and assumes the obligation to sell (for a call) or buy (for a put) the underlying futures contract at the exercise price for which they receive the option premium.

ENDNOTES

CHAPTER 1
UNDERSTANDING STOCK INDEX FUTURES

1. Melamed, Leo, "The Asian-Pacific Market: The New Millennium," *SIMEX Newsletter*, Issue 1, 1997.

2. Sutton, Jane, "Internet trading by uneducated bodes disaster," *Reuters Ltd.*, March 6, 1999.

3. Investment Company Institute, *Fundamentals: Investment Company Institute Research in Brief*, vol. 8, no. 1, March 1999.

4. Kawaller, Ira, "Determining the Relevant Fair Value(s) of S&P 500 Futures: A Case Study Approach," Chicago Mercantile Exchange, March 1996.

5. Hosking, Leslie V., "The Trouble With Circuit Breakers," *The Wall Street Journal*, October 31, 1997.

CHAPTER 2
WHAT MAKES STOCK INDEX FUTURES TICK?

1. Clements, Jonathan, "Risk-Adjusted Investment for the Meek: Making a New Case for the Dow Theory," averages.dowjones.com/ddrisk.html.

CHAPTER 4
WAYS TO USE STOCK INDEX FUTURES

1. Haugen, Robert A., and Lakonishok, Josef, *The Incredible January Effect*. Dow Jones-Irwin, 1988, p. 35.

2. Lucchetti, Aaron, "Traditional Small-Cap Rally Appears Earlier Than Ever," *The Wall Street Journal*, December 7, 1998.

3. Shalen, Catherine, "Turn-of-the-Year Performance of CBOT DJIA Spreads—A December Effect?" Chicago Board of Trade, December 15, 1997.

4. Ibid.

CHAPTER 5
KNOW YOUR STOCK INDEX: NORTH AMERICA

1. "22 Variations on a Theme," *Commodities* Magazine, May 1982, p. 34.

2. The Presidential Task Force on Market Mechanisms, *Report of The Presidential Task Force on Market Mechanisms*, January 1988, p. vi.

3. "Index Fever," *Commodities* Magazine, April 1982, p. 16.

4. Idaszak, Jerome, "CBOT-Dow fight likely to drag on," *Chicago Sun-Times*, May 20, 1982.

5. Idaszak, Jerome, "Dow Jones: Stock index will hurt us," *Chicago Sun-Times*, May 12, 1982.

6. "CBT wants DJIA," *Commodities* Magazine, April 1982, p. 18.

7. Idaszak, Jerome, "CBOT, Dow Jones clash over index trading rights," *Chicago Sun-Times*, May 4, 1982.

8. Idaszak, Jerome, "Dow Jones: Stock index will hurt us," *Chicago Sun-Times*, May 12, 1982.

9. "Missing link," *Commodities* Magazine, March 1983, p. 23.

10. "Missing link," *Commodities* Magazine, April 1983, p. 22.

11. Letter to Members, Chicago Board of Trade, April 1983.

12. "Dow look-alikes," *Futures* Magazine, November 1983, p. 28.

13. Lucchetti, Aaron and Ip, Greg, "Exchanges Plan Three Products," *The Wall Street Journal*, June 6, 1997.

14. Linton, Clifton, "SEC Contends Two Indexes Aren't Broad Enough," *Dow Jones News Service*, March 2, 1998.

15. Jacobs, Laura, "Futures leaders grapple with regulatory overhaul," *Reuters Ltd.*, March 15, 1999.

16. Falloon, William D., *Market Maker: A Sesquicentennial Look at the Chicago Board of Trade*, Board of Trade of the City of Chicago, 1998, p. 271–274.

17. Ibid., p. 273.

18. McHugh, Michael, "Lofty Expectations Await Launch of CBOT's DJIA Products," *Dow Jones News Service*, September 30, 1997.

19. Abbott, Susan, "Will OTC index contracts survive?" *Futures* Magazine, March 1986, p. 51.

CHAPTER 6
KNOW YOUR STOCK INDEX: ASIA/PACIFIC

1. "HK Futures Exchange: New Measures to Help Competitiveness," *Dow Jones News Services*, November 23, 1998.
2. Lucas, Louise, "Futures foray leads to profit," *The Financial Times*, December 3, 1998.
3. "HK Tsang: Merged Exchange Big Enough for Intl Alliances," *Dow Jones News Services*, March 4, 1999.
4. Kearney, Kathleen. "HK exchanges' merger plan mirrors global trend," *Reuters Ltd.*, March 4, 1999.
5. Borsuk, Richard, Ismail, Netty, and Rajendran, Joseph, "SIMEX to Merge with Equities in Singapore," *Dow Jones News Services*, November 4, 1998.
6. Tokyo Stock Exchange, *Outline of Tokyo Stock Price Index Futures*, October 1987.

CHAPTER 8
TRADING FROM THE BEACH

1. Burnham, Bill and Earle, Jamie, "Online Trading Quarterly: 4th Quarter 1998, The Online Trading Industry Comes of Age," Credit Suisse First Boston Corporation, March 1999.
2. Gasparino, Charles and Smith, Randall, "Web Trades Put Merrill on Horns of a Dilemma," *The Wall Street Journal*, February 12, 1999.
3. Ibid.
4. Ibid.
5. Schifrin, Matthew, with Malik, Om, "Amateur hour on Wall Street," *Forbes*, January 25, 1999, p. 82.
6. Burnham, Bill and Earle, Jamie. "Online Trading Quarterly: 4th Quarter 1998, The Online Trading Industry Comes of Age," Credit Suisse First Boston Corporation, March 1999.

INDEX